European Convention on Human Rights

Collected texts

Council of Europe Press, 1995

French edition:
Convention européene des Droits de l'Homme – Recueil de textes

ISBN 92-871-2507-4

Publishing and Documentation Service
Council of Europe
F-67075 Strasbourg Cedex

ISBN 92-871-2508-2
© Council of Europe, 1994
Réimpression 1995
Printed in the Netherlands

Contents

Introduction

The European Convention on Human Rights is undoubtedly the most concrete expression by the member States of the Council of Europe of their profound belief in the values of democracy, peace and justice and, through them, respect for the rights and fundamental freedoms of persons living in our society. Although this instrument is over forty years old, it has evolved and continues to do so, not only through the case-law of the European Commission and Court of Human Rights, but also through the addition of Protocols strengthening the rights and improving the protection mechanism.

The aim of this Collection is to give practising lawyers and any other interested persons clear and up-to-date information on all these instruments and on the texts relating to the working of the bodies set up by the Convention.

To this end, the Collection reproduces the text of the European Convention on Human Rights and its ten Protocols (Section 1) and, for each instrument, gives the state of signatures and ratifications as well as declarations and reservations (Section 2).

With regard to procedure before the bodies set up by the Convention, the European Agreement of 6 May 1969 contains rules relating to the immunity of persons participating in the proceedings of the

European Commission and Court of Human Rights. The text of this Agreement appears in Section 3.

The text of the Rules of procedure of the Commission and the texts of the revised Rules of the Court are set out respectively in Sections 4 and 5. Each text contains an appendix relating to legal aid for applicants and a list of the national authorities competent to certify the indigence of applicants.

By virtue of Articles 32 and 54 of the Convention, the Committee of Ministers is called upon to assume certain specific functions which are elaborated in the rules which it adopted in June 1969 and in February 1976. These rules are contained in Section 6.

Section 7 contains a selection of interesting texts of the Committee of Ministers of the Council of Europe concerning human rights.

In addition to the basic instruments and texts included in this brochure, a large amount of other information on more specific aspects of human rights is contained in publications prepared by the Council of Europe. A list of these publications may be obtained on request from the Human Rights Information Centre of the Directorate of Human Rights of the Council of Europe.

The basic texts relating to the Convention and to the Protocols, the principal decisions of the Commission, the Court and the Committee of Ministers, certain decisions of national courts relating to the Convention and other information on the Convention, the Commission and the Court are published in the Yearbook of the European Convention on Human Rights, of which 33 volumes have appeared to date covering the years 1958-1990. The Yearbook is obtainable from Martinus Nijhoff Publishers (P.O. Box 163, NL - 3300 AD Dordrecht).

Human Rights Information Centre
Council of Europe
Strasbourg, January 1994

European Convention on Human Rights

Convention for the Protection of Human Rights and Fundamental Freedoms

Rome, 4 November 1950[1]

Entry into force: 3 September 1953,
in accordance with Article 66

> Text amended according to the provisions of Protocol No. 3, which entered into force on 21 September 1970, of Protocol No. 5, which entered into force on 20 December 1971 and of Protocol No. 8, which entered into force on 1 January 1990, and comprising also the text of Protocol No. 2 which, in accordance with Article 5, paragraph 3, thereof, has been an integral part of the Convention since its entry into force on 21 September 1970.

The governments signatory hereto, being members of the Council of Europe,

Considering the Universal Declaration of Human Rights proclaimed by the General Assembly of the United Nations on 10th December 1948;

---

1 European Treaty Series, No. 5.

Considering that this declaration aims at securing the universal and effective recognition and observance of the rights therein declared;

Considering that the aim of the Council of Europe is the achievement of greater unity between its members and that one of the methods by which that aim is to be pursued is the maintenance and further realisation of human rights and fundamental freedoms;

Reaffirming their profound belief in those fundamental freedoms which are the foundation of justice and peace in the world and are best maintained on the one hand by an effective political democracy and on the other by a common understanding and observance of the human rights upon which they depend;

Being resolved, as the governments of European countries which are like-minded and have a common heritage of political traditions, ideals, freedom and the rule of law, to take the first steps for the collective enforcement of certain of the rights stated in the Universal Declaration;

Have agreed as follows:

Article 1

The High Contracting Parties shall secure to everyone within their jurisdiction the rights and freedoms defined in Section I of this Convention.

Section I

Article 2

1. Everyone's right to life shall be protected by law. No one shall be deprived of his life intentionally save in the execution of a sentence of a court following his conviction of a crime for which this penalty is provided by law.

2. Deprivation of life shall not be regarded as inflicted in contravention of this Article when it results from the use of force which is no more than absolutely necessary:

a. in defence of any person from unlawful violence;

b. in order to effect a lawful arrest or to prevent the escape of a person lawfully detained;

c. in action lawfully taken for the purpose of quelling a riot or insurrection.

Article 3

No one shall be subjected to torture or to inhuman or degrading treatment or punishment.

Article 4

1. No one shall be held in slavery or servitude.

2. No one shall be required to perform forced or compulsory labour.

3. For the purpose of this Article the term "forced or compulsory labour" shall not include:

a. any work required to be done in the ordinary course of detention imposed according to the provisions of Article 5 of this Convention or during conditional release from such detention;

b. any service of a military character or, in case of conscientious objectors in countries where they are recognised, service exacted instead of compulsory military service;

c. any service exacted in case of an emergency or calamity threatening the life or well-being of the community;

d. any work or service which forms part of normal civic obligations.

Article 5

1. Everyone has the right to liberty and security of person. No one shall be deprived of his liberty save in the following cases and in accordance with a procedure prescribed by law:

a. the lawful detention of a person after conviction by a competent court;

b. the lawful arrest or detention of a person for non-compliance with the lawful order of a court or in order to secure the fulfilment of any obligation prescribed by law;

c. the lawful arrest or detention of a person effected for the purpose of bringing him before the competent legal authority on reasonable suspicion of having committed an offence or when it is reasonably considered necessary to prevent his committing an offence or fleeing after having done so;

d. the detention of a minor by lawful order for the purpose of educational supervision or his lawful detention for the purpose of bringing him before the competent legal authority;

e. the lawful detention of persons for the prevention of the spreading of infectious diseases, of persons of unsound mind, alcoholics or drug addicts or vagrants;

f. the lawful arrest or detention of a person to prevent his effecting an unauthorised entry into the country or of a person against whom action is being taken with a view to deportation or extradition.

2. Everyone who is arrested shall be informed promptly, in a language which he understands, of the reasons for his arrest and of any charge against him.

3. Everyone arrested or detained in accordance with the provisions of paragraph 1.c of this Article shall be brought promptly before a judge or other officer authorised by law to exercise judicial power and shall be entitled to trial within a reasonable time or to release pending trial. Release may be conditioned by guarantees to appear for trial.

4. Everyone who is deprived of his liberty by arrest or detention shall be entitled to take proceedings by which the lawfulness of his detention shall be decided speedily by a court and his release ordered if the detention is not lawful.

5. Everyone who has been the victim of arrest or detention in contravention of the provisions of this Article shall have an enforceable right to compensation.

Article 6

1. In the determination of his civil rights and obligations or of any criminal charge against him, everyone is entitled to a fair and public hearing within a reasonable time by an independent and impartial tribunal established by law. Judgment shall be pronounced publicly but the press and public may be excluded from all or part of the trial in the interest of morals, public order or national security in a democratic society, where the interests of juveniles or the protection of the private life of the parties so require, or to the extent strictly necessary in the opinion of the court in special circumstances where publicity would prejudice the interests of justice.

2. Everyone charged with a criminal offence shall be presumed innocent until proved guilty according to law.

3. Everyone charged with a criminal offence has the following minimum rights:

    a. to be informed promptly, in a language which he understands and in detail, of the nature and cause of the accusation against him;

    b. to have adequate time and facilities for the preparation of his defence;

    c. to defend himself in person or through legal assistance of his own choosing or, if he has not sufficient means to pay for legal assistance, to be given it free when the interests of justice so require;

    d. to examine or have examined witnesses against him and to obtain the attendance and examination of witnesses on his behalf under the same conditions as witnesses against him;

    e. to have the free assistance of an interpreter if he cannot understand or speak the language used in court.

Article 7

1. No one shall be held guilty of any criminal offence on account of any act or omission which did not constitute a criminal offence under national or international law at the time when it was committed. Nor

shall a heavier penalty be imposed than the one that was applicable at the time the criminal offence was committed.

2. This Article shall not prejudice the trial and punishment of any person for any act or omission which, at the time when it was committed, was criminal according to the general principles of law recognised by civilised nations.

Article 8

1. Everyone has the right to respect for his private and family life, his home and his correspondence.

2. There shall be no interference by a public authority with the exercise of this right except such as is in accordance with the law and is necessary in a democratic society in the interests of national security, public safety or the economic well-being of the country, for the prevention of disorder or crime, for the protection of health or morals, or for the protection of the rights and freedoms of others.

Article 9

1. Everyone has the right to freedom of thought, conscience and religion; this right includes freedom to change his religion or belief and freedom, either alone or in community with others and in public or in private, to manifest his religion or belief, in worship, teaching, practice and observance.

2. Freedom to manifest one's religion or beliefs shall be subject only to such limitations as are prescribed by law and are necessary in a democratic society in the interests of public safety, for the protection of public order, health or morals, or for the protection of the rights and freedoms of others.

Article 10

1. Everyone has the right to freedom of expression. This right shall include freedom to hold opinions and to receive and impart information and ideas without interference by public authority and regardless of frontiers. This Article shall not prevent States from

requiring the licensing of broadcasting, television or cinema enterprises.

2. The exercise of these freedoms, since it carries with it duties and responsibilities, may be subject to such formalities, conditions, restrictions or penalties as are prescribed by law and are necessary in a democratic society, in the interests of national security, territorial integrity or public safety, for the prevention of disorder or crime, for the protection of health or morals, for the protection of the reputation or rights of others, for preventing the disclosure of information received in confidence, or for maintaining the authority and impartiality of the judiciary.

Article 11

1. Everyone has the right to freedom of peaceful assembly and to freedom of association with others, including the right to form and to join trade unions for the protection of his interests.

2. No restrictions shall be placed on the exercise of these rights other than such as are prescribed by law and are necessary in a democratic society in the interests of national security or public safety, for the prevention of disorder or crime, for the protection of health or morals or for the protection of the rights and freedoms of others. This Article shall not prevent the imposition of lawful restrictions on the exercise of these rights by members of the armed forces, of the police or of the administration of the State.

Article 12

Men and women of marriageable age have the right to marry and to found a family, according to the national laws governing the exercise of this right.

Article 13

Everyone whose rights and freedoms as set forth in this Convention are violated shall have an effective remedy before a national authority notwithstanding that the violation has been committed by persons acting in an official capacity.

Article 14

The enjoyment of the rights and freedoms set forth in this Convention shall be secured without discrimination on any ground such as sex, race, colour, language, religion, political or other opinion, national or social origin, association with a national minority, property, birth or other status.

Article 15

1. In time of war or other public emergency threatening the life of the nation any High Contracting Party may take measures derogating from its obligations under this Convention to the extent strictly required by the exigencies of the situation, provided that such measures are not inconsistent with its other obligations under international law.

2. No derogation from Article 2, except in respect of deaths resulting from lawful acts of war, or from Articles 3, 4 (paragraph 1) and 7 shall be made under this provision.

3. Any High Contracting Party availing itself of this right of derogation shall keep the Secretary General of the Council of Europe fully informed of the measures which it has taken and the reasons therefor. It shall also inform the Secretary General of the Council of Europe when such measures have ceased to operate and the provisions of the Convention are again being fully executed.

Article 16

Nothing in Articles 10, 11, and 14 shall be regarded as preventing the High Contracting Parties from imposing restrictions on the political activity of aliens.

Article 17

Nothing in this Convention may be interpreted as implying for any State, group or person any right to engage in any activity or perform any act aimed at the destruction of any of the rights and freedoms set forth herein or at their limitation to a greater extent than is provided for in the Convention.

Article 18

The restrictions permitted under this Convention to the said rights and freedoms shall not be applied for any purpose other than those for which they have been prescribed.

Section II

Article 19

To ensure the observance of the engagements undertaken by the High Contracting Parties in the present Convention, there shall be set up:

a. a European Commission of Human Rights, hereinafter referred to as "the Commission";

b. a European Court of Human Rights, hereinafter referred to as "the Court".

Section III

Article 20[1]

1. The Commission shall consist of a number of members equal to that of the High Contracting Parties. No two members of the Commission may be nationals of the same State.

2. The Commission shall sit in plenary session. It may, however, set up chambers, each composed of at least seven members. The chambers may examine petitions submitted under Article 25 of this Convention which can be dealt with on the basis of established case-law or which raise no serious question affecting the interpretation or application of the Convention. Subject to this restriction and to the provisions of paragraph 5 of this Article, the Chambers shall exercise all the powers conferred on the Commission by the Convention.

---

1 Text amended according to the provisions of Protocol No. 8 (European Treaty Series, No. 118) which entered into force on 1 January 1990.

The member of the Commission elected in respect of a High Contracting Party against which a petition has been lodged shall have the right to sit on a chamber to which that petition has been referred.

3. The Commission may set up committees, each composed of at least three members, with the power, exercisable by a unanimous vote, to declare inadmissible or strike from its list of cases a petition submitted under Article 25, when such a decision can be taken without further examination.

4. A chamber or committee may at any time relinquish jurisdiction in favour of the plenary Commission, which may also order the transfer to it of any petition referred to a chamber or committee.

5. Only the plenary Commission can exercise the following powers:

    a. the examination of applications submitted under Article 24;

    b. the bringing of a case before the Court in accordance with Article 48 a;

    c. the drawing up of rules of procedure in accordance with Article 36.

Article 21[1]

1. The members of the Commission shall be elected by the Committee of Ministers by an absolute majority of votes, from a list of names drawn up by the Bureau of the Consultative Assembly; each group of the Representatives of the High Contracting Parties in the Consultative Assembly shall put forward three candidates, of whom two at least shall be its nationals.

2. As far as applicable, the same procedure shall be followed to complete the Commission in the event of other States subsequently becoming Parties to this Convention, and in filling casual vacancies.

3. The candidates shall be of high moral character and must either possess the qualifications required for appointment to high judicial

1 Text amended according to the provisions of Protocol No. 8 (European Treaty Series, No. 118) which entered into force on 1 January 1990.

office or be persons of recognised competence in national or international law.

Article 22[1]

1. The members of the Commission shall be elected for a period of six years. They may be re-elected. However, of the members elected at the first election, the terms of seven members shall expire at the end of three years.

2. The members whose terms are to expire at the end of the initial period of three years shall be chosen by lot by the Secretary General of the Council of Europe immediately after the first election has been completed.

3. In order to ensure that, as far as possible, one half of the membership of the Commission shall be renewed every three years, the Committee of Ministers may decide, before proceeding to any subsequent election, that the term or terms of office of one or more members to be elected shall be for a period other than six years but not more than nine and not less than three years.

4. In cases where more than one term of office is involved and the Committee of Ministers applies the preceding paragraph, the allocation of the terms of office shall be effected by the drawing of lots by the Secretary General, immediately after the election.

5. A member of the Commission elected to replace a member whose term of office has not expired shall hold office for the remainder of his predecessor's term.

6. The members of the Commission shall hold office until replaced. After having been replaced, they shall continue to deal with such cases as they already have under consideration.

---

1 Text amended according to the provisions of Protocol No. 5 (European Treaty Series, No. 55) which entered into force on 20 December 1971.

Article 23[1]

The members of the Commission shall sit on the Commission in their individual capacity. During their term of office they shall not hold any position which is incompatible with their independence and impartiality as members of the Commission or the demands of this office.

Article 24

Any High Contracting Party may refer to the Commission, through the Secretary General of the Council of Europe, any alleged breach of the provisions of the Convention by another High Contracting Party.

Article 25

1. The Commission may receive petitions addressed to the Secretary General of the Council of Europe from any person, non-governmental organisation or group of individuals claiming to be the victim of a violation by one of the High Contracting Parties of the rights set forth in this Convention, provided that the High Contracting Party against which the complaint has been lodged has declared that it recognises the competence of the Commission to receive such petitions. Those of the High Contracting Parties who have made such a declaration undertake not to hinder in any way the effective exercise of this right.

2. Such declarations may be made for a specific period.

3. The declarations shall be deposited with the Secretary General of the Council of Europe who shall transmit copies thereof to the High Contracting Parties and publish them.

4. The Commission shall only exercise the powers provided for in this Article when at least six High Contracting Parties are bound by declarations made in accordance with the preceding paragraphs.

---

1 Text amended according to the provisions of Protocol No. 8 (European Treaty Series, No. 118) which entered into force on 1 January 1990.

Article 26

The Commission may only deal with the matter after all domestic remedies have been exhausted, according to the generally recognised rules of international law, and within a period of six months from the date on which the final decision was taken.

Article 27

1. The Commission shall not deal with any petition submitted under Article 25 which:

   a. is anonymous, or

   b. is substantially the same as a matter which has already been examined by the Commission or has already been submitted to another procedure of international investigation or settlement and if it contains no relevant new information.

2. The Commission shall consider inadmissible any petition submitted under Article 25 which it considers incompatible with the provisions of the present Convention, manifestly ill-founded, or an abuse of the right of petition.

3. The Commission shall reject any petition referred to it which it considers inadmissible under Article 26.

Article 28[1]

1. In the event of the Commission accepting a petition referred to it:

   a. it shall, with a view to ascertaining the facts, undertake together with the representatives of the parties an examination of the petition and, if need be, an investigation, for the effective conduct of which the States concerned shall furnish all necessary facilities, after an exchange of views with the Commission;

   b. it shall at the same time place itself at the disposal of the parties concerned with a view to securing a friendly settlement of the

---

1 Text amended according to the provisions of Protocol No. 8 (European Treaty Series, No. 118) which entered into force on 1 January 1990.

matter on the basis of respect for human rights as defined in this Convention.

2. If the Commission succeeds in effecting a friendly settlement, it shall draw up a report which shall be sent to the States concerned, to the Committee of Ministers and to the Secretary General of the Council of Europe for publication. This report shall be confined to a brief statement of the facts and of the solution reached.

Article 29[1] [2]

After it has accepted a petition submitted under Article 25, the Commission may nevertheless decide by a majority of two-thirds of its members to reject the petition if, in the course of its examination, it finds that the existence of one of the grounds for non-acceptance provided for in Article 27 has been established.

In such a case, the decision shall be communicated to the parties.

Article 30[1]

1. The Commission may at any stage of the proceedings decide to strike a petition out of its list of cases where the circumstances lead to the conclusion that:

a. the applicant does not intend to pursue his petition, or

b. the matter has been resolved, or

c. for any other reason established by the Commission, it is no longer justified to continue the examination of the petition.

However, the Commission shall continue the examination of a petition if respect for human rights as defined in this Convention so requires.

---

1 Text amended according to the provisions of Protocol No. 8 (European Treaty Series, No. 118) which entered into force on 1 January 1990.

2 Text amended according to the provisions of Protocol No. 3 (European Treaty Series, No. 45) which entered into force on 21 September 1970.

2. If the Commission decides to strike a petition out of its list after having accepted it, it shall draw up a report which shall contain a statement of the facts and the decision striking out the petition together with the reasons therefor. The report shall be transmitted to the parties, as well as to the Committee of Ministers for information. The Commission may publish it.

3. The Commission may decide to restore a petition to its list of cases if it considers that the circumstances justify such a course.

Article 31[1]

1. If the examination of a petition has not been completed in accordance with Article 28 (paragraph 2), 29 or 30, the Commission shall draw up a report on the facts and state its opinion as to whether the facts found disclose a breach by the State concerned of its obligations under the Convention. The individual opinions of members of the Commission on this point may be stated in the report.

2. The report shall be transmitted to the Committee of Ministers. It shall also be transmitted to the States concerned, who shall not be at liberty to publish it.

3. In transmitting the Report to the Committee of Ministers the Commission may make such proposals as it thinks fit.

Article 32

1. If the question is not referred to the Court in accordance with Article 48 of this Convention within a period of three months from the date of the transmission of the report to the Committee of Ministers, the Committee of Ministers shall decide by a majority of two-thirds of the members entitled to sit on the Committee whether there has been a violation of the Convention.

2. In the affirmative case the Committee of Ministers shall prescribe a period during which the High Contracting Party concerned must

---

1 Text amended according to the provisions of Protocol No. 8 (European Treaty Series, No. 118) which entered into force on 1 January 1990.

take the measures required by the decision of the Committee of Ministers.

3. If the High Contracting Party concerned has not taken satisfactory measures within the prescribed period, the Committee of Ministers shall decide by the majority provided for in paragraph 1 above what effect shall be given to its original decision and shall publish the report.

4. The High Contracting Parties undertake to regard as binding on them any decision which the Committee of Ministers may take in application of the preceding paragraphs.

Article 33

The Commission shall meet in camera.

Article 34[1]

Subject to the provisions of Articles 20 (paragraph 3) and 29, the Commission shall take its decisions by a majority of the members present and voting.

Article 35

The Commission shall meet as the circumstances require. The meetings shall be convened by the Secretary General of the Council of Europe.

Article 36

The Commission shall draw up its own rules of procedure.

Article 37

The secretariat of the Commission shall be provided by the Secretary General of the Council of Europe.

---

1 Text amended according to the provisions of Protocol No. 3 (European Treaty Series, No. 45) which entered into force on 21 September 1970 and of Protocol No. 8 (European Treaty Series, No. 118) which entered into force on 1 January 1990.

Section IV

Article 38

The European Court of Human Rights shall consist of a number of judges equal to that of the members of the Council of Europe. No two judges may be nationals of the same State.

Article 39

1. The members of the Court shall be elected by the Consultative Assembly by a majority of the votes cast from a list of persons nominated by the members of the Council of Europe; each member shall nominate three candidates, of whom two at least shall be its nationals.

2. As far as applicable, the same procedure shall be followed to complete the Court in the event of the admission of new members of the Council of Europe, and in filling casual vacancies.

3. The candidates shall be of high moral character and must either possess the qualifications required for appointment to high judicial office or be jurisconsults of recognised competence.

Article 40[1]

1. The members of the Court shall be elected for a period of nine years. They may be re-elected. However, of the members elected at the first election the terms of four members shall expire at the end of three years, and the terms of four more members shall expire at the end of six years.

2. The members whose terms are to expire at the end of the initial periods of three and six years shall be chosen by lot by the Secretary General immediately after the first election has been completed.

1 Text amended according to the provisions of Protocol No. 5 (European Treaty Series, No. 55) which entered into force on 20 December 1971 and of Protocol No. 8 (European Treaty Series, No. 118) which entered into force on 1 January 1990.

3. In order to ensure that, as far as possible, one third of the membership of the Court shall be renewed every three years, the Consultative Assembly may decide, before proceeding to any subsequent election, that the term or terms of office of one or more members to be elected shall be for a period other than nine years but not more than twelve and not less than six years.

4. In cases where more than one term of office is involved and the Consultative Assembly applies the preceding paragraph, the allocation of the terms of office shall be effected by the drawing of lots by the Secretary General immediately after the election.

5. A member of the Court elected to replace a member whose term of office has not expired shall hold office for the remainder of his predecessor's term.

6. The members of the Court shall hold office until replaced. After having been replaced, they shall continue to deal with such cases as they already have under consideration.

7. The members of the Court shall sit on the Court in their individual capacity. During their term of office they shall not hold any position which is incompatible with their independence and impartiality as members of the Court or the demands of this office.

Article 41[1]

The Court shall elect its President and one or two Vice-Presidents for a period of three years. They may be re-elected.

Article 42

The members of the Court shall receive for each day of duty a compensation to be determined by the Committee of Ministers.

---

1 Text amended according to the provisions of Protocol No. 8 (European Treaty Series, No. 118) which entered into force on 1 January 1990.

Article 43[1]

For the consideration of each case brought before it the Court shall consist of a Chamber composed of nine judges. There shall sit as an *ex officio* member of the Chamber the judge who is a national of any State Party concerned, or, if there is none, a person of its choice who shall sit in the capacity of judge; the names of the other judges shall be chosen by lot by the President before the opening of the case.

Article 44

Only the High Contracting Parties and the Commission shall have the right to bring a case before the Court.

Article 45

The jurisdiction of the Court shall extend to all cases concerning the interpretation and application of the present Convention which the High Contracting Parties or the Commission shall refer to it in accordance with Article 48.

Article 46

1. Any of the High Contracting Parties may at any time declare that it recognises as compulsory *ipso facto* and without special agreement the jurisdiction of the Court in all matters concerning the interpretation and application of the present Convention.

2. The declarations referred to above may be made unconditionally or on condition of reciprocity on the part of several or certain other High Contracting Parties or for a specified period.

3. These declarations shall be deposited with the Secretary General of the Council of Europe who shall transmit copies thereof to the High Contracting Parties.

---

1 Text amended according to the provisions of Protocol No. 8 (European Treaty Series, No. 118) which entered into force on 1 January 1990.

Article 47

The Court may only deal with a case after the Commission has acknowledged the failure of efforts for a friendly settlement and within the period of three months provided for in Article 32.

Article 48

The following may bring a case before the Court, provided that the High Contracting Party concerned, if there is only one, or the High Contracting Parties concerned, if there is more than one, are subject to the compulsory jurisdiction of the Court or, failing that, with the consent of the High Contracting Party concerned, if there is only one, or of the High Contracting Parties concerned if there is more than one:

  a. the Commission;

  b. a High Contracting Party whose national is alleged to be a victim;

  c. a High Contracting Party which referred the case to the Commission;

  d. a High Contracting Party against which the complaint has been lodged.

Article 49

In the event of dispute as to whether the Court has jurisdiction, the matter shall be settled by the decision of the Court.

Article 50

If the Court finds that a decision or a measure taken by a legal authority or any other authority of a High Contracting Party is completely or partially in conflict with the obligations arising from the present Convention, and if the internal law of the said Party allows only partial reparation to be made for the consequences of this decision or measure, the decision of the Court shall, if necessary, afford just satisfaction to the injured party.

Article 51

1. Reasons shall be given for the judgment of the Court.

2. If the judgment does not represent in whole or in part the unanimous opinion of the judges, any judge shall be entitled to deliver a separate opinion.

Article 52

The judgment of the Court shall be final.

Article 53

The High Contracting Parties undertake to abide by the decision of the Court in any case to which they are parties.

Article 54

The judgment of the Court shall be transmitted to the Committee of Ministers which shall supervise its execution.

Article 55

The Court shall draw up its own rules and shall determine its own procedure.

Article 56

1. The first election of the members of the Court shall take place after the declarations by the High Contracting Parties mentioned in Article 46 have reached a total of eight.

2. No case can be brought before the Court before this election.

Section V

Article 57

On receipt of a request from the Secretary General of the Council of Europe any High Contracting Party shall furnish an explanation of

the manner in which its internal law ensures the effective implementation of any of the provisions of this Convention.

Article 58

The expenses of the Commission and the Court shall be borne by
the Council of Europe.

Article 59

The members of the Commission and of the Court shall be entitled,
during the discharge of their functions, to the privileges and immunities provided for in Article 40 of the Statute of the Council of
Europe and in the agreements made thereunder.

Article 60

Nothing in this Convention shall be construed as limiting or derogating from any of the human rights and fundamental freedoms which
may be ensured under the laws of any High Contracting Party or
under any other agreement to which it is a Party.

Article 61

Nothing in this Convention shall prejudice the powers conferred on
the Committee of Ministers by the Statute of the Council of Europe.

Article 62

The High Contracting Parties agree that, except by special agreement, they will not avail themselves of treaties, conventions or declarations in force between them for the purpose of submitting, by
way of petition, a dispute arising out of the interpretation or application of this Convention to a means of settlement other than those
provided for in this Convention.

Article 63

1. Any State may at the time of its ratification or at any time thereafter declare by notification addressed to the Secretary General of
the Council of Europe that the present Convention shall extend to

all or any of the territories for whose international relations it is responsible.

2. The Convention shall extend to the territory or territories named in the notification as from the thirtieth day after the receipt of this notification by the Secretary General of the Council of Europe.

3. The provisions of this Convention shall be applied in such territories with due regard, however, to local requirements.

4. Any State which has made a declaration in accordance with paragraph 1 of this Article may at any time thereafter declare on behalf of one or more of the territories to which the declaration relates that it accepts the competence of the Commission to receive petitions from individuals, non-governmental organisations or groups of individuals in accordance with Article 25 of the present Convention.

Article 64

1. Any State may, when signing this Convention or when depositing its instrument of ratification, make a reservation in respect of any particular provision of the Convention to the extent that any law then in force in its territory is not in conformity with the provision. Reservations of a general character shall not be permitted under this article.

2. Any reservation made under this article shall contain a brief statement of the law concerned.

Article 65

1. A High Contracting Party may denounce the present Convention only after the expiry of five years from the date on which it became a Party to it and after six months' notice contained in a notification addressed to the Secretary General of the Council of Europe, who shall inform the other High Contracting Parties.

2. Such a denunciation shall not have the effect of releasing the High Contracting Party concerned from its obligations under this Convention in respect of any act which, being capable of constituting a

violation of such obligations, may have been performed by it before the date at which the denunciation became effective.

3. Any High Contracting Party which shall cease to be a member of the Council of Europe shall cease to be a Party to this Convention under the same conditions.

4. The Convention may be denounced in accordance with the provisions of the preceding paragraphs in respect of any territory to which it has been declared to extend under the terms of Article 63.

Article 66

1. This Convention shall be open to the signature of the members of the Council of Europe. It shall be ratified. Ratifications shall be deposited with the Secretary General of the Council of Europe.

2. The present Convention shall come into force after the deposit of ten instruments of ratification.

3. As regards any signatory ratifying subsequently, the Convention shall come into force at the date of the deposit of its instrument of ratification.

4. The Secretary General of the Council of Europe shall notify all the members of the Council of Europe of the entry into force of the Convention, the names of the High Contracting Parties who have ratified it, and the deposit of all instruments of ratification which may be effected subsequently.

Done at Rome, this 4th day of November 1950, in English and French, both texts being equally authentic, in a single copy which shall remain deposited in the archives of the Council of Europe. The Secretary General shall transmit certified copies to each of the signatories.

Protocol No. 2

to the Convention for the Protection of Human Rights and Fundamental Freedoms, conferring upon the European Court of Human Rights competence to give advisory opinions

Strasbourg, 6 May 1963

Entry into force: 21 September 1970,
in accordance with Article 5

The member States of the Council of Europe signatory hereto,

Having regard to the provisions of the Convention for the Protection of Human Rights and Fundamental Freedoms signed at Rome on 4th November 1950 (hereinafter referred to as "the Convention") and, in particular, Article 19 instituting, among other bodies, a European Court of Human Rights (hereinafter referred to as "the Court");

Considering that it is expedient to confer upon the Court competence to give advisory opinions subject to certain conditions,

Have agreed as follows:

Article 1

1. The Court may, at the request of the Committee of Ministers, give advisory opinions on legal questions concerning the interpretation of the Convention and the Protocols thereto.

2. Such opinions shall not deal with any question relating to the content or scope of the rights or freedoms defined in Section I of the Convention and in the Protocols thereto, or with any other question which the Commission, the Court or the Committee of Ministers might have to consider in consequence of any such proceedings as could be instituted in accordance with the Convention.

3. Decisions of the Committee of Ministers to request an advisory opinion of the Court shall require a two-thirds majority vote of the representatives entitled to sit on the Committee.

Article 2

The Court shall decide whether a request for an advisory opinion submitted by the Committee of Ministers is within its consultative competence as defined in Article 1 of this Protocol.

Article 3

1. For the consideration of requests for an advisory opinion, the Court shall sit in plenary session.

2. Reasons shall be given for advisory opinions of the Court.

3. If the advisory opinion does not represent in whole or in part the unanimous opinion of the judges, any judge shall be entitled to deliver a separate opinion.

4. Advisory opinions of the Court shall be communicated to the Committee of Ministers.

Article 4

The powers of the Court under Article 55 of the Convention shall extend to the drawing up of such rules and the determination of such procedure as the Court may think necessary for the purposes of this Protocol.

Article 5

1. This Protocol shall be open to signature by member States of the Council of Europe, signatories to the Convention, who may become Parties to it by:

a. signature without reservation in respect of ratification or acceptance;

b. signature with reservation in respect of ratification or acceptance, followed by ratification or acceptance.

Instruments of ratification or acceptance shall be deposited with the Secretary General of the Council of Europe.

2. This Protocol shall enter into force as soon as all States Parties to the Convention shall have become Parties to the Protocol, in accordance with the provisions of paragraph 1 of this article.

3. From the date of the entry into force of this Protocol, Articles 1 to 4 shall be considered an integral part of the Convention.

4. The Secretary General of the Council of Europe shall notify the member States of the Council of:

   a. any signature without reservation in respect of ratification or acceptance;

   b. any signature with reservation in respect of ratification or acceptance;

   c. the deposit of any instrument of ratification or acceptance;

   d. the date of entry into force of this Protocol in accordance with paragraph 2 of this article.

In witness whereof, the undersigned, being duly authorised thereto, have signed this Protocol.

Done at Strasbourg, this 6th day of May 1963, in English and in French, both texts being equally authoritative, in a single copy which shall remain deposited in the archives of the Council of Europe. The Secretary General shall transmit certified copies to each of the signatory States.

First Protocol

to the Convention for the Protection of Human Rights and Fundamental Freedoms securing certain rights and freedoms other than those already included in the Convention

Paris, 20 March 1952[1]

Entry into force: 18 May 1954,
in accordance with Article 6

The governments signatory hereto, being members of the Council of Europe,

Being resolved to take steps to ensure the collective enforcement of certain rights and freedoms other than those already included in Section I of the Convention for the Protection of Human Rights and Fundamental Freedoms signed at Rome on 4 November 1950 (hereinafter referred to as "the Convention"),

Have agreed as follows:

Article 1

Every natural or legal person is entitled to the peaceful enjoyment of his possessions. No one shall be deprived of his possessions except in the public interest and subject to the conditions provided for by law and by the general principles of international law.

The preceding provisions shall not, however, in any way impair the right of a State to enforce such laws as it deems necessary to control the use of property in accordance with the general interest or to secure the payment of taxes or other contributions or penalties.

---

1 European Treaty Series, No. 9.

Article 2

No person shall be denied the right to education. In the exercise of any functions which it assumes in relation to education and to teaching, the State shall respect the right of parents to ensure such education and teaching in conformity with their own religious and philosophical convictions.

Article 3

The High Contracting Parties undertake to hold free elections at reasonable intervals by secret ballot, under conditions which will ensure the free expression of the opinion of the people in the choice of the legislature.

Article 4

Any High Contracting Party may at the time of signature or ratification or at any time thereafter communicate to the Secretary General of the Council of Europe a declaration stating the extent to which it undertakes that the provisions of the present Protocol shall apply to such of the territories for the international relations of which it is responsible as are named therein.

Any High Contracting Party which has communicated a declaration in virtue of the preceding paragraph may from time to time communicate a further declaration modifying the terms of any former declaration or terminating the application of the provisions of this Protocol in respect of any territory.

A declaration made in accordance with this Article shall be deemed to have been made in accordance with paragraph 1 of Article 63 of the Convention.

Article 5

As between the High Contracting Parties the provisions of Articles 1, 2, 3 and 4 of this Protocol shall be regarded as additional articles to the Convention and all the provisions of the Convention shall apply accordingly.

Article 6

This Protocol shall be open for signature by the members of the Council of Europe, who are the signatories of the Convention; it shall be ratified at the same time as or after the ratification of the Convention. It shall enter into force after the deposit of ten instruments of ratification. As regards any signatory ratifying subsequently, the Protocol shall enter into force at the date of the deposit of its instrument of ratification.

The instruments of ratification shall be deposited with the Secretary General of the Council of Europe, who will notify all members of the names of those who have ratified.

Done at Paris, this 20th day of March 1952, in English and French, both texts being equally authentic, in a single copy which shall remain deposited in the archives of the Council of Europe. The Secretary General of the Council of Europe shall transmit certified copies to each of the signatory governments.

Protocol No. 4

to the Convention for the Protection of Human Rights and Fundamental Freedoms, securing certain rights and freedoms other than those already included in the Convention and in the First Protocol thereto

Strasbourg, 16 September 1963[1]

Entry into force: 2 May 1968,
in accordance with Article 7

The governments signatory hereto, being members of the Council of Europe,

Being resolved to take steps to ensure the collective enforcement of certain rights and freedoms other than those already included in Section I of the Convention for the Protection of Human Rights and Fundamental Freedoms signed at Rome on 4 November 1950 (hereinafter referred to as "the Convention") and in Articles 1 to 3 of the First Protocol to the Convention, signed at Paris on 20 March 1952,

Have agreed as follows:

Article 1

No one shall be deprived of his liberty merely on the ground of inability to fulfil a contractual obligation.

Article 2

1. Everyone lawfully within the territory of a State shall, within that territory, have the right to liberty of movement and freedom to choose his residence.

2. Everyone shall be free to leave any country, including his own.

---

1 European Treaty Series, No. 46.

3. No restrictions shall be placed on the exercise of these rights other than such as are in accordance with law and are necessary in a democratic society in the interests of national security or public safety, for the maintenance of *ordre public,* for the prevention of crime, for the protection of health or morals, or for the protection of the rights and freedoms of others.

4. The rights set forth in paragraph 1 may also be subject, in particular areas, to restrictions imposed in accordance with law and justified by the public interest in a democratic society.

Article 3

1. No one shall be expelled, by means either of an individual or of a collective measure, from the territory of the State of which he is a national.

2. No one shall be deprived of the right to enter the territory of the State of which he is a national.

Article 4

Collective expulsion of aliens is prohibited.

Article 5

1. Any High Contracting Party may, at the time of signature or ratification of this Protocol, or at any time thereafter, communicate to the Secretary General of the Council of Europe a declaration stating the extent to which it undertakes that the provisions of this Protocol shall apply to such of the territories for the international relations of which it is responsible as are named therein.

2. Any High Contracting Party which has communicated a declaration in virtue of the preceding paragraph may, from time to time, communicate a further declaration modifying the terms of any former declaration or terminating the application of the provisions of this Protocol in respect of any territory.

3. A declaration made in accordance with this article shall be deemed to have been made in accordance with paragraph 1 of Article 63 of the Convention.

4. The territory of any State to which this Protocol applies by virtue of ratification or acceptance by that State, and each territory to which this Protocol is applied by virtue of a declaration by that State under this article, shall be treated as separate territories for the purpose of the references in Articles 2 and 3 to the territory of a State.

Article 6

1. As between the High Contracting Parties the provisions of Articles 1 to 5 of this Protocol shall be regarded as additional articles to the Convention, and all the provisions of the Convention shall apply accordingly.

2. Nevertheless, the right of individual recourse recognised by a declaration made under Article 25 of the Convention, or the acceptance of the compulsory jurisdiction of the Court by a declaration made under Article 46 of the Convention, shall not be effective in relation to this Protocol unless the High Contracting Party concerned has made a statement recognising such right, or accepting such jurisdiction, in respect of all or any of Articles 1 to 4 of the Protocol.

Article 7

1. This Protocol shall be open for signature by the members of the Council of Europe who are the signatories of the Convention; it shall be ratified at the same time as or after the ratification of the Convention. It shall enter into force after the deposit of five instruments of ratification. As regards any signatory ratifying subsequently, the Protocol shall enter into force at the date of the deposit of its instrument of ratification.

2. The instruments of ratification shall be deposited with the Secretary General of the Council of Europe, who will notify all members of the names of those who have ratified.

In witness whereof, the undersigned, being duly authorised thereto, have signed this Protocol.

Done at Strasbourg, this 16th day of September 1963, in English and in French, both texts being equally authoritative, in a single copy which shall remain deposited in the archives of the Council of Europe. The Secretary General of the Council of Europe shall transmit certified copies to each of the signatory States.

Protocol No. 6

to the Convention for the Protection of Human Rights and Fundamental Freedoms concerning the abolition of the death penalty

Strasbourg, 28 April 1983[1]

Entry into force: 1 March 1985,
in accordance with Article 8

The member States of the Council of Europe, signatory to this Protocol to the Convention for the Protection of Human Rights and Fundamental Freedoms, signed at Rome on 4 November 1950 (hereinafter referred to as "the Conventio"),

Considering that the evolution that has occurred in several member States of the Council of Europe expresses a general tendency in favour of abolition of the death penalty,

Have agreed as follows:

Article 1

The death penalty shall be abolished. No one shall be condemned to such penalty or executed.

Article 2

A State may make provision in its law for the death penalty in respect of acts committed in time of war or of imminent threat of war; such penalty shall be applied only in the instances laid down in the law and in accordance with its provisions. The State shall communicate to the Secretary General of the Council of Europe the relevant provisions of that law.

---

1 European Treaty Series, No. 114.

Article 3

No derogation from the provisions of this Protocol shall be made under Article 15 of the Convention.

Article 4

No reservation may be made under Article 64 of the Convention in respect of the provisions of this Protocol.

Article 5

1. Any State may at the time of signature or when depositing its instrument of ratification, acceptance or approval, specify the territory or territories to which this Protocol shall apply.

2. Any State may at any later date, by a declaration addressed to the Secretary General of the Council of Europe, extend the application of this Protocol to any other territory specified in the declaration. In respect of such territory the Protocol shall enter into force on the first day of the month following the date of receipt of such a declaration by the Secretary General.

3. Any declaration made under the two preceding paragraphs may, in respect of any territory specified in such declaration, be withdrawn by a notification addressed to the Secretary General. The withdrawal shall become effective on the first day of the month following the date of receipt of such notification by the Secretary General.

Article 6

As between the States Parties the provisions of Articles 1 to 5 of this Protocol shall be regarded as additional articles to the Convention and all the provisions of the Convention shall apply accordingly.

Article 7

This Protocol shall be open for signature by the member States of the Council of Europe, signatories to the Convention. It shall be subject to ratification, acceptance or approval. A member State of the

Council of Europe may not ratify, accept or approve this Protocol unless it has, simultaneously or previously, ratified the Convention. Instruments of ratification, acceptance or approval shall be deposited with the Secretary General of the Council of Europe.

Article 8

1. This Protocol shall enter into force on the first day of the month following the date on which five member States of the Council of Europe have expressed their consent to be bound by the Protocol in accordance with the provisions of Article 7.

2. In respect of any member State which subsequently expresses its consent to be bound by it, the Protocol shall enter into force on the first day of the month following the date of the deposit of the instrument of ratification, acceptance or approval.

Article 9

The Secretary General of the Council of Europe shall notify the member States of the Council of:

    a. any signature;

    b. the deposit of any instrument of ratification, acceptance or approval;

    c. any date of entry into force of this Protocol in accordance with Articles 5 and 8;

    d. any other act, notification or communication relating to this Protocol.

In witness whereof the undersigned, being duly authorised thereto, have signed this Protocol.

Done at Strasbourg, this 28th day of April 1983, in English and French, both texts being equally authentic, in a single copy which shall be deposited in the archives of the Council of Europe. The Secretary General of the Council of Europe shall transmit certified copies to each member State of the Council of Europe.

Protocol No. 7

to the Convention for the Protection of Human Rights and Fundamental Freedoms

Strasbourg, 22 November 1984[1]

Entry into force: 1 November 1988,
in accordance with Article 9

The member States of the Council of Europe signatory hereto,

Being resolved to take further steps to ensure the collective enforcement of certain rights and freedoms by means of the Convention for the Protection of Human Rights and Fundamental Freedoms signed at Rome on 4 November 1950 (hereinafter referred to as "the Convention"),

Have agreed as follows:

Article 1

1. An alien lawfully resident in the territory of a State shall not be expelled therefrom except in pursuance of a decision reached in accordance with law and shall be allowed:

   a. to submit reasons against his expulsion,

   b. to have his case reviewed, and

   c. to be represented for these purposes before the competent authority or a person or persons designated by that authority.

2. An alien may be expelled before the exercise of his rights under paragraph 1. a, b and c of this Article, when such expulsion is necessary in the interests of public order or is grounded on reasons of national security.

---

1 European Treaty Series, No. 117.

Article 2

1. Everyone convicted of a criminal offence by a tribunal shall have the right to have his conviction or sentence reviewed by a higher tribunal. The exercise of this right, including the grounds on which it may be exercised, shall be governed by law.

2. This right may be subject to exceptions in regard to offences of a minor character, as prescribed by law, or in cases in which the person concerned was tried in the first instance by the highest tribunal or was convicted following an appeal against acquittal.

Article 3

When a person has by a final decision been convicted of a criminal offence and when subsequently his conviction has been reversed, or he has been pardoned, on the ground that a new or newly discovered fact shows conclusively that there has been a miscarriage of justice, the person who has suffered punishment as a result of such conviction shall be compensated according to the law or the practice of the State concerned, unless it is proved that the non-disclosure of the unknown fact in time is wholly or partly attributable to him.

Article 4

1. No one shall be liable to be tried or punished again in criminal proceedings under the jurisdiction of the same State for an offence for which he has already been finally acquitted or convicted in accordance with the law and penal procedure of that State.

2. The provisions of the preceding paragraph shall not prevent the reopening of the case in accordance with the law and penal procedure of the State concerned, if there is evidence of new or newly discovered facts, or if there has been a fundamental defect in the previous proceedings, which could affect the outcome of the case.

3. No derogation from this article shall be made under Article 15 of the Convention.

Article 5

Spouses shall enjoy equality of rights and responsibilities of a private law character between them, and in their relations with their children, as to marriage, during marriage and in the event of its dissolution. This article shall not prevent States from taking such measures as are necessary in the interests of the children.

Article 6

1. Any State may at the time of signature or when depositing its instrument of ratification, acceptance or approval, specify the territory or territories to which this Protocol shall apply and state the extent to which it undertakes that the provisions of this Protocol shall apply to such territory or territories.

2. Any State may at any later day, by a declaration addressed to the Secretary General of the Council of Europe, extend the application of this Protocol to any other territory specified in the declaration. In respect of such territory the Protocol shall enter into force on the first day of the month following the expiration of a period of two months after the date of receipt by the Secretary General of such declaration.

3. Any declaration made under the two preceding paragraphs may, in respect of any territory specified in such declaration, be withdrawn or modified by a notification addressed to the Secretary General. The withdrawal or modification shall become effective on the first day of the month following the expiration of a period of two months after the date of receipt of such notification by the Secretary General.

4. A declaration made in accordance with this article shall be deemed to have been made in accordance with paragraph 1 of Article 63 of the Convention.

5. The territory of any State to which this Protocol applies by virtue of ratification, acceptance or approval by that State, and each territory to which this Protocol is applied by virtue of a declaration by that State under this article, may be treated as separate territories for the purpose of the reference in Article 1 to the territory of a State.

Article 7

1. As between the States Parties, the provisions of Articles 1 to 6 of this Protocol shall be regarded as additional articles to the Convention, and all the provisions of the Convention shall apply accordingly.

2. Nevertheless, the right of individual recourse recognised by a declaration made under Article 25 of the Convention, or the acceptance of the compulsory jurisdiction of the Court by a declaration made under Article 46 of the Convention, shall not be effective in relation to this Protocol unless the State concerned has made a statement recognising such right, or accepting such jurisdiction in respect of Articles 1 to 5 of this Protocol.

Article 8

This Protocol shall be open for signature by member States of the Council of Europe which have signed the Convention. It is subject to ratification, acceptance or approval. A member State of the Council of Europe may not ratify, accept or approve this Protocol without previously or simultaneously ratifying the Convention. Instruments of ratification, acceptance or approval shall be deposited with the Secretary General of the Council of Europe.

Article 9

1. This Protocol shall enter into force on the first day of the month following the expiration of a period of two months after the date on which seven member States of the Council of Europe have expressed their consent to be bound by the Protocol in accordance with the provisions of Article 8.

2. In respect of any member State which subsequently expresses its consent to be bound by it, the Protocol shall enter into force on the first day of the month following the expiration of a period of two months after the date of the deposit of the instrument of ratification, acceptance or approval.

Article 10

The Secretary General of the Council of Europe shall notify all the member States of the Council of Europe of:

   a. any signature;

   b. the deposit of any instrument of ratification, acceptance or approval;

   c. any date of entry into force of this Protocol in accordance with Articles 6 and 9;

   d. any other act, notification or declaration relating to this Protocol.

In witness whereof the undersigned, being duly authorised thereto, have signed this Protocol.

Done at Strasbourg, this 22nd day of November 1984, in English and French, both texts being equally authentic, in a single copy which shall be deposited in the archives of the Council of Europe. The Secretary General of the Council of Europe shall transmit certified copies to each member State of the Council of Europe.

Protocol No. 9

to the Convention for the Protection of Human Rights and Fundamental Freedoms

Rome, 6 November 1990[1]

Entry into force: after ratification by ten member States, in accordance with Article 7

The member States of the Council of Europe, signatories to this Protocol to the Convention for the Protection of Human Rights and Fundamental Freedoms, signed at Rome on 4 November 1950 (hereinafter referred to as "the Convention"),

Being resolved to make further improvements to the procedure under the Convention,

Have agreed as follows:

Article 1

For Parties to the Convention which are bound by this Protocol, the Convention shall be amended as provided in Articles 2 to 5.

Article 2

Article 31, paragraph 2, of the Convention, shall read as follows:

"2. The Report shall be transmitted to the Committee of Ministers. The Report shall also be transmitted to the States concerned and, if it deals with a petition submitted under Article 25, the applicant. The States concerned and the applicant shall not be at liberty to publish it."

---

1 European Treaty Series, No. 140.

Article 3

Article 44 of the Convention shall read as follows:

"Only the High Contracting Parties, the Commission, and persons, non-governmental organisations or groups of individuals having submitted a petition under Article 25 shall have the right to bring a case before the Court."

Article 4

Article 45 of the Convention shall read as follows:

"The jurisdiction of the Court shall extend to all cases concerning the interpretation and application of the present Convention which are referred to it in accordance with Article 48."

Article 5

Article 48 of the Convention shall read as follows:

"1. The following may refer a case to the Court, provided that the High Contracting Party concerned, if there is only one, or the High Contracting Parties concerned, if there is more than one, are subject to the compulsory jurisdiction of the Court or, failing that, with the consent of the High Contracting Party concerned, if there is only one, or of the High Contracting Parties concerned if there is more than one:

a. the Commission;

b. a High Contracting Party whose national is alleged to be a victim;

c. a High Contracting Party which referred the case to the Commission;

d. a High Contracting Party against which the complaint has been lodged;

e. the person, non-governmental organisation or group of individuals having lodged the complaint with the Commission.

2. If a case is referred to the Court only in accordance with paragraph 1. e, it shall first be submitted to a panel composed of three members of the Court. There shall sit as an ex officio member of the panel the judge elected in respect of the High Contracting Party against which the complaint has been lodged, or, if there is none, a person of its choice who shall sit in the capacity of judge. If the complaint has been lodged against more than one High Contracting Party, the size of the panel shall be increased accordingly.

If the case does not raise a serious question affecting the interpretation or application of the Convention and does not for any other reason warrant consideration by the Court, the panel may, by a unanimous vote, decide that it shall not be considered by the Court. In that event, the Committee of Ministers shall decide, in accordance with the provisions of Article 32, whether there has been a violation of the Convention."

Article 6

1. This Protocol shall be open for signature by member States of the Council of Europe signatories to the Convention, which may express their consent to be bound by:

   a. signature without reservation as to ratification, acceptance or approval, or

   b. signature subject to ratification, acceptance or approval, followed by ratification, acceptance or approval.

2. The instruments of ratification, acceptance or approval shall be deposited with the Secretary General of the Council of Europe.

Article 7

1. This Protocol shall enter into force on the first day of the month following the expiration of a period of three months after the date on which ten member States of the Council of Europe have expressed their consent to be bound by the Protocol in accordance with the provisions of Article 6.

2. In respect of any member State which subsequently expresses its consent to be bound by it, the Protocol shall enter into force on the first day of the month following the expiration of a period of three months after the date of signature or of the deposit of the instrument of ratification, acceptance or approval.

Article 8

The Secretary General of the Council of Europe shall notify all the member States of the Council of Europe of:

a. any signature;

b. the deposit of any instrument of ratification, acceptance or approval;

c. any date of entry into force of this Protocol in accordance with Article 7;

d. any other act, notification or declaration relating to this Protocol.

In witness whereof, the undersigned, being duly authorised thereto, have signed this Protocol.

Done at Rome, this 6th day of November 1990, in English and French, both texts being equally authentic, in a single copy which shall be deposited in the archives of the Council of Europe. The Secretary General of the Council of Europe shall transmit certified copies to each member State of the Council of Europe.

Protocol No. 10

to the Convention for the Protection of Human Rights and Fundamental Freedoms

Strasbourg, 25 March 1992[1]

Entry into force: after ratification by all Parties to the Convention, in accordance with Article 3

The member States of the Council of Europe, signatories to this Protocol to the Convention for the Protection of Human Rights and Fundamental Freedoms, signed at Rome on 4 November 1950 (hereinafter referred to as "the Convention"),

Considering that it is advisable to amend Article 32 of the Convention with a view to the reduction of the two-thirds majority provided therein,

Have agreed as follows:

Article 1

The words "of two thirds" shall be deleted from paragraph 1 of Article 32 of the Convention.

Article 2

1. This Protocol shall be open for signature by member States of the Council of Europe signatories to the Convention, which may express their consent to be bound by:

    a. signature without reservation as to ratification, acceptance or approval; or

    b. signature subject to ratification, acceptance or approval, followed by ratification, acceptance or approval.

---

1 European Treaty Series, No. 146.

2. Instruments of ratification, acceptance or approval shall be deposited with the Secretary General of the Council of Europe.

Article 3

This Protocol shall enter into force on the first day of the month following the expiration of a period of three months after the date on which all Parties to the Convention have expressed their consent to be bound by the Protocol in accordance with the provisions of Article 2.

Article 4

The Secretary General of the Council of Europe shall notify the member States of the Council of:

a. any signature;

b. the deposit of any instrument of ratification, acceptance or approval;

c. the date of entry into force of this Protocol in accordance with Article 3;

d. any other act, notification or communication relating to this Protocol.

In witness whereof the undersigned, being duly authorised thereto, have signed this Protocol.

Done at Strasbourg, this 25th day of March 1992, in English and French, both texts being equally authentic, in a single copy which shall be deposited in the archives of the Council of Europe. The Secretary General of the Council of Europe shall transmit certified copies to each member State of the Council of Europe.

Signatures, ratifications, declarations and reservations relating to the Convention and its protocols

Signatures and ratifications

Convention for the Protection of Human Rights and Fundamental Freedoms[1]

Opening for signature: Rome, 04/11/50

Entry into force: 03/09/53 (Conditions: 10 ratifications)

Member States	Date of signature	Date of ratification	Entry into force
Austria	13/12/57	03/09/58	03/09/58 * R
Belgium	04/11/50	14/06/55	14/06/55 *
Bulgaria	07/05/92	07/09/92	07/09/92 *
Cyprus	16/12/61	06/10/62	06/10/62 *
Czech Republic	21/02/91	18/03/92	01/01/93 * ** R/D
Denmark	04/11/50	13/04/53	03/09/53 *
Estonia	14/05/93		
Finland	05/05/89	10/05/90	10/05/90 * R
France	04/11/50	03/05/74	03/05/74 * R/T
Germany	04/11/50	05/12/52	03/09/53 * R
Greece	28/11/50	28/11/74	28/11/74 *
Hungary	06/11/90	05/11/92	05/11/92 * R
Iceland	04/11/50	29/06/53	03/09/53 *
Ireland	04/11/50	25/02/53	03/09/53 * R

Member States	Date of signature	Date of ratification	Entry into force
Italy	04/11/50	26/10/55	26/10/55 *
Liechtenstein	23/11/78	08/09/82	08/09/82 * R
Lithuania	14/05/93		
Luxembourg	04/11/50	03/09/53	03/09/53 *
Malta	12/12/66	23/01/67	23/01/67 * D
Netherlands	04/11/50	31/08/54	31/08/54 * T
Norway	04/11/50	15/01/52	03/09/53 *
Poland	26/11/91	19/01/93	19/01/93 *
Portugal	22/09/76	09/11/78	09/11/78 * R
Romania	07/10/93		
San Marino	16/11/88	22/03/89	22/03/89 * R/D
Slovakia	21/02/91	18/03/92	01/01/93 * ** R
Slovenia	14/05/93		
Spain	24/11/77	04/10/79	04/10/79 * R/D
Sweden	28/11/50	04/02/52	03/09/53 *
Switzerland	21/12/72	28/11/74	28/11/74 * R/D
Turkey	04/11/50	18/05/54	18/05/54 *
United Kingdom	04/11/50	08/03/51	03/09/53 * T

1   Treaty open for signature by the member States.

*   State having made declarations pursuant to Articles 25 and 46 – see separate chart.

** The Czech and Slovak Federal Republic was a Contracting Party from 18.3.1992 to 31.12.1992. Following declarations made by the Czech Republic and Slovakia of their intention to succeed the Czech and Slovak Federal Republic and to consider themselves bound by the European Convention on Human Rights as of 1.1.1993, the Committee of Ministers decided on 30.6.1993 that these States are to be regarded as Parties to the Convention with effect from 1.1.1993. Similarly, these States are bound as of 1.1.1993 by the declarations made by the Czech and Slovak Federal Republic (18.3.1992) in respect of Articles 25 and 46 of the Convention

R: Reservations.

D: Declarations.

T: Territorial Declaration.

Protocol No. 2[1]

Opening for signature: Strasbourg, 06/05/63

Entry into force: 21/09/70

Member States	Date of signature	Date of ratification	Entry into force
Austria	06/05/63	29/05/67	21/09/70
Belgium	05/06/63	21/09/70	21/09/70
Bulgaria	07/05/92 a	07/09/92 b	07/09/92
Cyprus	19/09/67	22/01/69	21/09/70
Czech Republic	21/02/91 a	18/03/92 b	01/06/93 **
Denmark	06/05/63[2]	06/05/63[1]	21/09/70
Estonia	14/05/93 a		
Finland	05/05/89	10/05/90	10/05/90
France	02/10/81[2]	02/10/81[2]	02/10/81
Germany	06/05/63	03/01/69	21/09/70 D
Greece	28/11/74	08/01/75	28/11/74 D
Hungary	06/11/90	05/11/92 b	05/11/92
Iceland	16/11/67	16/11/67	21/09/70
Ireland	06/05/63	12/09/63	21/09/70
Italy	06/05/63	03/04/67	21/09/70
Liechtenstein	23/11/78	08/09/82	08/09/82
Lithuania	14/05/93 a		
Luxembourg	06/05/63	27/10/65	21/09/70
Malta	12/12/66	23/01/67	21/09/70
Netherlands	06/05/63	11/10/66	21/09/70 T
Norway	06/05/63	12/06/64	21/09/70
Poland	26/11/91 a	19/01/93 b	19/01/93
Portugal	27/01/77	09/11/78	09/11/78
Romania	07/10/93 a		
San Marino	01/03/89	22/03/89	22/03/89
Slovakia	21/02/91 a	18/03/92 b	01/06/93 **
Slovenia	14/05/93 a		
Spain	23/02/78	06/04/82	06/04/82
Sweden	06/05/63	13/06/64	21/09/70

Member States	Date of signature	Date of ratification	Entry into force
Switzerland	21/12/72	28/11/74	28/11/74
Turkey	06/05/63	25/03/68	21/09/70
United Kingdom	06/05/63[2]	06/05/63[2]	21/09/70

---

1 Treaty open for signature by the member States signatories to the Convention for the Protection of Human Rights and Fundamental Freedoms (European Treaty Series, No. 5).

2 Signature without reservation as to ratification.

a Date of signature of the Convention as completed by this Protocol.

b Date of ratification of the Convention as completed by this Protocol.

** The Czech and Slovak Federal Republic was a Contracting Party from 18.3.1992 to 31.12.1992. Following declarations made by the Czech Republic and Slovakia of their intention to succeed the Czech and Slovak Federal Republic and to consider themselves bound by the European Convention on Human Rights as of 1.1.1993, the Committee of Ministers decided on 30.6.1993 that these States are to be regarded as Parties to the Convention with effect from 1.1.1993. Similarly, these States are bound as of 1.1.1993 by the declarations made by the Czech and Slovak Federal Republic (18.3.1992) in respect of Articles 25 and 46 of the Convention.

D: Declarations.

T: Territorial Declaration.

First Protocol[1]

Opening for signature: Paris, 20/03/52
Entry into force: 18/05/54 (Conditions: 10 ratifications)

Member States	Date of signature	Date of ratification	Entry into force
Austria	13/12/57	03/09/58	03/09/58 * R
Belgium	20/03/52	14/06/55	14/06/55 *
Bulgaria	07/05/92	07/09/92	07/09/92 * R/D
Cyprus	16/12/61	06/10/62	06/10/62 *
Czech Republic	21/02/91	18/03/92	01/01/93 * **
Denmark	20/03/52	13/04/53	18/05/54 *
Estonia	14/05/93		
Finland	05/05/89	10/05/90	10/05/90 *
France	20/03/52	03/05/74	03/05/74 * T
Germany	20/03/52	13/02/57	13/02/57 * D
Greece	20/03/52	28/11/74	28/11/74 * R
Hungary	06/11/90	05/11/92	05/11/92 *
Iceland	20/03/52	29/06/53	18/05/54 *
Ireland	20/03/52	25/02/53	18/05/54 * D
Italy	20/03/52	26/10/55	26/10/55 *
Liechtenstein	07/05/87		
Lithuania	14/05/93		
Luxembourg	20/03/52	03/09/53	18/05/54 * R
Malta	12/12/66	23/01/67	23/01/67 * D
Netherlands	20/03/52	31/08/54	31/08/54 * D/T
Norway	20/03/52	18/12/52	18/05/54 *
Poland	14/09/92		
Portugal	22/09/76	09/11/78	09/11/78 *
Romania	04/11/93		
San Marino	01/03/89	22/03/89	22/03/89 * R
Slovakia	21/02/91	18/03/92	01/01/93 * **
Slovenia	14/05/93		
Spain	23/02/78	27/11/90	27/11/90 * R/D
Sweden	20/03/52	22/06/53	18/05/54 * R

Member States	Date of signature	Date of ratification	Entry into force
Switzerland	19/05/76		
Turkey	20/03/52	18/05/54	18/05/54 * R
United Kingdom	20/03/52	03/11/52	18/05/54 * R/T

---

1 Treaty open for signature by the member States signatories to the Convention for the Protection of Human Rights and Fundamental Freedoms (European Treaty Series, No. 5).

* State having made declarations pursuant to Articles 25 and 46 - see separate chart.

** The Czech and Slovak Federal Republic was a Contracting Party from 18.3.1992 to 31.12.1992. Following declarations made by the Czech Republic and Slovakia of their intention to succeed the Czech and Slovak Federal Republic and to consider themselves bound by the European Convention on Human Rights as of 1.1.1993, the Committee of Ministers decided on 30.6.1993 that these States are to be regarded as Parties to the Convention with effect from 1.1.1993. Similarly, these States are bound as of 1.1.1993 by the declarations made by the Czech and Slovak Federal Republic (18.3.1992) in respect of Articles 25 and 46 of the Convention.

R: Reservations.

D: Declarations.

T: Territorial Declaration.

Protocol No. 3[1]

Opening for signature: Strasbourg, 06/05/63

Entry into force: 21/09/70

Member States	Date of signature	Date of ratification	Entry into force
Austria	06/05/63	29/05/67	21/09/70
Belgium	05/06/63	21/09/70	21/09/70
Bulgaria	07/05/92 a	07/09/92 b	07/09/92
Cyprus	19/09/67	22/01/69	21/09/70
Czech Republic	21/02/91 a	18/03/92 b	01/06/93 **
Denmark	06/05/63[2]	06/05/63[2]	21/09/70
Estonia	14/05/93 a		
Finland	05/05/89 a	10/05/90 b	10/05/90
France	22/10/73	03/05/74	03/05/74
Germany	06/05/63	03/01/69	21/09/70 D
Greece	30/11/65	08/01/75	28/11/74 D
Hungary	06/11/90 a	05/11/92 b	05/11/92
Iceland	16/11/67	16/11/67	21/09/70
Ireland	06/05/63	12/09/63	21/09/70
Italy	06/05/63	03/04/67	21/09/70
Liechtenstein	23/11/78 a	08/09/82 b	08/09/82
Lithuania	14/05/93 a		
Luxembourg	06/05/63	27/10/65	21/09/70
Malta	12/12/66	23/01/67	21/09/70
Netherlands	06/05/63	11/10/66	21/09/70 T
Norway	06/05/63	12/06/64	21/09/70
Poland	26/11/91 a	19/01/93 b	19/01/93
Portugal	22/09/76 a	09/11/78 b	09/11/78
Romania	07/10/93 a		
San Marino	16/11/88 a	22/03/89 b	22/03/89
Slovakia	21/02/91 a	18/03/92 b	01/06/93 **
Slovenia	14/05/93 a		
Spain	24/11/77 a	04/10/79 b	04/10/79
Sweden	06/05/63	13/06/64	21/09/70

Member States	Date of signature	Date of ratification	Entry into force
Switzerland	21/12/72 a	28/11/74 b	28/11/74
Turkey	06/05/63	25/03/68	21/09/70
United Kingdom	06/05/63 [2]	06/05/63 [2]	21/09/70

---

1 Treaty open for signature by the member States signatories to the Convention for the Protection of Human Rights and Fundamental Freedoms (European Treaty Series, No. 5).

2 Signature without reservation as to ratification.

a Date of signature of the Convention as amended by this Protocol.

b Date of ratification of the Convention as amended by this Protocol.

** The Czech and Slovak Federal Republic was a Contracting Party from 18.3.1992 to 31.12.1992. Following declarations made by the Czech Republic and Slovakia of their intention to succeed the Czech and Slovak Federal Republic and to consider themselves bound by the European Convention on Human Rights as of 1.1.1993, the Committee of Ministers decided on 30.6.1993 that these States are to be regarded as Parties to the Convention with effect from 1.1.1993. Similarly, these States are bound as of 1.1.1993 by the declarations made by the Czech and Slovak Federal Republic (18.3.1992) in respect of Articles 25 and 46 of the Convention.

D: Declarations.

T: Territorial Declaration.

Protocol No. 4[1]

Opening for signature: Strasbourg, 16/09/63
Entry into force: 02/05/68

Member States	Date of signature	Date of ratification	Entry into force
Austria	16/09/63	18/09/69	18/09/69 * R
Belgium	16/09/63	21/09/70	21/09/70 *
Bulgaria			
Cyprus	06/10/88	03/10/89	03/10/89 * D
Czech Republic	21/02/91	18/03/92	01/01/93 * **
Denmark	16/09/63	30/09/64	02/05/68 *
Estonia	14/05/93		
Finland	05/05/89	10/05/90	10/05/90 *
France	22/10/73	03/05/74	03/05/74 * T
Germany	16/09/63	01/06/68	01/06/68 * D
Greece			
Hungary	06/11/90	05/11/92	05/11/92 *
Iceland	16/11/67	16/11/67	02/05/68 *
Ireland	16/09/63	29/10/68	29/10/68 * D
Italy	16/09/63	27/05/82	27/05/82 * D
Liechtenstein			
Lithuania	14/05/93		
Luxembourg	16/09/63	02/05/68	02/05/68 *
Malta			
Netherlands	15/11/63	23/06/82	23/06/82 * D/T
Norway	16/09/63	12/06/64	02/05/68 *
Poland	14/09/92		
Portugal	27/04/78	09/11/78	09/11/78 *
Romania	04/11/93		
San Marino	01/03/89	22/03/89	22/03/89 *
Slovakia	21/02/91	18/03/92	01/03/93 * **
Slovenia	14/05/93		
Spain	23/02/78		
Sweden	16/09/63	13/06/64	02/05/68 *

Member States	Date of signature	Date of ratification	Entry into force
Switzerland			
Turkey	19/10/92		
United Kingdom	16/09/63		

---

1 Treaty open for signature by the member States signatories to the Convention for the Protection of Human Rights and Fundamental Freedoms (European Treaty Series, No. 5).

* State having made declarations pursuant to Articles 25 and 46 - see separate chart.

** The Czech and Slovak Federal Republic was a Contracting Party from 18.3.1992 to 31.12.1992. Following declarations made by the Czech Republic and Slovakia of their intention to succeed the Czech and Slovak Federal Republic and to consider themselves bound by the European Convention on Human Rights as of 1.1.1993, the Committee of Ministers decided on 30.6.1993 that these States are to be regarded as Parties to the Convention with effect from 1.1.1993. Similarly, these States are bound as of 1.1.1993 by the declarations made by the Czech and Slovak Federal Republic (18.3.1992) in respect of Articles 25 and 46 of the Convention.

R: Reservations.

D: Declarations.

T: Territorial Declaration.

Protocol No. 5[1]

Opening for signature: Strasbourg, 20/01/66

Entry into force: 20/12/71

Member States	Date of signature	Date of ratification	Entry into force
Austria	25/01/66	09/10/69	20/12/71
Belgium	20/01/66	21/09/70	20/12/71
Bulgaria	07/05/92 a	07/09/92 b	07/09/92
Cyprus	19/09/67	22/01/69	20/12/71
Czech Republic	21/02/91 a	18/03/92 b	01/01/93 **
Denmark	20/01/66[2]	20/01/66[2]	20/12/71
Estonia	14/05/93 a		
Finland	05/05/89 a	10/05/90 b	10/05/90
France	22/10/73	03/05/74	03/05/74
Germany	03/03/66	03/01/69	20/12/71 D
Greece	28/11/74	08/01/75	28/11/74 D
Hungary	06/11/90 a	05/11/92 b	05/11/92
Iceland	16/11/67	16/11/67	20/12/71
Ireland	18/02/66[2]	18/02/66[2]	20/12/71
Italy	20/01/66	25/03/68	20/12/71
Liechtenstein	23/11/78 a	08/09/82 b	08/09/82
Lithuania	14/05/93 a		
Luxembourg	20/01/66	26/06/68	20/12/71
Malta	12/12/66	23/01/67	20/12/71
Netherlands	16/06/70	19/05/71	20/12/71 T
Norway	20/01/66[2]	20/01/66[2]	20/12/71
Poland	26/11/91 a	19/01/93 b	19/01/93
Portugal	22/09/76 a	09/11/78 b	09/11/78
Romania	07/10/93 a		
San Marino	16/11/88 a	22/03/89 b	22/03/89
Slovakia	21/02/91 a	18/03/92 b	01/06/93 **
Slovenia	14/05/93 a		
Spain	24/11/77 a	04/10/79 b	04/10/79
Sweden	20/01/66	27/09/66	20/12/71

Member States	Date of signature	Date of ratification	Entry into force
Switzerland	21/12/72 a	28/11/74 b	28/11/74
Turkey	14/05/71	20/12/71	20/12/71
United Kingdom	10/02/66	24/10/67	20/12/71

---

1 Treaty open for signature by the member States signatories to the Convention for the Protection of Human Rights and Fundamental Freedoms (European Treaty Series, No. 5).

2 Signature without reservation as to ratification.

a Date of signature of the Convention as amended by this Protocol.

b Date of ratification of the Convention as amended by this Protocol.

** The Czech and Slovak Federal Republic was a Contracting Party from 18.3.1992 to 31.12.1992. Following declarations made by the Czech Republic and Slovakia of their intention to succeed the Czech and Slovak Federal Republic and to consider themselves bound by the European Convention on Human Rights as of 1.1.1993, the Committee of Ministers decided on 30.6.1993 that these States are to be regarded as Parties to the Convention with effect from 1.1.1993. Similarly, these States are bound as of 1.1.1993 by the declarations made by the Czech and Slovak Federal Republic (18.3.1992) in respect of Articles 25 and 46 of the Convention.

D: Declarations.

T: Territorial Declaration.

Protocol No. 6[1]

Opening for signature: Strasbourg 28/04/83
Entry into force: 01/03/85

Member States	Date of signature	Date of ratification	Entry into force
Austria	28/04/83	05/01/84	01/03/85 *
Belgium	28/04/83		
Bulgaria			
Cyprus			
Czech Republic	21/02/91	18/03/92	01/01/93 **
Denmark	28/04/83	01/12/83	01/03/85 *
Estonia	14/05/93		
Finland	05/05/89	10/05/90	01/06/90 *
France	28/04/83	17/02/86	01/03/86 *
Germany	28/04/83	05/07/89	01/08/89 * D
Greece	02/05/83		
Hungary	06/11/90	05/11/92	01/12/92 *
Iceland	24/04/85	22/05/87	01/06/87 *
Ireland			
Italy	21/10/83	29/12/88	01/01/89 *
Liechtenstein	15/11/90	15/11/90	01/12/90 *
Lithuania			
Luxembourg	28/04/83	19/02/85	01/03/85 *
Malta	26/03/91	26/03/91	01/04/91 *
Netherlands	28/04/83	25/04/86	01/05/86 * D/T
Norway	28/04/83	25/10/88	01/11/88 *
Poland			
Portugal	28/04/83	02/10/86	01/11/86 *
Romania	15/12/93		
San Marino	01/03/89	22/03/89	01/04/89 *
Slovakia	21/02/91	18/03/92	01/01/93 **
Slovenia	14/05/93		
Spain	28/04/83	14/01/85	01/03/85 *
Sweden	28/04/83	09/02/84	01/03/85 *

Member States	Date of signature	Date of ratification	Entry into force
Switzerland	28/04/83	13/10/87	01/11/87 * D
Turkey			
United Kingdom			

---

1 Treaty open for signature by the member States signatories to the Convention for the Protection of Human Rights and Fundamental Freedoms (European Treaty Series, No. 5).

* State having made declarations pursuant to Articles 25 and 46 - see separate chart.

** The Czech and Slovak Federal Republic was a Contracting Party from 18.3.1992 to 31.12.1992. Following declarations made by the Czech Republic and Slovakia of their intention to succeed the Czech and Slovak Federal Republic and to consider themselves bound by the European Convention on Human Rights as of 1.1.1993, the Committee of Ministers decided on 30.6.1993 that these States are to be regarded as Parties to the Convention with effect from 1.1.1993. Similarly, these States are bound as of 1.1.1993 by the declarations made by the Czech and Slovak Federal Republic (18.3.1992) in respect of Articles 25 and 46 of the Convention.

D: Declarations.

T: Territorial Declaration.

Protocol No. 7[1]

Opening for signature: Strasbourg, 22/11/84

Entry into force: 01/11/88

Member States	Date of signature	Date of ratification	Entry into force
Austria	19/03/85	14/05/86	01/11/88 * D
Belgium			
Bulgaria	03/11/93		
Cyprus			
Czech Republic	21/02/91	18/03/92	01/01/93 * **
Denmark	22/11/84	18/08/88	01/11/88 * R/T
Estonia	14/05/93		
Finland	05/05/89	10/05/90	01/08/90 *
France	22/11/84	17/02/86	01/11/88 * R/D/T
Germany	19/03/85		D
Greece	22/11/84	29/10/87	01/11/88
Hungary	06/11/90	05/11/92	01/02/93 *
Iceland	19/03/85	22/05/87	01/11/88 *
Ireland	11/12/84		
Italy	22/11/84	07/11/91	01/02/92 D
Liechtenstein			
Lithuania	14/05/93		
Luxembourg	22/11/84	19/04/89	01/07/89 * R
Malta			
Netherlands	22/11/84		D
Norway	22/11/84	25/10/88	01/01/89 *
Poland	14/09/92		
Portugal	22/11/84		
Romania	04/11/93		
San Marino	01/03/89	22/03/89	01/06/89 * D
Slovakia	21/02/91	18/03/92	01/01/93 * **
Slovenia	14/05/93		
Spain	22/11/84		
Sweden	22/11/84	08/11/85	01/11/88 * D

Member States	Date of signature	Date of ratification	Entry into force
Switzerland	28/02/86	24/02/88	01/11/88 * R
Turkey	14/03/85		
United Kingdom			

---

1 Treaty open for signature by the member States signatories to the Convention for the Protection of Human Rights and Fundamental Freedoms (European Treaty Series, No. 5).

* State having made declarations pursuant to Articles 25 and 46 - see separate chart.

** The Czech and Slovak Federal Republic was a Contracting Party from 18.3.1992 to 31.12.1992. Following declarations made by the Czech Republic and Slovakia of their intention to succeed the Czech and Slovak Federal Republic and to consider themselves bound by the European Convention on Human Rights as of 1.1.1993, the Committee of Ministers decided on 30.6.1993 that these States are to be regarded as Parties to the Convention with effect from 1.1.1993. Similarly, these States are bound as of 1.1.1993 by the declarations made by the Czech and Slovak Federal Republic (18.3.1992) in respect of Articles 25 and 46 of the Convention.

D: Declarations.

T: Territorial Declaration.

Protocol No. 8[1]

Opening for signature: Vienna, 19/03/85
Entry into force: 01/01/90

Member States	Date of signature	Date of ratification	Entry into force
Austria	19/03/85	17/04/86	01/01/90
Belgium	19/03/85	08/11/85	01/01/90
Bulgaria	07/05/92 a	07/09/92 b	07/09/92
Cyprus	08/11/85	13/06/86	01/01/90
Czech Republic	21/02/91 a	18/03/92 b	01/01/93 **
Denmark	19/03/85[2]	19/03/85[2]	01/01/90
Estonia	14/05/93 a		
Finland	05/05/89	10/05/90 b	10/05/90
France	19/03/85	09/02/89	01/01/90 D
Germany	19/03/85	19/09/89	01/01/90 D
Greece	19/03/85	06/09/89	01/01/90
Hungary	06/11/90 a	05/11/92 b	05/11/92
Iceland	19/03/85	22/05/87	01/01/90
Ireland	20/03/85	21/03/88	01/01/90 D
Italy	19/03/85	29/12/88	01/01/90
Liechtenstein	19/03/85	28/08/85	01/01/90
Lithuania	14/05/93 a		
Luxembourg	19/03/85	04/11/87	01/01/90
Malta	07/03/88[2]	07/03/88[2]	01/01/90
Netherlands	20/03/85	11/12/86	01/01/90 T
Norway	19/03/85	25/10/88	01/01/90
Poland	26/11/91 a	19/01/93 b	19/01/93
Portugal	19/03/85	12/03/87	01/01/90
Romania	07/10/93 a		
San Marino	01/03/89	22/03/89	01/01/90
Slovakia	21/02/91 a	18/03/92 b	01/01/93 **
Slovenia	14/05/93 a		
Spain	19/03/85	23/06/89	01/01/90
Sweden	19/03/85	10/01/86	01/01/90

Member States	Date of signature	Date of ratification	Entry into force
Switzerland	19/03/85	21/05/87	01/01/90
Turkey	04/02/86	19/09/89	01/01/90
United Kingdom	19/03/85	21/04/86	01/01/90 D/T

---

1   Treaty open for signature by the member States signatories to the Convention for the Protection of Human Rights and Fundamental Freedoms (European Treaty Series, No. 5).

2   Signature without reservation as to ratification.

a   Date of signature of the Convention as amended by this Protocol.

b   Date of ratification of the Convention as amended by the Protocol.

**   The Czech and Slovak Federal Republic was a Contracting Party from 18.3.1992 to 31.12.1992. Following declarations made by the Czech Republic and Slovakia of their intention to succeed the Czech and Slovak Federal Republic and to consider themselves bound by the European Convention on Human Rights as of 1.1.1993, the Committee of Ministers decided on 30.6.1993 that these States are to be regarded as Parties to the Convention with effect from 1.1.1993. Similarly, these States are bound as of 1.1.1993 by the declarations made by the Czech and Slovak Federal Republic (18.3.1992) in respect of Articles 25 and 46 of the Convention.

D: Declarations.

T: Territorial Declaration.

Protocol No. 9[1]

Opening for signature: Rome, 06/11/90

Entry into force: 10 ratifications

Member States	Date of signature	Date of ratification	Entry into force
Austria	06/11/90	27/04/92	
Belgium	08/11/90		
Bulgaria			
Cyprus	06/11/90		
Czech Republic	21/02/91	18/03/92	**
Denmark	06/11/90		
Estonia	14/11/93		
Finland	06/11/90	11/12/92	
France	06/11/90		
Germany	22/05/92		
Greece	06/11/90		
Hungary	06/11/90	05/11/92	
Iceland			
Ireland			
Italy	06/11/90	13/12/93	
Liechtenstein	17/01/91		
Lithuania			
Luxembourg	06/11/90	09/07/92	
Malta	06/11/90		
Netherlands	11/05/92	23/11/92	T
Norway	10/12/90	15/01/92	
Poland	14/09/92		
Portugal	22/01/91		
Romania	04/11/93		
San Marino	06/11/90		
Slovakia	21/02/91	18/03/92	**
Slovenia	14/05/93		
Spain			
Sweden	06/11/90		

Member States	Date of signature	Date of ratification	Entry into force
Switzerland	06/11/90		
Turkey	06/11/90		
United Kingdom			

---

1   Treaty open for signature by the member States signatories to the Convention for the Protection of Human Rights and Fundamental Freedoms (European Treaty Series, No. 5).

** The Czech and Slovak Federal Republic was a Contracting Party from 18.3.1992 to 31.12.1992. Following declarations made by the Czech Republic and Slovakia of their intention to succeed the Czech and Slovak Federal Republic and to consider themselves bound by the European Convention on Human Rights as of 1.1.1993, the Committee of Ministers decided on 30.6.1993 that these States are to be regarded as Parties to the Convention with effect from 1.1.1993. Similarly, these States are bound as of 1.1.1993 by the declarations made by the Czech and Slovak Federal Republic (18.3.1992) in respect of Articles 25 and 46 of the Convention.

T: Territorial Declaration.

Protocol No. 10[1]

Opening for signature: Strasbourg, 25/03/92

Entry into force: Ratification by all parties to the Convention

Member States	Date of signature	Date of ratification	Entry into force
Austria	07/05/92	01/06/93	
Belgium	25/03/92	21/12/92	
Bulgaria		***	
Cyprus	25/03/92	***	
Czech Republic	21/02/91	18/03/92	**
Denmark	25/03/92	***	
Estonia	14/05/93		
Finland	25/03/92	21/07/92	
France	25/03/92	***	
Germany	25/03/92	***	
Greece	29/04/92	***	
Hungary	09/02/93	***	
Iceland		***	
Ireland		***	
Italy	25/03/92	***	
Liechtenstein		***	
Lithuania			
Luxembourg	25/03/92	***	
Malta	07/05/92[2]	07/05/92[2]	
Netherlands	25/03/92	23/11/92	T
Norway	25/03/92[2]	25/03/92[2]	
Poland	14/09/92	***	
Portugal	22/07/92	***	
Romania	04/11/93		
San Marino	07/07/92	***	
Slovakia	21/02/91	18/03/92	**
Slovenia	14/05/93		
Spain		***	
Sweden	09/04/92	19/10/92	

Member States	Date of signature	Date of ratification	Entry into force
Switzerland	25/03/92	***	
Turkey		***	
United Kingdom	25/03/92	09/03/93	T

---

1   Treaty open for signature by the member States signatories to the Convention for the Protection of Human Rights and Fundamental Freedoms (European Treaty Series, No. 5).

2   Signature without reservation as to ratification.

** The Czech and Slovak Federal Republic was a Contracting Party from 18.3.1992 to 31.12.1992. Following declarations made by the Czech Republic and Slovakia of their intention to succeed the Czech and Slovak Federal Republic and to consider themselves bound by the European Convention on Human Rights as of 1.1.1993, the Committee of Ministers decided on 30.6.1993 that these States are to be regarded as Parties to the Convention with effect from 1.1.1993. Similarly, these States are bound as of 1.1.1993 by the declarations made by the Czech and Slovak Federal Republic (18.3.1992) in respect of Articles 25 and 46 of the Convention.

*** State whose ratification is necessary for the entry into force of the Protocol.

T: Territorial Declaration.

Declarations made under Article 25[1]

Member States	First declarations	Current declarations	For a period of
Austria	03/09/58	03/09/91[2][3]	3 years
Belgium	05/07/55	30/06/92[2]	5 years
Bulgaria	07/09/92	07/09/92	3 years b
Cyprus	01/01/89	01/01/92[2]	3 years
Czech Republic	18/03/92 *	18/03/92[2][3]	5 years b
Denmark	13/04/53	05/04/92[2][3]	5 years
Estonia			
Finland	10/05/90	10/05/90[2][3]	a
France	02/10/81	25/09/89[2][3]	5 years
Germany	05/07/55	01/07/89[2]	5 years
Greece	20/11/85	20/11/91	3 years
Hungary	05/11/92	05/11/92[2][3]	5 years b
Iceland	29/03/55	25/03/60[2][3]	a
Ireland	25/02/53	25/02/53	a
Italy	01/08/73	01/01/91[2]	3 years
Liechtenstein	08/09/82	08/09/91	3 years
Lithuania			
Luxembourg	28/04/58	28/04/91[2][3]	5 years
Malta	01/05/87	01/05/92	5 years
Netherlands	28/06/90	01/09/79	a
Norway	10/12/55	29/06/92[2][3]	5 years
Poland	01/05/93	01/05/93	3 years b
Portugal	09/11/78	09/11/78[2]	2 years b
Romania			
San Marino	22/03/89	22/03/92[2][3]	3 years
Slovakia	18/03/92 *	18/03/92[2][3]	5 years b
Slovenia			
Spain	01/07/81	15/10/85	5 years b
Sweden	04/02/52	04/02/52[2][3]	a
Switzerland	28/11/74	28/11/92[2]	3 years
Turkey	28/01/87	28/01/90	3 years
United Kingdom	14/01/66	14/01/91	5 years

1 Declarations made under Articles 25 and 46 respectively of the Convention also apply to Articles 1 to 4 of the First Protocol (European Treaty Series, No. 9) and to Articles 1 to 5 of Protocol No. 6 (European Treaty Series, No. 114) in those States which have ratified either one or both of these Protocols.

2 Declarations also applying to Articles 1 to 4 of Protocol No. 4 (European Treaty Series, No. 46).

3 Declarations also applying to Articles 1 to 5 of Protocol No. 7 (European Treaty Series, No. 117).

a Until otherwise decided or for an indefinite period.

b Declaration renewable by tacit agreement.

* The Czech and Slovak Federal Republic was a Contracting Party from 18.3.1992 to 31.12.1992. Following declarations made by the Czech Republic and Slovakia of their intention to succeed the Czech and Slovak Federal Republic and to consider themselves bound by the European Convention on Human Rights as of 1.1.1993, the Committee of Ministers decided on 30.6.1993 that these States are to be regarded as Parties to the Convention with effect from 1.1.1993. Similarly, these States are bound as of 1.1.1993 by the declarations made by the Czech and Slovak Federal Republic (18.3.1992) in respect of Articles 25 and 46 of the Convention.

Declarations made under Article 46[1]

Member States	First declarations	Current declarations	For a period of
Austria	03/09/58	03/09/91[2][3]	3 years
Belgium	05/07/55	29/06/92[2]	5 years
Bulgaria	07/09/92	07/09/92	3 years b
Cyprus	24/01/80	24/01/92[2]	3 years
Czech Republic	18/03/92 *	18/03/92[2][3]	5 years b
Denmark	13/04/53	05/04/92[2][3]	5 years
Estonia			
Finland	10/05/90	10/05/90[2][3]	a
France	03/05/74	25/09/89[2][3]	5 years
Germany	05/07/55	01/07/89[2]	5 years
Greece	30/01/79	24/06/91	3 years
Hungary	05/11/92	05/11/92[2][3]	5 years b
Iceland	03/09/58	02/09/89[2][3]	5 years
Ireland	25/02/53	25/02/53[2]	a
Italy	01/08/73	01/01/91	3 years
Liechtenstein	08/09/82	08/09/91	3 years
Lithuania			
Luxembourg	28/04/58	28/04/91[2][3]	5 years
Malta	01/05/87	01/05/92	5 years
Netherlands	31/08/54	01/09/79[2]	a
Norway	30/06/64	29/06/92[2][3]	5 years
Poland	01/05/93	01/05/93	3 years b
Portugal	09/11/78	09/11/78[2]	2 years b
Romania			
San Marino	22/03/89	22/03/92[2][3]	3 years
Slovakia	18/03/93 *	18/03/92[2][3]	5 years b
Slovenia			
Spain	15/10/79	15/10/90	5 years b
Sweden	13/05/66	13/05/91[2][3]	5 years
Switzerland	28/11/74	28/11/74[2]	a
Turkey	22/01/90	22/01/93	3 years
United Kingdom	14/01/66	14/01/91	5 years

1 Declarations made under Articles 25 and 46 respectively of the Convention also apply to Articles 1 to 4 of the First Protocol (European Treaty Series, No. 9) and to Articles 1 to 5 of Protocol No. 6 (European Treaty Series, No. 114) in those States which have ratified either one or both of these Protocols.

2 Declarations also applying to Articles 1 to 4 of Protocol No. 4 (European Treaty Series, No. 46).

3 Declarations also applying to Articles 1 to 5 of Protocol No. 7 (Euorpean Treaty Series, No. 117).

a Until otherwise decided or for an indefinite period.

b Declaration renewable by tacit agreement.

* The Czech and Slovak Federal Republic was a Contracting Party from 18.3.1992 to 31.12.1992. Following declarations made by the Czech Republic and Slovakia of their intention to succeed the Czech and Slovak Federal Republic and to consider themselves bound by the European Convention on Human Rights as of 1.1.1993, the Committee of Ministers decided on 30.6.1993 that these States are to be regarded as Parties to the Convention with effect from 1.1.1993. Similarly, these States are bound as of 1.1.1993 by the declarations made by the Czech and Slovak Federal Republic (18.3.1992) in respect of Articles 25 and 46 of the Convention.

Reservations and other declarations relating to the Convention[1] (including declarations made under Article 63)

Austria
Reservations contained in the instrument of ratification deposited on 3 September 1958 (Or. Germ.)
The Federal President declares the Convention to be ratified with the reservation:

1. The provisions of Article 5 of the Convention shall be so applied that there shall be no interference with the measures for the deprivation of liberty prescribed in the laws on administrative procedure, BGBl No. 172/1950, subject to review by the Administrative Court or the Constitutional Court as provided for in the Austrian Federal Constitution;

2. The provisions of Article 6 of the Convention shall be so applied that there shall be no prejudice to the principles governing public court hearings laid down in Article 90 of the 1929 version of the Federal Constitution Law.

Czech and Slovak Federal Republic [2]

Reservation contained in the instrument of ratification deposited on 18 March 1992 and in a Note Verbale from the Federal Ministry of Foreign Affairs, dated 13 March 1992 and handed to the Secretary General at the time of deposit of the instrument of ratification (Or. Cze./Engl.)

The Czech and Slovak Federal Republic in accordance with Article 64 of the Convention for the Protection of Human Rights and Funda-

---

1 [...]: Reservations and Declarations withdrawn by the member States.

2 The Czech and Slovak Federal Republic was a Contracting Party from 18.3.1992 to 31.12.1992. Following declarations made by the Czech Republic and Slovakia of their intention to succeed the Czech and Slovak Federal Republic and to consider themselves bound by the European Convention on Human Rights as of 1.1.1993, the Committee of Ministers decided on 30.6.1993 that these States are to be regarded as Parties to the Convention with effect from 1.1.1993. Similarly, these States are bound as of 1.1.1993 by the declarations made by the Czech and Slovak Federal Republic (18.3.1992) in respect of Articles 25 and 46 of the Convention.

mental Freedoms makes a reservation in respect of Articles 5 and 6 to the effect that those articles shall not hinder to impose disciplinary penitentiary measures in accordance with Article 17 of the Act No. 76/1959 of Collection of Laws, on Certain Service Conditions of Soldiers.

Declarations contained in a Note Verbale *from the Federal Ministry of Foreign Affairs, dated 13 March 1992 and handed to the Secretary General at the time of the deposit of the instrument of ratification, on 18 March 1992* (Or. Engl.)

The Czech and Slovak Federal Republic declares that for a period of five years, which will be tacitly renewed for further periods of five years, unless the Czech and Slovak Federal Republic withdraws its declaration before the expiration of the appropriate term:

a. recognises the competence of the European Commission of Human Rights to receive, in accordance with Article 25 of the Convention, petitions from any person, non-governmental organisation or group of individuals claiming to be the victim of a violation of the rights set forth in the Convention for the Protection of Human Rights and Fundamental Freedoms, in Articles 1 to 4 of Protocol No. 4 and in Articles 1 to 5 of Protocol No. 7, in case the violation of the rights guaranteed in these documents occurred after these documents came into force for the Czech and Slovak Federal Republic,

b. recognises, on condition of reciprocity, the jurisdiction of the European Court of Human Rights, in accordance with Article 46 of the Convention for the Protection of Human Rights and Fundamental Freedoms to interpret and apply the Convention, Articles 1 to 4 of Protocol No. 4 and Articles 1 to 5 of Protocol No. 7, in case the violation of the rights guaranteed in these documents occurred after these documents came into force for the Czech and Slovak Federal Republic.

Declaration contained in a Note Verbale *from the Permanent Representation dated 8 April 1992, registered at the Secretariat General on the same day* (Or. Fr.)

The Czech and Slovak Federal Republic, referring to Article 64, paragraph 2 of the Convention for the Protection of Human Rights and

Fundamental Freedoms concluded in Rome on 4 November 1950 and ratified by the Czech and Slovak Federal Republic on 18 March 1992, has the honour to inform that the terms of section 17 of the Law on certain conditions of service of members of the armed forces, No. 76/1959 in the Compendium of Legislation, are as follows:

"Section 17

Disciplinary Sanctions

1. Disciplinary sanctions shall comprise: a reprimand, penalties for petty offences, custodial penalties, demotion by one rank, and in the case of non-commissioned officers, reduction to the ranks.

2. Disciplinary custodial penalties shall comprise: confinement after duty, light imprisonment and house arrest.

3. The maximum duration of a disciplinary custodial penalty shall be 21 days."

Czech Republic

Letter addressed to the Secretary General on 23 July 1993 by the Minister for Foreign Affairs of the Czech Republic concerning reservations and declarations made earlier by the Czech and Slovak Federal Republic in respect of the Convention for the Protection of Human Rights and Fundamental Freedoms.

Referring to the letter of 17 January 1993 in which the Government of the Czech Republic expressed its willingness to feel bound, among others, by the Convention for the Protection of Human Rights and Fundamental Freedoms, including reservations and declarations to its provisions made earlier by the Czech and Slovak Federal Republic, I have the honour to communicate to Your Excellency the following.

The Government of the Czech Republic confirms that the Czech Republic considers itself bound by the Convention for the Protection of Human Rights and Fundamental Freedoms, as amended by Protocols No. 3, 5, 8, and by Protocols No. 1, 2, 4, 6, 7, 9 and 10. At the same time, the Government of the Czech Republic wishes to reconfirm the reservation made according to Article 64 of the Convention in respect of Articles 5 and 6 to the effect that those articles shall not hinder to impose disciplinary penitentiary measures in accordance with Article 17 of the Act No. 76/1959 of Collection of Laws, on Certain Service Conditions of Soldiers.

Finland

Reservation contained in the instrument of ratification deposited on 10 May 1990 (Or. Engl.)

In accordance with Article 64 of the Convention, the government of Finland makes the following reservation in respect of the right to a public hearing guaranteed by Article 6, paragraph 1 of the Convention.

For the time being, Finland cannot guarantee a right to an oral hearing insofar as the current Finnish laws do not provide such a right. This applies to:

1. proceedings before the Courts of Appeal, the Supreme Court, the Water Courts and the Water Court of Appeal in accordance with Chapter 26 Sections 7 and 8, as well as Chapter 30 Section 20, of the Code of Judicial Procedure, and Chapter 15 Section 23, as well as Chapter 16 Sections 14 and 39, of the Water Act;

2. proceedings before the County Administrative Courts and the Supreme Administrative Court in accordance with Section 16 of the County Administrative Courts Act and section 15 of the Supreme Administrative Court Act;

3. proceedings, which are held before the Insurance Court as the Court of Final Instance, in accordance with Section 9 of the Insurance Court Act;

4. proceedings before the Appellate Board for Social Insurance in accordance with Section 8 of the Decree on the Appellate Board for Social Insurance.

The provisions of the Finnish laws referred to above are attached to this reservation as a separate annex.

France

Reservations and declarations contained in the instrument of ratification deposited on 3 May 1974 (Or. Fr.)

In depositing this instrument of ratification, the government of the Republic makes the following declaration:

Articles 5 and 6

The government of the Republic, in accordance with Article 64 of the Convention, makes a reservation in respect of Articles 5 and 6 thereof, to the effect that those articles shall not hinder the application of the provisions governing the system of discipline in the armed forces contained in Section 27 of Act No. 72-662 of 13 July 1972, determining the general legal status of military servicemen, nor of the provisions of Article 375 of the Code of Military Justice.

[Article 10[1]

The government of the Republic declares that it interprets the provisions of Article 10 as being compatible with the system established in France under Act No. 72-553 of 10 July 1972, determining the legal status of the French Radio and Television.]

Article 15, paragraph 1

The government of the Republic, in accordance with Article 64 of the Convention, makes a reservation in respect of paragraph 1 of Article 15, to the effect, firstly, that the circumstances specified in Article 16 of the Constitution regarding the implementation of that Article, in Section 1 of the Act of 3 April 1878 and in the Act of 9 August 1849 regarding proclamation of a state of siege, and in Sec-

---

1 Declaration withdrawn by *Note Verbale* from the Permanent Representation of France dated 24 March 1988, registered at the Secretariat General, on 29 March 1988 (Or. Fr.)

tion 1 of Act No. 55-385 of 3 April 1955 regarding proclamation of a state of emergency, and in which it is permissible to apply the provisions of those texts, must be understood as complying with the purpose of Article 15 of the Convention and that, secondly, for the interpretation and application of Article 16 of the Constitution of the Republic, the terms to the extent strictly required by the exigencies of the situation shall not restrict the power of the President of the Republic to take the measures required by the circumstances.

The government of the Republic further declares that the Convention shall apply to the whole territory of the Republic, having due regard, where the overseas territories are concerned, to local requirements, as mentioned in Article 63.

Federal Republic of Germany

Reservation contained in the instrument of ratification deposited on 13 November 1952 (Or. Engl.)

In conformity with Article 64 of the Convention the Federal Republic of Germany makes the reservation that it will only apply the provisions of Article 7, paragraph 2 of the Convention within the limits of Article 103 clause 2 of the Basic Law of the Federal Republic of Germany. This provides that any act is only punishable if it was so by law before the offence was committed.

The territory to which the Convention shall apply extends also to Western Berlin.

Hungary

Reservation contained in the instrument of ratification, deposited on 5 November 1992 (Or. Engl.)

In accordance with Article 64 of the Convention, the Republic of Hungary makes the following reservation in respect of the right to access to courts guaranteed by Article 6, paragraph 1 of the Convention:

For the time being in proceedings for regulatory offences before the administrative authorities, Hungary cannot guarantee the right to access to courts, because the current Hungarian laws do not provide such right, the decision of the administrative authorities being final.

The relevant provisions of the Hungarian law referred to above are:

– Section 4 of Act IV of 1972 on courts, modified several times, which provides, that the courts, unless an Act stipulates otherwise, may review the legality of the decisions taken by the administrative authorities;

– An exception is contained in Section 71/A of Act I of 1968 on proceedings for regulatory offences, modified several times, which allows for the offender to request judicial review solely against the measures taken by the administrative authority to commute to confinements the fine the offender had been sentenced to pay; no other access to court against final decisions taken in proceedings for regulatory offences is permitted.

Ireland

Reservation contained in the instrument of ratification deposited on 25 February 1953 (Or. Engl.)

The government of Ireland do hereby confirm and ratify the aforesaid Convention and undertake faithfully to perform and carry out all the stipulations therein contained, subject to the reservation that they do not interpret Article 6, paragraph 3.c, of the Convention as requiring the provision of free legal assistance to any wider extent than is now provided in Ireland.

Liechtenstein

Reservations contained in the instrument of ratification deposited on 8 September 1982 (Or. Fr.)

[*Article 2*

In accordance with Article 64 of the Convention, the Principality of Liechtenstein makes the reservation that the principle of self-defence, as laid down in Article 2[1], paragraph 2, sub-paragraph a of the Convention, shall in the Principality of Liechtenstein also apply to the defence of property and freedom in accordance with the principles at present embodied in Article 2, paragraph g of the Liechtenstein Criminal Code of 27 May 1852.]

Article 6

In accordance with Article 64 of the Convention, the Principality of Liechtenstein makes the reservation that the principle that hearings must be held and judgments pronounced in public, as laid down in Article 6, paragraph 1 of the Convention, shall apply only within the limits deriving from the principles at present embodied in the following Liechtenstein laws:

– Act of 10 December 1912 on civil procedure, LGBl. 1912 No. 9/1

– Act of 10 December 1912 on the exercise of jurisdiction and the competence of the courts in civil cases, LGBl. 1912 No. 9/2

– Act of 31 December 1913 on the introduction of a code of criminal procedure, LGBl. 1914 No. 3

– Act of 21 April 1922 on non-contentious procedure, LGBl. 1922 No. 19

– Act of 21 April 1922 on national administrative justice, LGBl. 1922 No. 24

– Act of 5 November 1925 on the Supreme Court ("Haute Cour"), LGBl. 1925 No. 8

– Act of 30 January 1961 on national and municipal taxes, LGBl. 1961 No. 7

– Act of 13 November 1974 on the acquisition of immovable property, LGBl 1975 No. 5.

The statutory provisions of criminal procedure relating to juvenile delinquency, as contained in:

---

1 The withdrawal of this reservation was notified by letter from the head of the government dated 22 April 1991, registered at the Secretariat General on 26 April 1991 (Or. Fr.).

– the Criminal Code of 27 May 1852, Official Collection of Liechtenstein Acts and Regulations up to the year 1863
– the Act of 7 April 1922 on the organisation of the courts, LGBl. 1922 No. 16
– the Act of 1 June 1922 concerning the amending of the Criminal Act, the Code of Criminal Procedure and their additional and subordinate acts, LGBl. 1922 No. 21
– the Act of 23 December 1958 on the protection of young persons and social assistance for young persons, LGBl. 1959 No. 8.

Declaration dated 23 May 1991

On behalf of my government, I have the honour to inform you of the following modifications which have to be made in respect of Liechtenstein laws listed in the reservation made by the Principality of Liechtenstein on Article 6 paragraph 1 of the Convention:

Act of 31 December 1913 on the Introduction of a Code of Criminal Procedure, LGBl. 1914 No. 3 has been replaced by the Code of Criminal Procedure of 18 October 1988, LGBl. 1988 No. 62.

The statutory provisions of criminal procedure relating to juvenile delinquency have been enacted in the Act on Criminal Procedure in Matters of Junvenile Delinquency of 20 May 1987, LGBl. 1988 No. 39.

[Article 8[1]

In accordance with Article 64 of the Convention, the Principality of Liechtenstein makes the reservation that the right to respect for private life, as guaranteed by Article 8 of the Convention, shall be exercised, with regard to homosexuality, in accordance with the principles at present embodied in paragraphs 129 and 130 of the Liechtenstein Criminal Code of 27 May 1852.

In accordance with Article 64 of the Convention, the Principality of Liechtenstein makes the reservation that the right to respect for

---

1 The withdrawal of this reservation was notified by letter from the head of the government dated 22 April 1991, registered at the Secretariat General on 26 April 1991 (Or. Fr.).

family life, as guaranteed by Article 8 of the Convention, shall be exercised, with regard to the status of illegitimate children, in accordance with the principles at present embodied in the third chapter of the first part and the thirteenth chapter of the second part of the Liechtenstein Civil Code of 1 June 1811 and, with regard to the status of women in matrimonial and family law, in accordance with the principles at present embodied in the fifth chapter of the second part of the Marriage Act of 13 December 1973 (LGBl. 1974 No. 20) and the fourth chapter of the first part of the Liechtenstein Civil Code.

In accordance with Article 64 of the Convention, the Principality of Liechtenstein makes the reservation that the right to respect for family life, as guaranteed by Article 8 of the Convention, shall be exercised, with regard to aliens, in accordance with the principles at present embodied in the Ordinance of 9 September 1980 (LGBl. 1980 No. 66).]

Malta

Declaration made at the time of signature, on 12 December 1966 and contained in the instrument of ratification deposited on 23 January 1967 (Or. Engl.)

1. Declaration of interpretation

The government of Malta declares that it interprets paragraph 2 of Article 6 of the Convention in the sense that it does not preclude any particular law from imposing upon any person charged under such law the burden of proving particular facts.

2. The government of Malta, having regard to Article 64 of the Convention, and desiring to avoid any uncertainty as regards the application of Article 10 of the Convention declares that the Constitution of Malta allows such restrictions to be imposed upon public officers in regard to their freedom of expression as are reasonably justifiable in a democratic society. The Code of conduct of public officers in Malta precludes them from taking an active part in political discussions or other political activity during working hours or on official premises.

3. The government of Malta, having regard to Article 64 of the Convention declares that the principle of lawful defence admitted under sub-paragraph a of paragraph 2 of Article 2 of the Convention shall apply in Malta also to the defence of property to the extent required by the provisions of paragraphs a and b of section 238 of the Criminal Code of Malta, the text whereof, along with the text of the preceding section 237, is as follows:

"237. No offence is committed when a homicide or a bodily harm is ordered or permitted by law or by a lawful authority, or is imposed by actual necessity either in lawful self-defence or in the lawful defence of another person.

238. Cases of actual necessity of lawful defence shall include the following:

  a. where the homicide or bodily harm is committed in the act of repelling, during the night-time, the scaling or breaking of enclosures, walls, or the entrance doors of any house or inhabited apartment, or of the appurtenances thereof having a direct or an indirect communication with such house or apartment;

  b. where the homicide or bodily harm is committed in the act of defence against any person committing theft or plunder, with violence, or attempting to commit such theft or plunder;

  c. where the homicide or bodily harm is imposed by the actual necessity of the defence of one's own chastity or of the chastity of another person."

Netherlands

[*Declaration*[1] [2] *contained in the letter from the Permanent Representative of the Netherlands, and handed to the Secretary General*

---

1 By letter of 10 December 1980 from the Permanent Representative of the Netherlands, the reservation relating to Article 6 with regard to the Netherlands Antilles was withdrawn.

2 The Convention no longer applies to Surinam since this territory became independent on 25 November 1975.

at the time of the instrument of ratification on 1 December 1955 (Or. Fr.)

The Convention shall apply to Surinam and the Netherlands Antilles except as regards the provisions of free legal assistance under Article 6 (3) c.]

Declaration contained in a letter from the Permanent Representative of the Netherlands, dated 24 December 1985, registered at the Secretariat General on 3 January 1986 (Or. Engl.)

The island of Aruba, which is at present still part of the Netherlands Antilles, will obtain internal autonomy as a country within the Kingdom of the Netherlands as of 1 January 1986. Consequently the Kingdom will from then on no longer consist of two countries, namely the Netherlands (the Kingdom in Europe) and the Netherlands Antilles (situated in the Caribbean region), but will consist of three countries, namely the said two countries and the country Aruba.

As the changes being made on 1 January 1986 concern a shift only in the internal constitutional relations within the Kingdom of the Netherlands, and as the Kingdom as such will remain the subject under international law with which treaties are concluded, the said changes will have no consequences in international law regarding to treaties concluded by the Kingdom which already apply to the Netherlands Antilles, including Aruba. These treaties will remain in force for Aruba in its new capacity of country within the Kingdom. Therefore these treaties will as of 1 January 1986, as concerns the Kingdom of the Netherlands, apply to the Netherlands Antilles (without Aruba) and Aruba.

Consequently the treaties referred to in the annex, to which the Kingdom of the Netherlands is a Party and which apply to the Netherlands Antilles, will as of 1 January 1986 as concerns the Kingdom of the Netherlands apply to the Netherlands Antilles and Aruba.

Norway

[Reservation contained in the instrument of ratification deposited on 15 January 1952 (Or. Fr.)

Whereas Article 2 of the Norwegian Constitution of 17 May 1814 contains a provision under which Jesuits are not tolerated, a corresponding reservation is made with regard to the application of Article 9 of the Convention.][1]

Portugal

Reservations contained in the letter from the Permanent Representative of Portugal, dated 8 November 1978, handed to the Secretary General at the time of deposit of the instrument of ratification, on 9 November 1978 (Or. Fr.)

In pursuance of Article 64 of the Convention, the government of the Portuguese Republic formulates the following reservations:

I. Article 5 of the Convention will be applied subject to Articles 27 and 28 of the Military Discipline Regulations, which provide for the placing under arrest of members of the armed forces.

Articles 27 and 28 of the Military Discipline Regulations read as follows:

"Article 27

1. Arrests consist of the detention of the offender in a building intended for the purpose, in an appropriate place, barracks or military establishment, in suitable quarters on board ship or, failing these, in a place determined by the competent authority.

2. Between the reveille and sundown, during the period of detention, the members of the armed forces can perform the duties assigned to them.

---

1 On 4 December 1956 this reservation was withdrawn as a result of the abrogation of the constitutional provision in question.

Article 28

Close arrest consists of the detention of the offender in a building intended for the purpose."

II. Article 7 of the Convention will be applied subject to Article 309 of the Constitution of the Portuguese Republic, which provides for the indictment and trial of officers and personnel of the State Police Force (PIDE-DGS).

Article 309 of the Constitution reads as follows:

"Article 309

1. Law No. 8/75 of 25 July shall remain in force with the amendments made by Law No. 16/75 of 23 December and Law No. 18/75 of 28 December.

2. The offences referred to in Articles 2 (2), 3, 4 b and 5 of the Law referred to in the foregoing paragraph may be further defined by law.

3. The exceptional extenuating circumstances as provided for in Article 7 of the said Law may be specifically regulated by law.

(Act No. 8/75 lays down the penalties applicable to officers, officials and associates of the former General Directorate of Security (beforehand the International and State Defence Police), disbanded after 25 April 1974, and stipulates that the military courts have jurisdiction in such cases)."

[III.[1] Article 10 of the Convention will be applied subject to Article 38 (6) of the Constitution of the Portuguese Republic, which provides that the television may not be privately owned.

---

1 Reservation withdrawn by letter from the Permanent Representative of Portugal registered at the Secretariat General on 11 May 1987 (Or. Fr.).

Article 38 (6) of the Constitution reads as follows:

"Article 38

6. The television shall not be privately owned."

IV.[1] Article 11 of the Convention will be applied subject to Article 60 of the Constitution of the Portuguese Republic, which prohibits lock-outs.

Article 60 of the Constitution reads as follows:

"Article 60

Lock-outs shall be prohibited."

V.[1] Article 4 (3) b of the Convention will be applied subject to Article 276 of the Constitution of the Portuguese Republic, which provides for compulsory civic service.

Article 276 of the Constitution reads as follows:

"Article 276

1. The defence of the country is a fundamental duty of every Portuguese.

2. Military service shall be compulsory, for a period and on conditions to be laid down by law.

3. Persons considered unfit for armed military service and conscientious objectors shall perform unarmed military service or civic service suited to their situations.

4. Civic service may be established as a substitute for or as a complement to military service and may be made compulsory by law for citizens not subject to military service.

5. No citizen shall keep or obtain any office in the state or in any other public body if he fails to perform his military service or civic service, if compulsory.

---

1 Reservation withdrawn by letter from the Permanent Representative of Portugal registered at the Secretariat General on 11 May 1987 (Or. Fr.).

6. Performance by a citizen of military service or compulsory civic service shall be without prejudice to his post, social security benefits or permanent career."

VI.[1] Article 11 of the Convention will be applied subject to Article 46 (4) of the Constitution of the Portuguese Republic, which prohibits organisations with allegiance to a fascist ideology.

Article 46 (4) of the Constitution reads as follows:

"Article 46

4. Armed, military-type, militarised or para-military associations outside the state and the Armed Forces and organisations which adopt Fascist ideology shall not be permitted."]

San Marino

Declaration contained in the instrument of ratification deposited on 22 March 1989 (Or. It.)

The government of the Republic of San Marino, although confirming its firm undertaking neither to foresee nor to authorise derogations of any kind from the obligations subscribed, feels compelled to stress that the fact of being a State of limited territorial dimensions calls for particular care in matters of residence, work and social measures for foreigners even if they are not covered by the European Convention for the Protection of Human Rights and Fundamental Freedoms and the Protocols thereto.

Reservation contained in the instrument of ratification deposited on 22 March 1989 (Or. It.)

With regard to the provisions of Article 11 of the Convention on the right to form trade unions, the government of the Republic of San

---

1 Reservation withdrawn by letter from the Permanent Representative of Portugal registered at the Secretariat General on 11 May 1987 (Or. Fr.).

Marino declares that in San Marino two trade unions exist and are active, that Articles 2 and 4 of Law No. 7 of 17 February 1961 on the protection of employment and employees foresee that associations or trade unions must register with the Law Court and that such registration may be obtained provided the association includes at least six categories of employees and a minimum of 500 members.

Spain

Reservations and declarations made at the time of deposit of the instrument of ratification, on 4 October 1979 (Or. Sp.)

I. Reservations

In pursuance of Article 64 of the Convention, Spain makes reservations in respect of the application of the following provisions:

1. Articles 5 and 6, insofar as they may be incompatible with the disciplinary provisions concerning the Armed Forces, as they appear in Book 2, Part XV and Book 3, Part XXIV of the Code of Military Justice.

Brief statement of the relevant provisions:

The Code of Military Justice provides that the punishment of minor offences may be ordered directly by an offender's official superior, after having elucidated the facts. The punishment of serious offences is subject to an investigation of a judicial character, in the course of which the accused must be given a hearing. The penalties and the power to impose them are defined by law. In any case, the accused can appeal against the punishment to his immediate superior and so on, up to the Head of State.

(These provisions have been replaced by Basic Law 12/1985 of 27 November — Chapter II of Part III and Chapters II, III and IV of Part IV — concerning the disciplinary regime of the Armed Forces, which entered into force on 1 June 1986.

The new legislation amended the former provisions by reducing the duration of the sanctions imposing deprivation of liberty which can be applied without judicial intervention by increasing the guarantees of persons during the preliminary investigation.

By letter of 28 May 1986 the Permanent Representative of Spain nevertheless confirmed Spain's reservation to Articles 5 and 6 to the extent to which those articles might be incompatible with the latter law.)

2. Article 11, insofar as it may be incompatible with Articles 28 and 127 of the Spanish Constitution.

Brief statement of the relevant provisions:

Article 28 of the Constitution recognises the right to organise, but provides that legislation may restrict the exercise of this right or make it subject to exception in the case of the armed forces or other corps subject to military discipline and shall regulate the manner of its exercise in the case of civil servants.

Article 127, paragraph 1, specifies that serving judges, law officers and prosecutors may not belong to either political parties or trade unions and provides that legislation shall lay down the system and modalities as to the professional association of these groups.

II. *Interpretative Declarations*

Spain declares that it interprets:

1. The provisions of the last sentence in Article 10, paragraph 1, as being compatible with the present system governing the organisation of radio and television broadcasting in Spain.

2. The provisions of Articles 15 and 17 to the effect that they permit the adoption of the measures contemplated in Articles 55 and 116 of the Spanish Constitution.

At the time of deposit of the instrument of ratification of the Convention for the Protection of Human Rights and Fundamental

Freedoms, on 29 September 1979, Spain formulated a reservation to Articles 5 and 6 to the extent to which those Articles might be incompatible with the provisions of the Code of Military Justice — Chapter XV of Part II and Chapter XXIV of Part III — concerning the disciplinary regime of the Armed Forces.

I have the honour to inform you, for communication to the Parties to the Convention, that these provisions have been replaced by Basic Law 12/1985 of 27 November — Chapter II of Part III and Chapters II, III and IV of Part IV — concerning the disciplinary regime of the Armed Forces, which will enter into force on 1 June 1986.

The new legislation amends the former provisions by reducing the duration of the sanctions imposing deprivation of liberty which can be applied without judicial intervention by increasing the guarantees of persons during the preliminary investigation.

Spain confirms nevertheless its reservation to Articles 5 and 6 to the extent to which those Articles might be incompatible with the provisions of Basis Law 12/1985 of 27 November — Chapter II of Part III and Chapters II, III and IV of Part IV — concerning the disciplinary regime of the Armed Forces, which will enter into force on 1 June 1986.

Switzerland

Reservations and Declarations contained in the instrument of ratification deposited on 28 November 1974 (Or. Fr.)

[Reservation in respect of Article 5[1]

The provisions of Article 5 of the Convention shall not affect the operation of the cantonal legislation authorising the detention of certain categories of persons by decision of an administrative authority or cantonal provisions governing the procedure for placing a child or ward in an institution in accordance with federal legislation on

---

1 The withdrawal of this reservation was notified by letter from the Head of the Federal Department for Foreign Affairs dated 26 January 1982, with effect from 1 January 1982.

paternal authority or guardianship (Articles 284, 386, 406 and 421.13 of the Swiss Civil Code).]

Reservation in respect of Article 6

The rule contained in Article 6, paragraph 1, of the Convention that hearings shall be public shall not apply to proceedings relating to the determination of civil rights and obligations or of any criminal charge which, in accordance with cantonal legislation, are heard before an administrative authority.

The rule that judgment must be pronounced publicly shall not affect the operation of cantonal legislation on civil or criminal procedure providing that judgment shall not be delivered in public but notified to the parties in writing.

Declaration on the interpretation of Article 6, paragraph 1[1]

The Swiss Federal Council considers that the guarantee of fair trial in Article 6, paragraph 1 of the Convention, in the determination of civil rights and obligations or any criminal charge against the person in question is intended solely to ensure ultimate control by the judiciary over the acts or decisions of the public authorities relating to such rights or obligations or the determination of such a charge.

Declaration on the interpretation of Article 6, paragraph 3, sub-paragraphs c and e

The Swiss Federal Council declares that it interprets the guarantee of free legal assistance and the free assistance of an interpreter, in Article 6, paragraph 3, c and e of the Convention, as not permanently absolving the beneficiary from payment of the resulting costs.

---

1 See below.

Declaration contained in a letter from the Head of the Federal Department for Foreign Affairs dated 16 May 1988, registered at the Secretariat General on 19 May 1988 (Or. Fr.)

The declaration on the interpretation of Article 6, paragraph 1, contained in the instrument of ratification deposited by Switzerland on 28 November 1974 has been considered invalid in the context of a case concerning the determination of a criminal charge; further to the judgment delivered by the European Court of Human Rights on 29 April 1988 in the Belilos case (20/1986/118/167) the scope of the declaration is limited solely to the determination of civil rights and obligations, under the said provision.

As of 29 April 1988 the above-mentioned declaration shall read as follows:

"The Swiss Federal Council considers that the guarantee of fair trial in Article 6, paragraph 1 of the Convention in the determination of civil rights and obligations is intended solely to ensure ultimate control by the judiciary over the acts or decisions of the public authorities relating to such rights or obligations. For the purpose of the present declaration, ultimate control by the judiciary" shall mean a control by the judiciary limited to the application of the law, such as a cassation control."

Declaration appended to a letter from the Federal Department for Foreign Affairs dated 23 December 1988, registered at the Secretariat General on 28 December 1988 and modified[1] by a letter from the Permanent Representation dated 13 February 1989 (Or. Fr.)

Submission pursuant to Article 64, paragraph 2 of the European Convention on Human Rights, of a list and brief statement of the federal and cantonal legislative provisions covered, with effect from 29 April 1988, by the interpretative declaration on Article 6, paragraph 1 of the Convention issued by the Swiss Federal Council on 28 November 1974 and clarified on 16 May 1988 following the Beli-

---

1 Note from the Secretariat: The amendment concerned the text with regard to Article 79 of the federal Law on administrative procedure of 20 December 1968.

los judgment delivered on 29 April 1988 by the European Court of Human Rights.

As announced on 16 May 1988 upon submission of the clarification of the interpretative on Article 6, paragraph 1 of the European Convention on Human Rights to the Secretary General of the Council of Europe, Switzerland pursuant to Article 64, paragraph 2 of the Convention submits the following list of federal and cantonal legislative provisions covered with effect from 29 April 1988, by the interpretative declaration issued by the Swiss Federal Council on 28 November 1974 and clarified on 16 May 1988.

In view of the continuing uncertainty under the case-law of the European Court of Human Rights concerning the scope of Article 6, paragraph 1 of the Convention where the concept of the "determination of civil rights and obligations" is concerned, the Federal Council is unable to give an exhaustive list of the federal and cantonal legislative provisions it wishes to be covered by the above-mentioned interpretative declaration. Pending clarification by the European Court of Human Rights or the Committee of Ministers by way of case-law or in prescriptive form, the Swiss Federal Council believes that this list cannot be regarded as exhaustive and in no way predetermines the standpoint the Federal Council might adopt in a particular case as to the scope of the concept of the "determination of civil rights and obligations".

United Kingdom

Declaration contained in a letter from the Permanent Representative dated 23 October 1953, registered at the Secretariat General on 23 October 1953 (Or. Engl.)

Her Majesty's Government have considered the extension of the European Convention of Human Rights to those territories for whose international relations they are responsible and in which that Convention would be applicable.

In accordance with the provisions of Article 63 of the Convention, Her Majesty's Government in the United Kingdom declare that the European Convention on Human Rights signed in Rome on the 4th

November 1950 shall extend to those territories on the enclosed list for whose international relations they are responsible.

Aden Colony
The Bahamas
Barbados
Basutoland
Bechuanaland
Bermuda
British Guiana
British Honduras
British Solomon Islands
Channel Islands:
   The Bailiwick of Jersey
   The Bailiwick of Guernsey
Cyprus
Falklands Islands
Fiji
Gambia
Gilbert and Ellice Islands
Gold Coast
Jamaica
Kenya
Gibraltar
Leeward Islands
Federation of Malaya

Malta
Isle of Man
Mauritius
Nigeria
Northern Rhodesia
North Borneo
Nyassaland
St Helena
Sarawak
Seychelles
Sierra Leone
Singapore
Somaliland
Swaziland
Tanganyika
Trinidad
Uganda
Windward Islands:
   Dominica
   Grenada
   St Lucia
   St Vincent
Zanzibar

and at the request of the government of that Kingdom, for whose international relations Her Majesty's Government in the United Kingdom is responsible, Kingdom of Tonga.

Declaration contained in a letter from the Permanent Representative dated 9 June 1964, registered at the Secretariat General on 10 June 1964 (Or. Engl.)

I have the honour to inform you, with reference to Mr Scarlett's letter (61/48/53) of October 23, 1953 on the extension of the European Human Rights Convention to certain territories for whose international relations Her Majesty's Government were responsible, that of the territories named in that declaration, the following have since become independent:

Cyprus, August 16, 1960
Gold Coast (Ghana), March 6, 1957
Jamaica, August 6, 1962
Kenya, December 12, 1963
Federation of Malaya, August 31, 1957
Federation of Nigeria, including North and South Cameroons, October 1, 1960
South Cameroons, June 1, 1961
North Cameroons, October 1, 1961

> (These two territories were under United Kingdom Trustee-ship and administered with Nigeria until Nigerian independence. A plebiscite was then held and North Cameroons opted to join Nigeria and South Cameroons to join the Cameroon Republic.)

North Borneo, September 16, 1963
Sarawak, September 16, 1963
Sierra Leone, April 27, 1961
Singapore, September 16, 1963
Somaliland, June 26, 1960
Tanganyika, December 9, 1961
Trinidad and Tobago, August 31, 1962
Uganda, October 9, 1962
Zanzibar, December 10, 1963

2. The responsibilities which Her Majesty's Government assumed under the European Human Rights Convention on behalf of these countries lapsed on the dates indicated.

3. I enclose a revised list of the territories for whose international relations Her Majesty's Government are now responsible, and to which the European Convention on Human Rights has been extended.

List of territories for whose international relations Her Majesty's Government in the United Kingdom are responsible and to which the European Convention on Human Rights has been extended:

State of Aden
The Bahamas
Barbados
Basutoland
Bechuanaland
Bermuda
British Guiana
British Honduras
British Solomon Islands
Channel Islands:
    The Bailiwick of Jersey
    The Bailiwick of Guernsey
Falkland Islands
Fiji
Gambia
Gilbert and Ellice Islands

Gibraltar
Leeward Islands
Malta
Isle of Man
Mauritius
Northern Rhodesia
Nyassaland
St Helena
Seychelles
Kingdom of Tonga
Windward Islands:
    Dominica
    Grenada
    St Lucia
    St Vincent

Foreign Office - May 1964

Declaration contained in a letter from the Permanent Representative dated 12 August 1964, registered at the Secretariat General on 14 August 1964 (Or. Engl.)

In my letter of June 9th, 1964, I enclosed a list of territories for whose international relations Her Majesty's Government are responsible and to which the European Convention on Human Rights has been extended.

I regret that certain omissions were made in this list and I therefore have the honour to transmit to you the enclosed revised list of the territories in question. I should be grateful if you would circulate this to member governments as an amendment. I should also be grateful if, following its independence dating from July 6th, Malawi could be added to the list of territories which have become independent since the 1953 declaration.

List of territories for whose international relations Her Majesty's Government in the United Kingdom are responsible and to which the European Convention on Human Rights has been extended:

State of Aden
The Bahamas
Barbados
Basutoland
Bechuanaland
Bermuda
British Guiana
British Honduras
British Solomon Islands
Cayman Islands
Channel Islands:
  The Bailiwick of Jersey
  The Bailiwick of Guernsey
Falkland Islands
Fiji
Gambia
Gilbert and Ellice Islands
Gibraltar
Leeward Islands:

Antigua
British Virgin Islands
Montserrat
St Christopher-Nevis-
  Anguilla
Malta
Isle of Man
Mauritius
Northern Rhodesia
St Helena
Seychelles
Kingdom of Tonga
Turks and Caicos Islands
Windward Islands:
  Dominica
  Grenada
  St Lucia
  St Vincent

Foreign Office - August 1964

*Declaration contained in a letter from the Permanent Representa-
tive dated 5 August 1966, registered at the Secretariat General on
5 August 1966 (Or. Engl.)*

I have the honour to inform you that since May 1964 the following
territories have become independent and that as a consequence Her
Majesty's Government's responsibilities in respect of them under the
European Human Rights Convention lapsed on the dates indicated:

Malta, 21 September, 1964
Northern Rhodesia (now Zambia), 24 October, 1964
The Gambia, 18 February, 1965
British Guiana (now Guyana) 26 May, 1966

I have also been instructed to transmit to you the enclosed revised
list of the territories for whose international relations Her Majesty's
Government are still responsible, and to which the European Convention on Human Rights was extended in their declaration of the
23rd of October 1953.

List of territories for whose international relations Her Majesty's Government in the United Kingdom are responsible and to which the European Convention on Human Rights has been extended:

State of Aden
The Bahamas
Barbados
Basutoland
Bechuanaland
Bermuda
British Honduras
British Solomon Islands
Cayman Islands
Channel Islands:
   The Bailiwick of Jersey
   The Bailiwick of Guernsey
Falkland Islands
Fiji
Gilbert and Ellice Islands
Gibraltar
Leeward Islands:

Antigua
British Virgin Islands
Montserrat
St Christopher-Nevis-
   Anguilla
Isle of Man
Mauritius
St Helena
Seychelles
Swaziland
Kingdom of Tonga
Turks and Caicos Islands
Windward Islands:
   Dominica
   Grenada
   St Lucia
   St Vincent

Foreign Office - August 1966

Declaration contained in a letter from the Permanent Representative dated 12 January 1967, registered at the Secretariat General on 13 January 1967 (Or. Engl.)

I have the honour to inform you that since July 1966 the following territories have become independent, and that as a consequence Her Majesty's Government's responsibilities in respect of them under the European Human Rights Convention lapsed on the dates indicated:

Bechuanaland (now Botswana), 30 September, 1966
Basutoland (now Lesotho), 4 October, 1966
Barbados, 30 November, 1966

Declaration contained in a letter from the Permanent Representative dated 12 September 1967, registered at the Secretariat General on 12 September 1967 (Or. Engl.)

On instructions from Her Majesty's Principal Secretary of State for Foreign Affairs I have the honour to declare, in accordance with the provisions of Article 63(1) of the Convention for the Protection of Human Rights and Fundamental Freedoms, signed at Rome on the 4th November 1950, that the Convention shall hereby extend to the State of Brunei.

Declaration contained in a letter from the Permanent Representative dated 12 June 1969, registered at the Secretariat General, on 13 June 1969 (Or. Engl.)

I have the honour to inform you that since January 1967 the following territories have become independent, and that as a consequence Her Majesty's Government responsabilities in respect of them under the European Human Rights Convention lapsed on the dates indicated:

State of Aden, 30 November 1967
Mauritius, 12 March 1968
Swaziland, 6 September 1968

Declaration contained in a letter from the Permanent Representative dated 30 June 1969, registered at the Secretariat General, on 1 July 1969 (Or. Engl.)

List of territories for whose international relations Her Majesty's Government in the United Kingdom are responsible and to which the European Convention on Human Rights has been extended:

The Bahamas
Bermuda
British Honduras
British Solomon Islands
Cayman Islands
Channel Islands:
   The Bailiwick of Jersey
   The Bailiwick of Guernsey
Falkland Islands
Fiji
Gilbert and Ellice Islands
Gibraltar
Leeward Islands:
   Antigua
   British Virgin Islands

Montserrat
St Christopher-Nevis-
   Anguilla
Isle of Man
St Helena
Seychelles
State of Brunei
Kingdom of Tonga
Turks and Caicos Islands
Windward Islands:
   Dominica
   Grenada
   St Lucia
   St Vincent

June 1969

Declaration contained in a Note Verbale *from the Permanent Representative dated 17 January 1979, registered at the Secretariat General, on 18 January 1979* (Or. Engl.)

Her Majesty's Government in the United Kingdom ceased to be responsible on the dates shown below for the international relations of the following territories, to which the European Convention on Human Rights had been extended under Article 63:

British Solomon Islands, 7 July 1978
Seychelles, 28 June 1976
Tuvalu, 1 October 1978
Dominica, 3 November 1978

Declaration contained in a Note Verbale *from the Permanent Representative dated 29 March 1979, registered at the Secretariat General, on 30 March 1979* (Or. Engl.)

Her Majesty's Government in the United Kingdom ceased to be responsible on 22 February 1979 for the international relations of the territory of St Lucia, to which the European Convention on Human Rights had been extended under Article 63.

Declaration contained in a Note Verbale *from the Permanent Representative dated 27 July 1979, registered at the Secretariat General, on 30 July 1979* (Or. Engl.)

Her Majesty's Government in the United Kingdom ceased to be responsible on 12 July 1979 for the international relations of the Gilbert Islands (Kiribati), to which the European Convention on Human Rights had been extended under Article 63.

Declaration contained in a Note Verbale *from the Permanent Representative dated 22 February 1980, registered at the Secretariat General, on 27 February 1980* (Or. Engl.)

Her Majesty's Government in the United Kingdom ceased to be responsible on 27 October 1979 for the international relations of the territory of St. Vincent, to which the Convention on Human Rights had been extended under Article 63.

Declaration contained in a letter from the Permanent Representative dated 30 September 1981, registered at the Secretariat General, on 1 October 1981 (Or. Engl.)

I have the honour to refer to Article 63 of the Convention for the Protection of Human Rights and Fundamental Freedoms, under which the Convention was extended to Belize in 1953.

On instructions from Her Majesty's Principal Secretary of State for Foreign and Commonwealth Affairs, I now have the honour to inform you that since the independence of Belize from 21 September 1981, the government of the United Kingdom is no longer responsible for this territory.

Declaration contained in a letter from the Permanent Representative dated 2 December 1981, registered at the Secretary General, 14 December 1981 (Or. Engl.)

I have the honour to refer to Article 63 of the Convention for the Protection of Human Rights and Fundamental Freedoms, under which the Convention was extended to the Leeward Islands (including Antigua) in 1953.

On instructions from Her Majesty's Principal Secretary of State for Foreign and Commonwealth Affairs, I now have the honour to inform you that since the independence of Antigua and Barbuda (as Antigua is now known) from 1 November 1981, the government of the United Kingdom is no longer responsible for this territory.

Declaration contained in a letter from the Permanent Representative dated 8 November 1983, registered at the Secretariat General, on 9 November 1983 (Or. Engl.)

I have the honour to refer to Article 63 of the Convention for the Protection of Human Rights and Fundamental Freedoms, under which the Convention was extended to the Leeward Islands (including St Kitts-Nevis) in 1953.

On instructions from Her Majesty's Principal Secretary of State for Foreign and Commonwealth Affairs, I now have the honour to inform you that since the independence of St Kitts-Nevis from 19 September 1983, the government of the United Kingdom is no longer responsible for this territory.

Declaration contained in a letter from the Permanent Representative dated 3 April 1984, registered at the Secretariat General, on 3 April 1984 (Or. Engl.)

I have the honour to refer to Article 63 of the Convention for the Protection of Human Rights and Fundamental Freedoms, under which the Convention was extended to Brunei on 12 September 1967.

On instructions from Her Majesty's Principal Secretary of State for Foreign and Commonwealth Affairs, I now have the honour to inform you that since Brunei Darussalam resumed full international responsibility as a sovereign and independent state on 31 December 1983, the government of the United Kingdom is no longer responsible for her external affairs.

List of territories for whose international relations Her Majesty's Government in the United Kingdom are responsible and to which the European Convention on Human Rights has been extended:

Anguilla	Guernsey
Bermuda	Isle of Man
British Virgin Islands	Jersey
Cayman Islands	Montserrat
Falkland Islands	St Helena
Gibraltar	Turks and Caicos Islands

April 1984

Reservations and other declarations relating to Protocol No. 2

Federal Republic of Germany

Declaration contained in a letter from the Permanent Representative of the Federal Republic of Germany, dated 3 January 1969, handed to the Secretary General at the time of deposit of the instrument of ratification on the same day (Or. Germ.)

I have the honour to declare, on behalf of the government of the Federal Republic of Germany and on the occasion of the deposit, that Protocols No. 2, No. 3 and No. 5 to the Convention on the Protection of Human Rights and Fundamental Freedoms, shall also apply to the Land Berlin with effect from the date on which they enter into force in respect of the Federal Republic of Germany.

Greece

Declaration made at the time of deposit of the instrument of ratification, on 8 January 1975 (Or. Fr.)

In depositing this instrument of ratification, the Permanent Representative stated that Protocols Nos. 2, 3 and 5 shall enter into force in respect of Greece with effect from 28 November 1974, date of the deposit of the instrument of ratification of the Convention of 4 November 1950 and of the Protocol of 20 March 1952. He recalled the declaration made by the Minister for Foreign Affairs of Greece on 28 November 1974, at the time of deposit of the instrument of ratification of the Convention and the said Protocol and at the occasion of signature of Protocol No. 5 of 20 January 1966, according to which Greece should complete with a minimum of delay the whole set of instruments relating to the Convention with effect from 28 November 1974.

Netherlands

Declaration contained in the instrument of ratification, deposited on 11 October 1966 (Or. Fr.)

We approve herewith, for the Kingdom of Europe, Surinam and the Dutch West Indies, in respect of all the provisions contained therein, the Protocol reproduced above.

Declaration contained in a letter from the Permanent Representative of the Netherlands, dated 24 December 1985, registered at the Secretariat General on 3 January 1986 (Or. Engl.)

The island of Aruba, which is at present still part of the Netherlands Antilles, will obtain internal autonomy as a country within the Kingdom of the Netherlands as of 1 January 1986. Consequently the Kingdom will from then on no longer consist of two countries, namely the Netherlands (the Kingdom in Europe) and the Netherlands Antilles (situated in the Caribbean region), but will consist of three countries, namely the said two countries and the country Aruba.

As the changes being made on 1 January 1986 concern a shift only in the internal constitutional relations within the Kingdom of the Netherlands, and as the Kingdom as such will remain the subject under international law with which treaties are concluded, the said changes will have no consequences in international law regarding to treaties concluded by the Kingdom which already apply to the Netherlands Antilles, including Aruba. These treaties will remain in force for Aruba in its new capacity of country within the Kingdom. Therefore these treaties will as of 1 January 1986, as concerns the Kingdom of the Netherlands, apply to the Netherlands Antilles (without Aruba) and Aruba.

Consequently the treaties referred to in the annex, to which the Kingdom of the Netherlands is a Party and which apply to the Netherlands Antilles, will as of 1 January 1986 as concerns the Kingdom of the Netherlands apply to the Netherlands Antilles and Aruba.

Reservations and other declarations relating to the First Protocol to the Convention

Austria

Reservation contained in the instrument of ratification deposited on 3 September 1958 (Or. Germ.)

... being desirous of avoiding any uncertainty concerning the application of Article 1 of the Protocol in connection with the State Treaty of 15 May 1955 for the Restoration of an Independent and Democratic Austria, (the Federal President) declares the Protocol ratified with the reservations that there shall be no interference with the provisions of Part IV "Claims arising out of the War" and Part V "Property, Rights and Interests" of the above-mentioned State Treaty.

Bulgaria

Reservation and Declaration contained in the instrument of ratification deposited on 7 September 1992 (Or.Fr.)

Reservation

The terms of the second provision of Article 1 of the Protocol shall not affect the scope or content of Article 22, paragraph 1, of the Constitution of the Republic of Bulgaria, which states that: "No foreign physical person or foreign legal entity shall acquire ownership over land, except through legal inheritance. Ownership thus acquired shall be duly transferred."

Declaration

The second provision of Article 2 of the Protocol must not be interpreted as imposing on the State additional financial commitments relating to educational establishments with a specific philosophical or religious orientation other than the commitments of the Bulgarian State provided for in the Constitution and in legislation in force in the country.

France

Declaration contained in the instrument of ratification deposited on 3 May 1974 (Or. Fr.)

In depositing this instrument of ratification, the government of the Republic declares that the Protocol shall apply to the whole territory of the Republic, having due regard, where the overseas territories are concerned, to local requirements, as mentioned in Article 63 of the Convention for the Protection of Human Rights and Fundamental Freedoms.

Federal Republic of Germany

Declarations made at the time of ratification on 13 February 1957 (Or. Germ.)

The Federal Republic of Germany adopts the opinion according to which the second sentence of Article 2 of the (First) Protocol entails no obligation on the part of the State to finance schools of a religious or philosophical nature, or to assist in financing such schools, since this question, as confirmed by the concurring declaration of the Legal Committee of the Consultative Assembly and the Secretary General of the Council of Europe, lies outside the scope of the Convention for the Protection of Human Rights and Fundamental Freedoms and of its Protocol.

The Protocol of the Convention for the Protection of Human Rights and Fundamental Freedoms, signed at Paris on 20 March 1952, applies also to the Land Berlin with effect from 13 February 1957, the date on which the Protocol entered into force in respect of the Federal Republic of Germany.

Greece

Reservation contained in the instrument of ratification deposited on 28 November 1974 (Or. Fr.)

For the application of Article 2 of the 1952 Protocol, the government of Greece, in view of certain provisions of the Education Acts in force in Greece, formulates a reservation according to which the principle affirmed in the second sentence of Article 2, is accepted only so far as it is compatible with the provision of efficient instruction and training, and the avoidance of unreasonable public expenditure.

[*Reservation[1] contained in a letter from the Permanent Representative of Greece, dated 23 August 1979, registered at the Secretariat General on 24 August 1979* (Or. Fr.)

The application of the word "philosophical" which is the penultimate word of the sentence of Article 2, will, in Greece, conform with the relevant provisions of internal legislation.]

Ireland

Declaration contained in the instrument of ratification deposited on 25 February 1953 (Or. Engl.)

At the time of signing the (First) Protocol the Irish Delegate puts on record that, in the view of the Irish government, Article 2 of the Protocol is not sufficiently explicit in ensuring to parents the right to provide education for their children in their homes or in schools of the parents' own choice, whether or not such schools are private schools or are schools recognised or established by the State.

Luxembourg

Reservation made at the time of deposit of the instrument of ratification on 3 September 1953 (Or. Fr.)

The government of the Grand Duchy of Luxembourg, having regard to Article 64 of the Convention and desiring to avoid any uncertainty as regards the application of Article 1 of the Protocol in relation to the Luxembourg Law of 26 April 1951 concerning the liquidation of certain ex-enemy property, rights and interests subject to measures

---

1 Reservation withdrawn with effect from 1 January 1984, by a Declaration from the President of the Greek Republic, dated 26 January 1985.

of sequestration, makes a reservation relating to the provisions of the above-mentioned Law of 26 April 1951.

Malta

Declaration made at the time of signature, on 12 December 1966, and contained in the instrument of ratification deposited on 23 January 1967 (Or. Engl.)

The government of Malta, having regard to Article 64 of the Convention, declares that the principle affirmed in the second sentence of Article 2 of the Protocol is accepted by Malta only in so far as it is compatible with the provision of efficient instruction and training, and the avoidance of unreasonable public expenditure, having regard to the fact that the population of Malta is overwhelmingly Roman Catholic.

Netherlands

Declaration contained in a letter from the Permanent Representative of the Netherlands, dated 29 November 1955 handed to the Secretary General at the time of deposit of the instrument of ratification on 1 December 1955 (Or. Fr.)

In the opinion of the Netherlands government, the State should not only respect the rights of parents in the matter of education but, if need be, ensure the possibility of exercising those rights by appropriate financial measures.

The Protocol shall apply to Surinam and the Netherlands Antilles.[1]

Declaration contained in a letter from the Permanent Representative of the Netherlands, dated 24 December 1985, registered at the Secretariat General on 3 January 1986 (Or. Engl.)

The island of Aruba, which is at present still part of the Netherlands Antilles, will obtain internal autonomy as a country within the King-

---

1 The Protocol no longer applies to Surinam since this territory became independent on 25 November 1975.

dom of the Netherlands as of 1 January 1986. Consequently the Kingdom will from then on no longer consist of two countries, namely the Netherlands (the Kingdom in Europe) and the Netherlands Antilles (situated in the Caribbean region), but will consist of three countries, namely the said two countries and the country Aruba.

As the changes being made on 1 January 1986 concern a shift only in the internal constitutional relations within the Kingdom of the Netherlands, and as the Kingdom as such will remain the subject under international law with which treaties are concluded, the said changes will have no consequences in international law regarding to treaties concluded by the Kingdom which already apply to the Netherlands Antilles, including Aruba. These treaties will remain in force for Aruba in its new capacity of country within the Kingdom. Therefore these treaties will as of 1 January 1986, as concerns the Kingdom of the Netherlands, apply to the Netherlands Antilles (without Aruba) and Aruba.

Consequently the treaties referred to in the annex, to which the Kingdom of the Netherlands is a Party and which apply to the Netherlands Antilles, will as of 1 January 1986 as concerns the Kingdom of the Netherlands apply to the Netherlands Antilles and Aruba.

Portugal

[Reservations[1] contained in the letter from the Permanent Representative of Portugal, dated 8 November 1978 handed to the Secretary General at the time of deposit of the instrument of ratification on 9 November 1978 (Or. Fr.)

As regards the Protocol, the government of the Portuguese Republic formulates the following reservations:

---

1 Reservations withdrawn by letter from the Permanent Representative of Portugal registered at the Secretariat General on 11 May 1987 (Or. Fr.).

VII. Article 1 of the Protocol will be applied subject to Article 82 of the Constitution of the Portuguese Republic, which provides that expropriations of large landowners, big property owners and entrepreneurs or shareholders may be subject to no compensation under the conditions to be laid down by the law.

Article 82 of the Constitution reads as follows:

"*Article 82*

1. The law shall determine the methods and forms of intervention, nationalisation and socialisation of the means of production and criteria for fixing compensation.

2. The law may stipulate that expropriations of large landowners, big property owners and entrepreneurs or shareholders shall not be subject to any compensation whatsoever."

VIII. Article 2 of the Protocol will be applied subject to Articles 43 and 75 of the Constitution of the Portuguese Republic, which provide for the non-denominationality of public education, the supervision of private education by the State and the validity of legal provisions concerning the setting-up of private educational establishments.

Articles 43 and 75 of the Constitution read as follows:

"*Article 43*

1. The freedom to learn and teach shall be safeguarded.

2. The State shall not arrogate to itself the right to plan education and culture in accordance with any philosophical, aesthetic, political, ideological or religious guidelines.

3. Public education shall not be denominational."

"Article 75

1. The State shall establish a network of official education institutions to meet the needs of the whole population.
2. The State shall supervise private education which is complementary to public education."

San Marino

Reservation contained in the instrument of ratification deposited on 22 March 1989 (Or. It.)

The government of the Republic of San Marino declares that having regard to the provisions of law in force which govern the use of goods in conformity with the general interest, the principle set forth in Article 1 of the Additional Protocol to the Convention for the Protection of Human Rights and Fundamental Freedoms, opened for signature, in Paris, on 20 March 1952, has no bearing on the regulations in force concerning the real estate of foreign citizens.

Spain

Reservation and Declaration contained in the instrument of ratification deposited on 27 November 1990 (Or. Sp./Fr.)

Reservation

In accordance with Article 64 of the Convention for the Protection of Human Rights and Fundamental Freedoms, in order to avoid any uncertainty as to the application of Article 1 of the Protocol, Spain expresses a Reservation in the light of Article 33 of the Spanish Constitution, which stipulates the following:

"1. The right to private property and to inheritance is recognised.
2. The social function of these rights shall determine their scope, as provided for by law.
3. No person shall be deprived of their property or their rights except for a cause recognised as being in the public interest or in the interest of society and in exchange for fitting compensation as provided for by law."

Declaration

In accordance with Article 5 of the Protocol, Spain reiterates its previous declarations concerning Articles 25 and 46 of the European Convention on Human Rights and accordingly recognises the competence of the European Commission of Human Rights and the jurisdiction of the European Court of Human Rights in connection with applications concerning facts subsequent to the date of deposit of the instrument of ratification of the Protocol, and in particular internal expropriation procedures set in motion subsequent to that date.

Sweden

Reservation made at the time of the deposit of the instrument of ratification on 22 June 1953 (Or. Fr.)

... We do ratify, approve and accept the Protocol (First) with all its Articles and clauses with the reservation in respect of Article 2 of the Protocol, to the effect that Sweden could not grant to parents the right to obtain, by reason of their philosophical convictions, dispensation for their children from the obligation of taking part in certain parts of the education in the public schools, and also to the effect that the dispensation from the obligation of taking part in the teaching of Christianity in these schools could only be granted for children of another faith than the Swedish church in respect of whom a satisfactory religious instruction had been arranged. This reservation is based on the provisions of the new rule of 17 March 1933 for the establishment of secondary education within the Kingdom and also on the analogous provisions concerning other educational establishments.

Turkey

Reservation made at the time of deposit of the instrument of ratification on 18 May 1954 (Or. Fr.)

Having seen and examined the Convention and the Protocol (First), we have approved the same with the reservation set out in respect of Article 2 of the Protocol by reason of the provisions of Law No. 6366 voted by the National Grand Assembly of Turkey dated 10 March 1954.

Article 3 of the said Law No. 6366 reads:

Article 2 of the Protocol shall not affect the provisions of Law No. 430 of 3 March 1924 relating to the unification of education.

United Kingdom

Reservation made at the time of signature on 20 March 1952 (Or. Engl.)

At the time of signing the present (First) Protocol, I declare that, in view of certain provisions of the Education Acts in the United Kingdom, the principle affirmed in the second sentence of Article 2 is accepted by the United Kingdom only so far as it is compatible with the provision of efficient instruction and training, and the avoidance of unreasonable public expenditure.

Declaration contained in a letter from the Permanent Representative of the United Kingdom, dated 22 February 1988 registered at the Secretariat General on 25 February 1988 (Or. Engl.)

In accordance with Article 4 of the said Protocol I hereby declare, on behalf of the government of the United Kingdom, that the Protocol shall apply to:

The Bailiwick of Guernsey
The Bailiwick of Jersey
Anguilla
British Virgin Islands
Cayman Islands
Gibraltar
Montserrat
St Helena

St Helena Dependencies
Turks and Caicos Islands,

being territories for whose international relations the government of the United Kingdom are responsible, subject to the following reservations:

1. In view of certain provisions of the Education (Guernsey) Laws and of the Education Ordinance of Gibraltar, the principle affirmed in the second sentence of Article 2 is accepted by the United Kingdom only so far as it is compatible with the provision of efficient instruction and training, and the avoidance of unreasonable public expenditure in Guernsey and Gibraltar.

2. The principle affirmed in the second sentence of Article 2 is accepted by the United Kingdom only insofar as it does not affect the application of the following legal provisions:

   i. the common law of Anguilla which permits the imposition by teachers of moderate and reasonable corporal punishment;

   ii. section 26 of the Education Act 1977 of the British Virgin Islands (which permits the administration of corporal punishment to a pupil only where no other punishment is considered suitable or effective and only by the principal or any teacher appointed by the principal for that purpose);

   iii. section 30 of the Education Law 1983 of the Cayman Islands (which permits the administration of corporal punishment to a pupil only where no other punishment is considered suitable or effective and only by the principal or any teacher appointed in writing by him for that purpose);

   iv. the common law of Montserrat which permits the imposition by teachers of moderate and reasonable corporal punishment;

   v. the law of St Helena, which permits the administration by teachers of reasonable corporal punishment; and section 6 of the Children and Young Persons Ordinance 1965 of St Helena (which states that the right of a teacher to administer such punishment is not affected by the provisions of that section which relate to the offence of cruelty to children);

vi. the law of St Helena Dependencies, which permits the administration by teachers of reasonable corporal punishment; and section 6 of the Children and Young Persons Ordinance 1965 of St Helena (which states that the right of a teacher to administer such punishment is not affected by the provisions of that section which relate to the offence of cruelty to children);

vii. the common law of the Turks and Caicos Islands which permits the administration by teachers of reasonable corporal punishment; and section 5 of the Juveniles Ordinance (Chapter 28) of the Turks and Caicos Islands (which states that the right of a teacher to administer such punishment is not affected by the provisions of that section which relate to the offence of cruelty to juveniles).

Reservations and other declarations relating to Protocol No. 3

(The provisions of Protocol No. 3, which entered into force on 21 September 1970, have been integrated into the text of the Convention)

Federal Republic of Germany

Declaration contained in a letter from the Permanent Representative of the Federal Republic of Germany, dated 3 January 1969, handed to the Secretary General at the time of deposit of the instrument of ratification on the same day (Or. Germ.)

I have the honour to declare, on behalf of the government of the Federal Republic of Germany and on the occasion of the deposit, that Protocols No. 2, No. 3 and No. 5 to the Convention on the Protection of Human Rights and Fundamental Freedoms, shall also apply to the Land Berlin with effect from the date on which they enter into force in respect of the Federal Republic of Germany.

Greece

Declaration made at the time of deposit of the instrument of ratification, on 8 January 1975 (Or. Fr.)

In depositing this instrument of ratification, the Permanent Representative stated that Protocols Nos. 2, 3 and 5 shall enter into force in respect of Greece with effect from 28 November 1974, date of the deposit of the instrument of ratification of the Convention of 4 November 1950 and of the Protocol of 20 March 1952. He recalled the declaration made by the Minister for Foreign Affairs of Greece on 28 November 1974, at the time of deposit of the instrument of ratification of the Convention and the said Protocol and at the occasion of signature of Protocol No. 5 of 20 January 1966, according to which Greece should complete with a minimum of delay the whole set of instruments relating to the Convention with effect from 28 November 1974.

Netherlands

Declaration contained in the instrument of ratification, deposited on 11 October 1966 (Or. Fr.)

We approve herewith, for the Kingdom in Europe, Surinam[1] and the Dutch West Indies, in respect of all the provisions contained therein, the Protocol reproduced above.

Declaration contained in a letter from the Permanent Representative of the Netherlands, dated 24 December 1985, registered at the Secretariat General on 3 January 1986 (Or. Engl.)

The island of Aruba, which is at present still part of the Netherlands Antilles, will obtain internal autonomy as a country within the Kingdom of the Netherlands as of 1 January 1986. Consequently the Kingdom will from then on no longer consist of two countries, namely the Netherlands (the Kingdom in Europe) and the Netherlands

---

1 Protocol No. 3 no longer applies to Surinam since this territory became independent on 25 November 1975.

Antilles (situated in the Caribbean region), but will consist of three countries, namely the said two countries and the country Aruba.

As the changes being made on 1 January 1986 concern a shift only in the internal constitutional relations within the Kingdom of the Netherlands, and as the Kingdom as such will remain the subject under international law with which treaties are concluded, the said changes will have no consequences in international law regarding to treaties concluded by the Kingdom which already apply to the Netherlands Antilles, including Aruba. These treaties will remain in force for Aruba in its new capacity of country within the Kingdom. Therefore these treaties will as of 1 January 1986, as concerns the Kingdom of the Netherlands, apply to the Netherlands Antilles (without Aruba) and Aruba.

Consequently the treaties referred to in the annex, to which the Kingdom of the Netherlands is a Party and which apply to the Netherlands Antilles, will as of 1 January 1986 as concerns the Kingdom of the Netherlands apply to the Netherlands Antilles and Aruba.

Reservations and other declarations relating to Protocol No. 4

Austria

Reservation made at the time of signature, on 16 September 1963, and renewed at the time of deposit of the instrument of ratification, on 18 September 1969 (Or. Fr.)

Protocol No. 4 is signed with the reservation that Article 3 shall not apply to the provisions of the Law of 3 April 1919, StGBl. No. 209 concerning the banishment of the House of Habsbourg-Lorraine and the confiscation of their property, as set out in the Act of 30 October 1919, StGBl. No. 501, in the Constitutional Law of 30 July 1925, BGBl. No. 292, in the Federal Constitutional Law of 26 January 1928, BGBl. No. 30, and taking account of the Federal Constitutional Law of 4 July 1963, BGBl. No. 172.

Cyprus

Declaration made at the time of signature on 6 October 1988 and confirmed at the time of deposit of the instrument of ratification on 3 October 1989 (Or. Engl.)

The government of the Republic of Cyprus adopts the position that, according to a proper interpretation of the provisions of Article 4 of the Protocol, they are not applicable to aliens unlawfully in the Republic of Cyprus as a result of the situation created by the continuing invasion and military occupation of part of the territory of the Republic of Cyprus by Turkey.

France

Declaration contained in the instrument of ratification, deposited on 3 May 1974 (Or. Fr.)

The Protocol shall apply to the whole territory of the Republic, having due regard, where the overseas territories are concerned, to local requirements, as mentioned in Article 63 of the Convention for the Protection of Human Rights and Fundamental Freedoms.

Federal Republic of Germany

Declaration made at the time of deposit of the instrument of ratification, on 1 June 1968 (Or. Fr.)

This Protocol applies also to the Land Berlin with effect from the date on which it entered into force in respect of the Federal Republic of Germany.

Ireland

Declaration made at the time of signature, on 16 September 1963 (Or. Engl.)

The reference to extradition contained in paragraph 21 of the Report of the Committee of Experts on this Protocol and concerning paragraph 1 of Article 3 of the Protocol includes also laws providing for the execution in the territory of one Contracting party of warrants of arrest issued by the authorities of another Contracting Party.

Italy

Declaration made at the time of deposit of the instrument of ratification, on 27 May 1982 (Or. Fr.)

Paragraph 2 of Article 3 cannot prevent the application of the transitory disposition XIII of the Italian Constitution concerning the interdiction of entry and residence of some members of the House of Savoy on the territory of the State.

Netherlands

Declaration contained in the instrument of ratification, deposited on 23 June 1982 (Or. Fr.)

We approve herewith, for the Kingdom in Europe and the Netherlands Antilles, the said Protocol.

Declaration contained in a letter from the Minister of Foreign Affairs, dated 9 June 1982, handed to the Secretary General at the time of deposit of the instrument of ratification, on 23 June 1982 (Or. Fr.)

Since, following ratification by the Kingdom of the Netherlands, Protocol No. 4 to the Convention on Human Rights and Fundamental Freedoms, securing certain rights and freedoms other than those already specified in the Convention and the first Protocol, applies to the Netherlands and to the Netherlands Antilles, the Netherlands and the Netherlands Antilles are regarded as separate territories for the application of Articles 2 and 3 of the Protocol, in accordance with Article 5, paragraph 4. Under Article 3, no-one may be expelled from or deprived of the right to enter the territory of the state of which he is a national. There is, however, only one nationality (Netherlands) for the whole of the Kingdom. Accordingly, nationality cannot be used as a criterion in making a distinction between the citizens of the Netherlands and those of the Netherlands Antilles, a distinction which is unavoidable since Article 3 applies separately to each of the parts of the Kingdom.

This being so, the Netherlands reserve the right to make a distinction in law, for purpose of the application of Article 3 of the Protocol, between Netherlands nationals residing in the Netherlands and Netherlands nationals residing in the Netherlands Antilles.

Declaration contained in a letter from the Permanent Representative of the Netherlands, dated 24 December 1985, registered at the Secretariat General on 3 January 1986 (Or. Engl.)

The island of Aruba, which is at present still part of the Netherlands Antilles, will obtain internal autonomy as a country within the Kingdom of the Netherlands as of 1 January 1986. Consequently the Kingdom will from then on no longer consist of two countries, namely the Netherlands (the Kingdom in Europe) and the Netherlands Antilles (situated in the Caribbean region), but will consist of three countries, namely the said two countries and the country Aruba.

As the changes being made on 1 January 1986 concern a shift only in the internal constitutional relations within the Kingdom of the Netherlands, and as the Kingdom as such will remain the subject under international law with which treaties are concluded, the said changes will have no consequences in international law regarding treaties concluded by the Kingdom which already apply to the Netherlands Antilles, including Aruba. These treaties will remain in force for Aruba in its new capacity of country within the Kingdom. Therefore these treaties will as of 1 January 1986, as concerns the Kingdom of the Netherlands, apply to the Netherlands Antilles (without Aruba) and Aruba.

Consequently the treaties referred to in the annex, to which the Kingdom of the Netherlands is a Party and which apply to the Netherlands Antilles, will as of 1 January 1986 as concerns the Kingdom of the Netherlands apply to the Netherlands Antilles and Aruba.

Reservations and other declarations relating to Protocol No. 5

(The provisions of Protocol No. 5, which entered into force on 20 December 1971, have been integrated into the text of the Convention)

Federal Republic of Germany

Declaration contained in a letter from the Permanent Representative of the Federal Republic of Germany, dated 3 January 1969, handed to the Secretary General at the time of deposit of the instrument of ratification on the same day (Or. Germ.)

I have the honour to declare, on behalf of the government of the Federal Republic of Germany and on the occasion of the deposit, that Protocols No. 2, No. 3 and No. 5 to the Convention on the Protection of Human Rights and Fundamental Freedoms, shall also apply to the Land Berlin with effect from the date on which they enter into force in respect of the Federal Republic of Germany.

Greece

Declaration made at the time of deposit of the instrument of ratification, on 8 January 1975 (Or. Fr.)

In depositing this instrument of ratification, the Permanent Representative stated that Protocols Nos. 2, 3 and 5 shall enter into force in respect of Greece with effect from 28 November 1974, date of the deposit of the instrument of ratification of the Convention of 4 November 1950 and of the Protocol of 20 March 1952. He recalled the declaration made by the Minister for Foreign Affairs of Greece on 28 November 1974, at the time of deposit of the instrument of ratification of the Convention and the said Protocol and at the occasion of signature of Protocol No. 5 of 20 January 1966, according to which Greece should complete with a minimum of delay the whole set of instruments relating to the Convention with effect from 28 November 1974.

Netherlands

Declaration contained in the instrument of ratification, deposited on 19 May 1971 (Or. Fr.)

We approve herewith, for the Kingdom in Europe, Surinam[1] and the Dutch West Indies, in respect of all the provisions contained therein, the Protocol reproduced above.

Declaration contained in a letter from the Permanent Representative of the Netherlands, dated 24 December 1985, registered at the Secretariat General on 3 January 1986 (Or. Engl.)

The island of Aruba, which is at present still part of the Netherlands Antilles, will obtain internal autonomy as a country within the Kingdom of the Netherlands as of 1 January 1986. Consequently the Kingdom will from then on no longer consist of two countries, namely the Netherlands (the Kingdom in Europe) and the Netherlands Antilles (situated in the Caribbean region), but will consist of three countries, namely the said two countries and the country Aruba.

As the changes being made on 1 January 1986 concern a shift only in the internal constitutional relations within the Kingdom of the Netherlands, and as the Kingdom as such will remain the subject under international law with which treaties are concluded, the said changes will have no consequences in international law regarding to treaties concluded by the Kingdom which already apply to the Netherlands Antilles, including Aruba. These treaties will remain in force for Aruba in its new capacity of country within the Kingdom. Therefore these treaties will as of 1 January 1986, as concerns the Kingdom of the Netherlands, apply to the Netherlands Antilles (without Aruba) and Aruba.

Consequently the treaties referred to in the annex, to which the Kingdom of the Netherlands is a Party and which apply to the Netherlands Antilles, will as of 1 January 1986 as concerns the Kingdom of the Netherlands apply to the Netherlands Antilles and Aruba.

---

1 Protocol No. 5 no longer applies to Surinam since this territory became independent on 25 November 1975.

Communication and other declarations relating to Protocol No. 6

Federal Republic of Germany

Declaration contained in a letter from the Permanent Representative of the Federal Republic of Germany dated 5 July 1989, handed to the Secretary General at the time of deposit of the instrument of ratification (Or. Ger./Engl./Fr.)

In connection with the deposit of the instrument of ratification to Protocol No. 6 of 28 April 1983 to the Convention for the Protection of Human Rights and Fundamental Freedoms concerning the Abolition of the Death Penalty I have the honour to declare on behalf of the government of the Federal Republic of Germany that, in its view, the obligations deriving from Protocol No. 6 are confined to the abolition of the death penalty within the Protocol's area of application in the respective State and that national non-criminal legislation is not affected. The Federal Republic of Germany has already met its obligations under the Protocol by means of Article 102 of the Basic Law.

Declaration contained in a letter from the Permanent Representative of the Federal Republic of Germany dated 5 July 1989, handed to the Secretary General at the time of deposit of the instrument of ratification (Or. Ger./Engl./Fr.)

In connection with the deposit of the instrument of ratification to Protocol No. 6 of 28 April 1983 to the Convention for the Protection of Human Rights and Fundamental Freedoms concerning the Abolition of the Death Penalty I have the honour to declare on behalf of the government of the Federal Republic of Germany that Protocol No. 6 shall also apply to Land Berlin with effect from the date on which it enters into force for the Federal Republic of Germany.

Netherlands

Declaration contained in the instrument of acceptance, deposited on 25 April 1986 (Or. Engl.)

The Netherlands accept the Protocol for the Kingdom in Europe, the Netherlands Antilles and Aruba.

Declaration contained in a letter from the Permanent Representation of the Netherlands, dated 25 April 1986, handed to the Secretary General at the time of deposit of the instrument of acceptance, on 25 April 1986 (Or. Engl.)

On the occasion of the deposit today of the instrument of acceptance by the Kingdom of the Netherlands of Protocol No. 6 to the Convention for the Protection of Human Rights and Fundamental Freedoms concerning the Abolition of the Death Penalty, done at Strasbourg on 28 April 1983, I have the honour to state, on behalf of the government of the Kingdom of the Netherlands, that the bills for the abolition of capital punishment, insofar as it is still provided for under Dutch military law and Dutch regulations governing wartime offences, have been before Parliament since 1981. It should be noted, however, that under the provisions of the Constitution of the Netherlands, which came into force on 17 February 1983, capital punishment may not be imposed.

Furthermore I have the honour to communicate herewith, in accordance with Article 2 of the said Protocol, Sections 103 and 108 of the criminal Code of the Netherlands Antilles and Aruba.

Sections 103 and 108 of the criminal Code of the Netherlands Antilles and Aruba:

"103. Any person who enters into an understanding with a foreign power with a view to inducing that power to engage in hostilities or wage war against the State, to strengthening its resolve to do so, or to promising or providing assistance in the preparation of such acts, shall be liable to a prison sentence of a maximum of fifteen years.

If the hostilities are carried out or a state of war occurs, the death sentence, life imprisonment, or a determinate prison sentence of a maximum of twenty years shall be imposed."

"108. Any person who, in time of war, intentionally aids an enemy of the State or disadvantages the State in relation to an enemy, shall be liable to a determinate prison sentence of a maximum of fifteen years. Life imprisonment or a determinate prison sentence of a maximum of twenty years shall be imposed if the offender:

1. informs or gives the enemy possession of any maps, plans, drawings or descriptions of military facilites or supplies any information relating to military operations or plans; or

2. acts as a spy for the enemy or assists, shelters or conceals an enemy spy.

The death penalty, life imprisonment or a determinate prison sentence of a maximum of twenty years shall be imposed if the offender:

1. destroys, renders unusable or betrays to the enemy or puts the enemy in possession of any fortified or manned location or post, any means of communication, any depot, any military supplies, any war funds, any restricted area (PB1965,69), or the navy or army or any part thereof, or if he hinders, impedes or sabotages any defensive or offensive flooding operations, whether planned or executed, or any other military operation.

2. causes or incites insurrection, mutiny or desertion among service personnel."

Switzerland

Communication contained in a letter from the Federal Department of Foreign Affairs, dated 28 September 1987, handed to the Secretary General at the time of deposit of the instrument of ratification, on 13 October 1987 (Or. Fr.)

In connection with the deposit of the instrument of ratification of Protocol No. 6 to the Convention for the Protection of Human Rights and Fundamental Freedoms, concerning the abolition of the death penalty, we wish to notify you of the following on behalf of the Swiss Federal Council in respect of Article 2 of the Protocol:

The Swiss legal system allows the death penalty to be reintroduced in time of war or in the event of an imminent threat of war, in pursuance of Articles 5 and 27 of the Military Criminal Code of 13 June 1927.

The Swiss legal system also allows the death penalty to be reintroduced on grounds of necessity *(droit de nécessité)*. The Federal Council did this on 28 May 1940 by legislating on the basis of an ordinance issued in pursuance of the full powers conferred on it by the Federal Assembly on 30 August 1939, at the outbreak of the Second World War.

Consequently, in time of war or of imminent threath of war, within the meaning of Article 2 of Protocol No. 6, the death penalty could be applied in Switzerland in the cases provided for in ordinary legislation (Articles 5 and 27 of the Military Criminal Code) or in legislation adopted by the Federal Council on grounds of necessity *(droit de nécessité)*.

Copies of the following provisions of the relevant Swiss legislation are attached:[1]

– Article 5 of the Military Criminal Code of 13 June 1927,

– Article 27 of the Military Criminal Code of 13 June 1927,

– Section 6 of the Federal Council Ordinance of 28 May 1940 amending and supplementing the Military Criminal Code (this legislative ordinance was abrogated with effect from 21 August 1945).

To indicate the background to this last-named provision, copies are also attached of the Federal Council's message of 29 August 1939 to the Federal Assembly on measures for ensuring the security of the country and maintaining its neutrality (FF 1939 II 217); the Federal Assembly's Order of 30 August 1939 on measures for ensuring the security of the country and maintaining its neutrality (Full Powers'

---

1 Note by the Secretariat: Copies of the (French) text of this legislation are available upon request to the Directorate of Legal Affairs of the Council of Europe.

Federal Order, RO 55 (1939), p. 781); the 3rd report of 19 November 1940 from the Federal Council to the Federal Assembly on measures taken by it in pursuance of its extraordinary powers (FF 1940 I 1226, spec. 1233); and the Federal Council's Order of 3 August 1945 terminating active service and abrogating the legislative ordinance of 28 May 1940 (RO 61 (1945), p. 561).

Where appropriate, the Federal Council would notify you immediately of the entry into force of the above-mentioned statutory provisions....

Reservations and other declarations relating to Protocol No. 7

Austria

Declarations contained in the instrument of ratification, deposited on 14 May 1986 (Or. Engl./Fr.)

The Republic of Austria declares:

1. Higher Tribunals in the sense of Article 2, paragraph 1, include the Administrative Court and the Constitutional Court.

2. Articles 3 and 4 exclusively relate to criminal proceedings in the sense of the Austrian code of criminal procedure.

Denmark

Reservation contained in a letter from the Chargé d'affaires a.i. *of Denmark, dated 18 August 1988, handed to the Secretary General at the time of deposit of the instrument of ratification, on 18 August 1988* (Or. Engl.)

The government of Denmark declares that Article 2, paragraph 1 does not bar the use of rules of the Administration of Justice Act *(Lov om rettens pleje)* according to which the possibility of review by a higher court — in cases subject to prosecution by the lower instance of the prosecution *(politisager)* — is denied.

a. when the prosecuted, having been duly notified, fails to appear in court;

b. when the court has repealed the punishment; or

c. in cases where only sentences of fines or confiscations of objects below the amount or value established by law are imposed.

Declaration contained in a letter from the Permanent Representative of Denmark, dated 9 September 1988, registered at the Secretariat General on 12 September 1988 (see enclosed explanatory Note) (Or. Fr.)

Under the terms of Article 6, paragraph 1, of Protocol No. 7 to the Convention for the Protection of Human Rights and Fundamental Freedoms, the government of Denmark hereby declares that the said Protocol shall not apply to the Faroe Islands.

Explanatory note

On 25 July 1988, the government of Denmark addressed to the Majesty the Queen a recommendation aiming at obtaining the authorisation to ratify Protocol No. 7 to the Convention for the Protection of Human Rights and Fundamental Freedoms. This recommendation provided for the formulation of the following declaration concerning the territorial application:

"Under the terms of Article 6, paragraph 1, of Protocol No. 7 to the Convention for the Protection of Human Rights and Fundamental Freedoms, the government of Denmark hereby declares that the said Protocol shall not apply to the Faroe Islands."

Due to an omission, the declaration was not made to the Secretary General, depository of the Convention, upon deposit of the instrument of ratification on 18 August 1988, as it should have been under the terms of Article 6, paragraph 1, of the Protocol.

The government of Denmark corrects today this clerical mistake by forwarding to the Secretary General the text of the above mentioned declaration, to take effect at the date of entry into force of the Protocol in respect of the Kingdom of Denmark.

France

Declaration made at the time of signature, on 22 November 1984 and confirmed at the time of deposit of the instrument of ratification on 17 February 1986 (Or. Fr.)

The government of the French Republic declares that, in accordance with the meaning of Article 2, paragraph 1, the review by a higher court may be limited to a control of the application of the law, such as an appeal to the Supreme Court.

Reservations made at the time of signature, on 22 November 1984 (Or. Fr.)

The government of the French Republic declares that only those offences which under French law fall within the jurisdiction of the French criminal courts should be considered as offences within the meaning of Articles 2 to 4 of the present Protocol.

The government of the French Republic declares that:

a. Article 5 must not prevent the application of the provisions of Chapter II, Title V of the Third Book of the Civil Code or the application of Article 383 of the Civil Code;

b. Article 5 should not be interpreted as implying that parental authority may be exercised in common in situations where the French law would recognise the exercise of such authority by only one of the parents.

Reservations contained in the instrument of ratification, deposited on 17 February 1986 (Or. Fr.)

The government of the French Republic declares that only those offences which under French law fall within the jurisdiction of the French criminal courts may be regarded as offences within the meaning of Articles 2 to 4 of this Protocol;

The government of the French Republic declares that Article 5 may not impede the application of the rules of the French legal system concerning the transmission of the patronymic name.

Article 5 may not impede the application of provisions of local law in the territorial collectivity of Mayotte and the territories of New Caledonia and of the Wallis and Futuna Archipelago.

Protocol No. 7 to the Convention for the Protection of Human Rights and Fundamental Freedoms shall apply to the whole territory of the Republic, due regard being had where the overseas territories and the territorial collectivity of Mayotte are concerned, to the local requirements referred to in Article 63 of the European Convention on Human Rights and Fundamental Freedoms.

Federal Republic of Germany

Declarations made at the time of signature, on 19 March 1985 (Or. Engl.)

1. By "criminal offence" and "offence" in Articles 2 to 4 of the present Protocol, the Federal Republic of Germany understands only such acts as are criminal offences under its law.

2. The Federal Republic of Germany applies Article 2(1) to convictions or sentences in the first instance only, it being possible to restrict review to errors in law and to hold such reviews in camera; in addition, it understands that the application of Article 2(1) is not dependent on the written judgment of the previous instance being translated into a language other than the language used in court.

3. The Federal Republic of Germany understands the words "according to the law or the practice of the State concerned" to mean that Article 3 refers only to the retrial provided for in Sections 359 et seq. of the Code of Criminal Procedure (*Strafprozessordnung*).

Italy

Declaration contained in a letter dated 7 November 1991 handed to the Secretary General at the time of deposit of the instrument of ratification, on 7 November 1991 (Or. Fr.)

The Italian Republic declares that Articles 2 to 4 of the Protocol apply only to offences, procedures and decisions qualified as criminal by Italian law.

Luxembourg

Reservation made at the time of deposit of the instrument of ratification, on 19 April 1989 (Or. Fr.)

The Grand Duchy of Luxembourg declares that Article 5 of the Protocol must not prevent the application of the rules of the Luxembourg legal system concerning transmission of the patronymic name.

Netherlands

Declaration made at the time of signature, on 22 November 1984 (Or. Engl.)

The Netherlands government interprets paragraph 1 of Article 2 thus that the right conferred to everyone convicted of a criminal offence to have conviction or sentence reviewed by a higher tribunal relates only to convictions or sentences given in the first instance by tribunals which according to Netherlands law are in charge of jurisdiction in criminal matters.

San Marino

Declaration contained in the instrument of ratification deposited on 22 March 1989 (Or. It.)

With regard to the provisions of Article 3 on the compensation of the victim of a miscarriage of justice, the government of San Marino declares that although the principle is applied in practice, it is not enshrined in any legislative provisions. Therefore the government of the Republic undertakes to embody the principle and its regulation into a relevant legislative provision to be adopted within two years from today.

Sweden

Declaration made at the time of deposit of the instrument of ratification, on 8 November 1985 (Or. Engl.)

Article 1

The government of Sweden declares that an alien who is entitled to appeal against an expulsion order, may, pursuant to Section 70 of the Swedish Aliens Act (1980:376), make a statement (termed a declaration of acceptance) in which he renounces his right of appeal against the decision. A declaration of acceptance may not be revoked. If the alien has appealed against the order before making a declaration of acceptance, his appeal shall be deemed withdrawn by reason of the declaration.

Switzerland

Reservations contained in the instrument of ratification deposited on 24 February 1988 (Or. Fr.)

Article 1

When expulsion takes place in pursuance of a decision of the Federal Council taken in accordance with Article 70 of the Constitution on the grounds of a threat to the internal or external security of Switzerland, the person concerned does not enjoy the rights listed in paragraph 1 even after the execution of the expulsion.

Article 5

Following the entry into force of the revised provisions of the Swiss Civil Code of 5 October 1984, the provisions of Article 5 of the Additional Protocol No. 7 shall apply subject to, on the one hand, the provisions of Federal law concerning the family name (Article 160 CC and 8a final section, CC) and, on the other hand, to the provisions concerning the acquisition of the right of citizenship (Articles 161, 134, paragraph 1, 149, paragraph 1, CC and 8b final section, CC). Furthermore, the present reservation also concerns certain provisions of transitional law on marriage settlement (Articles 9, 9a, 9c, 9d, 9e, 10 and 10a final section, CC).

Reservations and other declarations relating to Protocol No. 8

(The provisions of Protocol No. 8, which entered into force on 1 January 1990, have been integrated into the text of the Convention)

France

Declaration made at the time of signature, on 19 March 1985 (Or. Fr.)

The procedure for approval by France of Protocol No. 8 to the Convention for the Protection of Human Rights and Fundamental Freedoms will be instituted in the light of the measures to be taken in the Council of Europe for the implementation of this instrument.

Federal Republic of Germany

Declaration made at the time of deposit of the instrument of ratification on 19 September 1989 (Or. Ger./Engl./Fr.)

In connection with the deposit today of the instrument of ratification of Protocol No. 8 to the Convention for the Protection of Human Rights and Fundamental Freedoms of 19 March 1985, I have the honour to declare on behalf of the government of the Federal Republic of Germany that Protocol No. 8 shall apply to the Land Berlin with effect from the date on which it enters into force for the Federal Republic of Germany.

Ireland

Declaration contained in a letter from the Department of Foreign Affairs, dated 18 March 1988, handed to the Secretary General at the time of deposit of the instrument of ratification (Or. Engl.)

At the time of deposit of the Instrument of Ratification, I have been directed by the *Tánaiste* (Deputy Prime Minister and Minister for

Foreign Affairs of Ireland) to state that the government of Ireland attach importance to the establishment by the European Commission of Human Rights, in their Rules of Procedure, of a provision that before any application is referred to a Chamber of the Commission, as provided for by Protocol No. 8, the member State against which such an application has been lodged shall be given the opportunity to express an opinion as to whether the application should be referred to a Chamber or to the plenary Commission. It is the clear understanding of the government of Ireland that such a consultation process is to be provided for by the European Commission of Human Rights.

Netherlands

Declaration contained in the instrument of acceptance, deposited on 11 December 1986 (Or. Engl.)

The Kingdom of the Netherlands accepts the said Protocol for the Kingdom in Europe, the Netherlands Antilles **and** Aruba.

United Kingdom

Declaration contained in a letter from the Permanent Representative of the United Kingdom, dated 18 April 1986, handed to the Secretary General at the time of deposit of the instrument of ratification, on 21 April 1986 (Or. Engl.)

In connection with the implementation of the new procedures provided for by the Protocol, I have been directed by Her Majesty's Principal Secretary of State for Foreign and Commonwealth Affairs to place on record that it is the understanding of the United Kingdom government that the European Commission of Human Rights will establish in its Rules of Procedure or otherwise a practice of consultation between the Commission and the member State against which an application is brought on the question whether that application should be considered by a Chamber or by the full Commission.

The United Kingdom attaches considerable importance to the establishment of such a consultation process.

Declaration contained in the instrument of ratification, deposited on 21 April 1986 (Or. Engl.)

The Protocol is ratified on behalf of:

The United Kingdom of Great Britain and Northern Ireland, The Bailiwick of Jersey, The Bailiwick of Guernsey, The Isle of Man, Anguilla, Bermuda, British Virgin Islands, Cayman Islands, Falkland Islands, South Georgia and the South Sandwich Islands, Gibraltar, Montserrat, Saint Helena, Saint Helena Dependencies, Turks and Caicos Islands.

Reservations and other declarations relating to Protocol No. 9

Netherlands

Declaration contained in the instrument of acceptance, deposited on 23 November 1992 (Or. Engl.)

The Kingdom of the Netherlands accepts the said Protocol for the Kingdom in Europe, for the Netherlands Antilles and for Aruba.

Reservations and other declarations relating to Protocol No. 10

Netherlands

Declaration contained in the instrument of acceptance, deposited on 23 November 1992 (Or. Engl.)

The Kingdom of the Netherlands accepts the said Protocol for the Kingdom in Europe, for the Netherlands Antilles **and** for Aruba.

United Kingdom

Declaration contained in the instrument of ratification, deposited on 9 March 1993 (Or. Engl.)

The Protocol is ratified on behalf of the United Kingdom of Great Britain and Northern Ireland, the Bailiwick of Jersey, the Bailiwick of Guernsey, the Isle of Man, Anguilla, Bermuda, British Virgin Islands, Cayman Islands, Falkland Islands, South Georgia and the South Sandwich Islands, Gibraltar, Montserrat, St Helena Dependencies, Turks and Caicos Islands.

European Agreement
relating to persons
participating in
proceedings of the
European Commission
and Court of Human Rights

European Agreement relating to persons participating in proceedings of the European Commission and Court of Human Rights

London, 6 May 1969

Entry into force: 17 April 1971,
in accordance with Article 8

The member States of the Council of Europe, signatory hereto,

Having regard to the Convention for the Protection of Human Rights and Fundamental Freedoms, signed at Rome on 4 November 1950 (hereinafter referred to as "the Convention");

Considering that it is expedient for the better fulfilment of the purposes of the Convention that persons taking part in proceedings before the European Commission of Human Rights (hereinafter referred to as the "Commission") or the European Court of Human Rights (hereinafter referred to as the "Court") shall be accorded certain immunities and facilities;

Desiring to conclude an Agreement for this purpose,

Have agreed as follows:

Article 1

1. The persons to whom this Agreement applies are:

  a. agents of the Contracting Parties and advisers and advocates assisting them;

  b. persons taking part in proceedings instituted before the Commission under Article 25 of the Convention, whether in their own name or as representatives of one of the applicants enumerated in the said Article 25;

  c. barristers, solicitors or professors of law, taking part in proceedings in order to assist one of the persons enumerated in subparagraph b above;

  d. persons chosen by the delegates of the Commission to assist them in proceedings before the Court;

  e. witnesses, experts and other persons called upon by the Commission or the Court to take part in proceedings before the Commission or the Court.

2. For the purposes of this Agreement, the terms "Commission" and "Court" shall include a Sub-Commission or Chamber, or members of either body carrying out their duties under the terms of the Convention or of the rules of the Commission or of the Court, as the case may be; and the term "taking part in proceedings" shall include making communications with a view to a complaint against a State which has recognised the right of individual petition under Article 25 of the Convention.

3. In the course of the exercise by the Committee of Ministers of its functions under Article 32 of the Convention, any person mentioned in paragraph 1 of this Article is called upon to appear before, or to submit written statements to the Committee of Ministers, the provisions of this agreement shall apply in relation to him.

Article 2

1. The persons referred to in paragraph 1 of Article 1 of this Agreement shall have immunity from legal process in respect of oral or written statements made, or documents or other evidence submitted by them before or to the Commission or the Court.

2. This immunity does not apply to the communication, outside the Commission or the Court, by or on behalf of any person entitled to immunity under the preceding paragraph, of any such statements, documents or evidence or any part thereof submitted by that person to the Commission or the Court.

Article 3

1. The Contracting Parties shall respect the right of the persons referred to in paragraph 1 of Article 1 of this agreement to correspond freely with the Commission and the Court.

2. As regards persons under detention, the exercise of this right shall in particular imply that:

   a. if their correspondence is examined by the competent authorities, its despatch and delivery shall nevertheless take place without undue delay and without alteration;

   b. such persons shall not be subject to disciplinary measures in any form on account of any communication sent through the proper channels to the Commission or the Court;

   c. such persons shall have the right to correspond, and consult out of hearing of other persons, with a lawyer qualified to appear before the courts of the country where they are detained in regard to an application to the Commission, or any proceedings resulting therefrom.

3. In application of the preceding paragraphs, there shall be no interference by a public authority except such as is in accordance with the law and is necessary in a democratic society in the interests of national security, for the detection or prosecution of a criminal offence or for the protection of health.

Article 4

1. a. The Contracting Parties undertake not to hinder the free movement and travel, for the purpose of attending and returning from proceedings before the Commission or the Court, of persons referred to in paragraph 1 of Article 1 of this Agreement whose presence has in advance been authorised by the Commission or the Court.

b. No restrictions shall be placed on their movement and travel other than such as are in accordance with the law and necessary in a democratic society in the interests of national security or public safety, for the maintenance of *ordre public,* for the prevention of crime, for the protection of health or morals, or for the protection of the rights and freedoms of others.

2. a. Such persons shall not, in countries of transit and in the country where the procedings take place, be prosecuted or detained or be subjected to any other restriction of their personal liberty in respect of acts or convictions prior to the commencement of the journey.

b. Any Contracting Party may at the time of signature or ratification of this Agreement declare that the provisions of this paragraph will not apply to its own nationals. Such a declaration may be withdrawn at any time by means of a notification addressed to the Secretary General of the Council of Europe.

3. The Contracting Parties undertake to re-admit on his return to their territory any such person who commenced his journey in the said territory.

4. The provisions of paragraphs 1 and 2 of this Article shall cease to apply when the person concerned has had for a period of 15 consecutive days from the date when his presence is no longer required by the Commission or the Court the opportunity of returning to the country from which his journey commenced.

5. Where there is any conflict between the obligations of a Contracting Party resulting from paragraph 2 of this article and those resulting from a Council of Europe convention or from an extradition treaty or other treaty concerning mutual assistance in criminal matters with other Contracting Parties, the provisions of paragraph 2 of this article shall prevail.

Article 5

1. Immunities and facilities are accorded to the persons referred to in paragraph 1 of Article 1 of this agreement solely in order to ensure for them the freedom of speech and the independence necessary for the discharge of their functions, tasks or duties, or the exercise of their rights in relation to the Commission and the Court.

2. a. The Commission or the Court, as the case may be, shall alone be competent to waive, in whole or in part, the immunity provided for in paragraph 1 of Article 2 of this Agreement; they have not only the right but the duty to waive immunity in any case where, in their opinion, such immunity would impede the course of justice and waiver in whole or in part would not prejudice the purpose defined in paragraph 1 of this article.

   b. The immunity may be waived by the Commission or by the Court, either *ex officio* or at the request, addressed to the Secretary General of the Council of Europe, of any Contracting Party or of any person concerned.

   c. Decisions waiving immunity or refusing the waiver shall be accompanied by a statement of reasons.

3. If a Contracting Party certifies that waiver of the immunity provided for in paragraph 1 of Article 2 of this Agreement is necessary for the purpose of proceedings in respect of an offence against national security, the Commission or the Court shall waive immunity to the extent specified in the certificate.

4. In the event of the discovery of a fact which might, by its nature, have a decisive influence and which at the time of the decision refusing waiver of immunity was unknown to the author of the request, the latter may make a new request to the Commission or the Court.

Article 6

Nothing in this Agreement shall be construed as limiting or derogating from any of the obligations assumed by the Contracting Parties under the Convention.

Article 7

1. This Agreement shall be open to signature by the member States of the Council of Europe, who may become Parties to it either by:

   a. signature without reservation in respect of ratification or acceptance, or

   b. signature with reservation in respect of ratification or acceptance, followed by ratification or acceptance.

2. Instruments of ratification or acceptance shall be deposited with the Secretary General of the Council of Europe.

Article 8

1. This agreement shall enter into force one month after the date on which five member States of the Council shall have become Parties to the Agreement, in accordance with the provisions of Article 7.

2. As regards any member States who shall subsequently sign the Agreement without reservation in respect of ratification or acceptance or who shall ratify or accept it, the Agreement shall enter into force one month after the date of such signature or after the date of deposit of the instrument of ratification or acceptance.

Article 9

1. Any Contracting Party may at the time of signature or when depositing its instrument of ratification or acceptance, specify the territory or territories to which this Agreement shall apply.

2. Any Contracting Party may, when depositing its instrument of ratification or acceptance or at any later date, by declaration addressed to the Secretary General of the Council of Europe, extend this Agreement to any other territory or territories specified in the declaration and for whose international relations it is responsible or on whose behalf it is authorised to give undertakings.

3. Any declaration made in pursuance of the preceding paragraph may, in respect of any territory mentioned in such declaration, be

withdrawn according to the procedure laid down in Article 10 of this Agreement.

Article 10

1. This Agreement shall remain in force indefinitely.

2. Any Contracting Party may, insofar as it is concerned, denounce this Agreement by means of a notification addressed to the Secretary General of the Council of Europe.

3. Such denunciation shall take effect six months after the date of receipt by the Secretary General of such notification. Such a denunciation shall not have the effect of releasing the Contracting Parties concerned from any obligation which may have arisen under this Agreement in relation to any person referred to in paragraph 1 of Article 1.

Article 11

The Secretary General of the Council of Europe shall notify the member States of the Council of:

a. any signature without reservation in respect of ratification or acceptance;

b. any signature with reservation in respect of ratification or acceptance;

c. the deposit of any instrument of ratification or acceptance;

d. any date of entry into force of this Agreement in accordance with Article 8 thereof;

e. any declaration received in pursuance of the provisions of paragraph 2 of Article 4 and of paragraphs 2 and 3 of Article 9;

f. any notification of withdrawal of a declaration in pursuance of the provisions of paragraph 2 of Article 4 and any notification received in pursuance of the provisions of Article 10 and the date on which any denunciation takes effect.

In witness whereof the undersigned, being duly authorised thereto, have signed this Agreement.

Done at London, this 6th day of May 1969, in the English and French languages, both texts being equally authoritative, in a single copy which shall remain deposited in the archives of the Council of Europe. The Secretary General of the Council of Europe shall transmit certified copies to each of the signatory States.

Signatures and ratifications[1]

Opening for signature: London 06/05/69

Entry into force: 17/04/71

Member States	Date of signature	Date of ratification	Entry into force
Austria	14/01/81	17/07/81	18/08/81
Belgium	06/05/69	16/03/71	17/04/71
Bulgaria			
Cyprus	02/07/70	23/11/70	17/04/71
Czech Republic			
Denmark	06/05/69	07/03/84	08/04/84
Estonia			
Finland	28/09/90	27/02/91	28/03/91
France	10/06/82	27/02/84	28/03/84 D
Germany	06/05/69	03/04/78	04/05/78 R/D
Greece			
Hungary	09/02/93		
Iceland			
Ireland	12/12/69	09/11/71	10/12/71
Italy	08/01/74	06/01/81	07/02/81 D
Liechtenstein	27/09/82	26/01/84	27/02/84 D
Lithuania			
Luxembourg	06/05/69	10/09/70	17/04/71
Malta	06/05/69	30/04/71	31/05/71

Member States	Date of signature	Date of ratification	Entry into force
Netherlands	15/12/70	28/01/72	29/02/72 T
Norway	06/05/69	01/07/70	17/04/71
Poland			
Portugal	23/02/79	23/07/81	24/08/81
Romania			
San Marino	01/03/89	22/03/89	23/04/89
Slovakia			
Slovenia	23/11/93		
Spain	16/07/87	23/06/89	24/07/89 D
Sweden	06/05/69	20/12/71	21/01/72
Switzerland	21/12/72	28/11/74	29/12/74 D
Turkey			
United Kingdom	06/05/69	24/02/71	17/04/71 T

1   Treaty open for signature by the member States.

R: Reservations.

D: Declarations.

T: Territorial Declaration.

Declarations and reservations

France

Declarations contained in the instrument of ratification deposited on 27 February 1984 (Or. Fr.)

1. The government of the French Republic declares that it interprets paragraph 1a of Article 4 as not applying to detained persons.

2. In respect of the application of paragraph 1 of Article 4, the foreign nationals referred to in paragraph 1 of Article 1 of the Agreement must be in possession of the circulation documents required for entry into France and obtain if appropriate the necessary visa. A

visa known as a "special visa" must additionally be obtained by foreigners expelled from French territory.

Those visas will be issued within the briefest periods by the competent French consular representatives, subject to the provisions of paragraph 1 b of Article 4 of the Agreement.

3. The government of the French Republic declares that, regard being had to the terms of paragraph 4 of Article 4, it interprets paragraph 2 a of that article as not applying on French territory to persons ordinarily resident in France.

Federal Republic of Germany

Reservations and Declaration contained in two letters from the Permanent Representative of the Federal Republic of Germany dated 3 April 1978 and handed to the Secretary General at the time of deposit of the instrument of ratification on the same day (Or. Engl.)

Reservations

When depositing this instrument of ratification, the Permanent Representative declares that the government of the Federal Republic of Germany makes the following reservations with regard to the Agreement:

1. In application of paragraphs 1 and 2 of Article 3 of the Agreement, there may be interference by a public authority beyond the scope of paragraph 3 of Article 3 provided that it is in accordance with the law and necessary in a democratic society for the prevention of a criminal offence.

2. The provision of sub-paragraph a of paragraph 2 of Article 4 of the Agreement shall not apply to Germans within the meaning of the Basic Law of the Federal Republic of Germany.

Declaration

The said Agreement shall also apply to Land Berlin with effect from the date on which it enters into force for the Federal Republic of Germany.

Italy

Declaration contained in a letter from the Permanent Representative of Italy dated 17 December 1980 handed to the Secretary General at the time of deposit of the instrument of ratification on 6 January 1981 (Or. Fr.)

The provision of sub-paragraph a of paragraph 2 of Article 4 of the Agreement shall not apply to Italian nationals.

Liechtenstein

Declaration contained in the instrument of ratification deposited on 26 January 1984 (Or. Fr.)

The Principality of Liechtenstein shall not apply the provisions of paragraph 2, sub-paragraph a, of Article 4 of this Agreement to the nationals of Liechtenstein.

Netherlands

Declaration contained in the instrument of acceptance deposited on 28 January 1972 (Or. Fr.)

The government of the Kingdom of the Netherlands accepts the said Agreement for the Kingdom in Europe, Surinam and the Netherlands Antilles.

Declaration contained in a letter from the Permanent Representative of the Netherlands, dated 24 December 1985, registered at the Secretariat General on 3 January 1986 (Or. Engl.)

The island of Aruba, which is at present still part of the Netherlands Antilles, will obtain internal autonomy as a country within the Kingdom of the Netherlands as of 1 January 1986. Consequently the Kingdom will from then on no longer consist of two countries, namely the Netherlands (the Kingdom in Europe) and the Netherlands Antilles (situated in the Caribbean region), but will consist of three countries, namely the said two countries **and** the country Aruba.

As the changes being made on 1 January 1986 concern a shift only in the internal constitutional relations within the Kingdom of the Netherlands, and as the Kingdom as such will remain the subject under international law with which treaties are concluded, the said changes will have no consequences in international law regarding to treaties concluded by the Kingdom which already apply to the Netherlands Antilles, including Aruba. These treaties will remain in force for Aruba in its new capacity of country within the Kingdom. Therefore these treaties will as of 1 January 1986, as concerns the Kingdom of the Netherlands, apply to the Netherlands Antilles (without Aruba) **and** Aruba.

Consequently the treaties referred to in the annex, to which the Kingdom of the Netherlands is a Party and which apply to the Netherlands Antilles, will as of 1 January 1986 as concerns the Kingdom of the Netherlands apply to the Netherlands Antilles **and** Aruba.

Spain

Declaration contained in a letter from the Permanent Representation of Spain dated 26 June 1987 registered at the Secretariat General on 30 June 1987 and renewed at the time of deposit of the instrument of ratification, on 23 June 1989 (Or. Fr./Span.)

The Kingdom of Spain declares that the provisions of paragraph 2 of Article 4 shall not apply to its own nationals.

Switzerland

Declaration contained in the instrument of ratification deposited on 28 November 1974 (Or. Fr.)

The Swiss Federal Council declares that the provisions of Article 4, paragraph 2 a of the Agreement shall not apply to Swiss nationals charged or convicted in Switzerland of a serious crime against the State, national defence or the defensive capacity of the country.

United Kingdom

Declaration contained in a letter from the Permanent Representative of the United Kingdom dated 19 October 1971 registered at the Secretariat General on 20 October 1971 (Or. Engl.)

In accordance with Article 9 (2) of the European Agreement relating to Persons participating in Proceedings of the European Commission and Court of Human Rights, I have the honour to declare on behalf of the United Kingdom of Great Britain and Northern Ireland that the provisions of this Agreement shall hereby extend to the following territories: the Bailiwick of Jersey, the Bailiwick of Guernsey and the Isle of Man.

**European Commission
of Human Rights**

A. Rules of procedure of the European Commission of Human Rights

Entry into force: 28 June 1993

> Revised version as adopted by the Commission on 12 February and 6 May 1993

The Commission,

Having regard to the Convention for the Protection of Human Rights and Fundamental Freedoms and Protocols hereinafter called the Convention;

Pursuant to Article 36 of the Convention,

Adopts the present Rules:

Title I — Organisation of the Commission

Chapter I — The Commission

Rule 1

1. The Commission sits in plenary session, in Chambers and in Committees set up under Article 20, paragraphs 2 and 3, of the Convention.

2. Unless otherwise stated, the terms "Commission" and "President" in these Rules shall mean "Chamber" and "President of the Chamber" in relation to cases referred to Chambers, and "Committee" and "President of the Committee" in relation to cases referred to Committees.

Chapter II — Members of the Commission

Rule 2

1. The duration of the term of office of members of the Commission elected on 18 May 1954 shall be calculated as from this date. Similarly, the duration of the term of office of any member elected as a consequence of a State becoming a Party to the Convention after 18 May 1954 shall be calculated as from the election.

2. However, when members are re-elected on the expiry of their terms of office or are elected to replace a member whose term of office has expired or is about to expire, the duration of their term of office shall, in either case, be calculated as from the date of such expiry.

Rule 3

Before taking up their duties, members of the Commission shall, at the first meeting of the Commission at which they are present after their election, make the following solemn declaration:

"I solemnly declare that I will exercise all my powers and duties honourably and faithfully, impartially and conscientiously and that I will keep secret all Commission proceedings."

Rule 4

1. Members of the Commission shall take precedence after the President of the Commission and Presidents of Chambers according to the length of time they have been in office.

2. Members having the same length of time in office shall take precedence according to age.

3. Re-elected members shall take precedence having regard to the duration of their previous terms of office.

Rule 5

Resignation of a member shall be notified to the President of the Commission who shall transmit it to the Secretary General of the Council of Europe.

Chapter III — Presidency of the Commission

Rule 6

1. The Commission shall elect its President in plenary session not later than the second session after the date of the entry into office of members elected at periodical elections of part of the Commission in accordance with Article 22, paragraph 1, of the Convention.

2. The term of office of the President of the Commission shall be three years.

3. If the President of the Commission, before the normal expiry of his term of office, ceases to be a member of the Commission or resigns from office, the Commission shall as soon as possible elect a successor to hold office for the remainder of the said term.

4. Each Chamber, voting separately, shall elect its President and Vice-President as soon as the Chambers have been constituted according to Rule 24, paragraph 3.

5. The term of office of the President of a Chamber shall be eighteen months. On the expiry of this term the presidency of the Chamber shall be assumed by the Vice-President for the remainder of the period for which the Chamber has been constituted. At the same time the Chamber concerned shall elect a new Vice-President.

6. A member of the Commission who has served as the President of a Chamber shall not be eligible for re-election as President or Vice-President of a Chamber until eighteen months have elapsed since the end of his previous term of office.

7. The elections referred to in this Rule shall be by secret ballot; only the members present shall take part. Election shall be by an absolute majority of the members of the Commission or of the members of the Chamber concerned, as appropriate.

8. If no member receives such a majority, a second ballot shall take place. The member receiving the most votes shall then be elected. In the case of equal voting the member having precedence under Rule 4 shall be elected.

Rule 7

1. The President of the Commission shall direct the work of the Commission and preside at its plenary sessions.

2. The Presidents of Chambers shall preside at the meetings of the Chamber which has elected them.

3. Each Committee shall be presided over by the member taking precedence under Rule 4 of these Rules.

4. The term "President" shall in these Rules, where appropriate, include also any member acting as president.

Rule 8

1. The Presidents of Chambers, according to the order of precedence laid down in Rule 4, shall take the place of the President of the Commission if the latter is prevented from carrying out the duties of President or if the office of President is vacant.

2. The Vice-President of a Chamber shall take the place of the President of the Chamber which has elected him if the latter is prevented from carrying out his duties or if the office of President of Chamber is vacant.

3. The President of the Commission may delegate certain functions to the President of either Chamber.

Rule 9

1. If the President of the Commission and the Presidents of Chambers are at the same time prevented from carrying out their duties, or if their offices are at the same time vacant, the duties of President of the Commission shall be carried out by another member according to the order of precedence laid down in Rule 4.

2. If the President and Vice-President of the Chamber are prevented from carrying out their duties in respect of that Chamber, or if their offices are at the same time vacant, the duties of President shall be carried out by another member according to the order of precedence laid down in Rule 4.

Rule 10

Members of the Commission shall not preside in cases to which the High Contracting Party, of which they are nationals or in respect of which they were elected, is a party.

Rule 11

Where the President of the Commission or the Presidents of the Chambers for some special reason consider that they should not act as President in a particular case, they shall be replaced in accordance with the provisions of Rule 8, paragraph 1, and Rule 9.

Chapter IV — Secretariat of the Commission

Rule 12

1. The Secretariat of the Commission shall consist of the Secretary, the Deputy Secretary, and other staff members appointed under Article 37 of the Convention.

2. The Secretary and the Deputy Secretary to the Commission shall be appointed by the Secretary General of the Council of Europe on the proposal of the Commission.

3. The officials of the Secretariat of the Commission, other than the Secretary and the Deputy Secretary, shall be appointed by the

Secretary General, with the agreement of the President of the Commission or the Secretary acting on the President's instructions.

Rule 13

1. The Secretary to the Commission shall, under the general direction of the President, be responsible for the work of the Secretariat and, in particular:

   a. shall assist the Commission and its members in the fulfilment of their duties,

   b. shall be the channel for all communications concerning the Commission,

   c. shall have custody of the archives of the Commission.

2. The Secretary shall be responsible for the publication of:

   a. the decisions of the Commission,

   b. minutes of the Commission's sessions,

   c. any other document

insofar as their publication in the official languages or in any other language is considered useful by the President.

Rule 14

A special register shall be kept at the Secretariat in which shall be entered the date of registration of each application and the date of the termination of the relevant proceedings before the Commission.

Title II — The functioning of the Commission

Chapter I — General Rules

Rule 15

1. The seat of the Commission shall be in Strasbourg.

2. The Commission may decide, at any stage of the examination of an application, that it is necessary that an investigation or any other of its functions be carried out elsewhere by it or one or more of its members.

Rule 16

1. The Commission shall meet during at least sixteen weeks in each year.

2. The Commission shall, at the last session of each year at the latest, fix its sessions for the following year. It shall meet at other times by decision of the President as circumstances may require. It shall also meet if at least one third of the members so request.

3. Members who are prevented by illness or other serious reason from attending all or part of any session of the Commission or from fulfilling any other duty shall, as soon as possible, give notice thereof to the Secretary who shall inform the President.

Rule 17

1. All deliberations of the Commission shall be and shall remain confidential. Only the Secretary to the Commission, members of its Secretariat, interpreters, and persons providing technical or secretarial assistance to the Commission may be present at its meetings, unless the Commission decides otherwise.

2. The contents of all case-files, including all pleadings, shall be confidential. However, the decisions of the Commission on admissibility shall be available to the public, provided that the name or other means of identification of an applicant shall not be indicated, unless the Commission decides otherwise.

3. At any stage in the examination of an application, the Secretary may communicate information to the press to an extent compatible with the legitimate interests of the parties and subject to any special directions by the Commission.

Rule 18

1. After any deliberations and before a vote is taken on any matter in the Commission, the President may request members to state their opinions thereon, in the order of precedence laid down in Rule 4, starting with the junior member. The vote may also be taken in the same manner.

2. If the voting is equal, a roll call vote shall then be taken as provided in paragraph 1 of this Rule and the President shall have a casting vote.

3. In decisions on the admissibility of an application, or in expressing an opinion on a breach of the Convention, members shall not abstain.

Rule 19

1. The records of deliberations shall be limited to a record of the subject of the discussions, the votes taken, the names of those voting for and against a motion and any statements expressly made for insertion therein.

2. The records of hearings shall contain the names of the members present and of any persons appearing; they shall give a brief account of the course of the hearing and of any decision taken.

3. The draft minutes of the Commission's sessions shall be circulated to members and if no comments are received within a prescribed time-limit they shall be deemed to be adopted. Any such comments will be taken up at the next session.

Rule 20

1. Members shall not take part in the examination of an application before the Commission, where they

   a. have any personal interest in the case;

   b. have participated in any decision on the facts on which the application is based as adviser to any of the parties or as a member of any tribunal or body of enquiry.

2. If, in any case of doubt with regard to paragraph 1 of this Rule, or in any other circumstances which might appear to affect the impartiality of members in their examination of an application, they or the President consider that they should not take part, the Commission shall decide.

Rule 21

When, for any special reason other than under Rule 20, members consider that they should not take part or continue to take part in the examination of a case, they shall inform the President.

Rule 22

Any member who, under the provisions of Rule 20 or Rule 21, does not take part in the examination of an application, shall not form part of the quorum during such examination.

Chapter II — The Plenary Commission

Rule 23

1. A quorum of the Commission shall consist of a number of members equal to the majority of the members of the Commission.

2. However, seven members shall constitute a quorum when the Commission examines an application submitted under Article 25 of the Convention and:

a. decides to act as provided in Rule 48, paragraph 2, or

b. declares the application inadmissible or decides to strike it off its list of cases provided that notice of the application has not been given to the High Contracting Party concerned under Rule 48, paragraph 2 b.

3. Seven members shall also constitute a quorum when the Commission acts in pursuance of the Addendum to the present Rules (Legal aid).

Chapter III — The Chambers

Rule 24

1. There shall be two Chambers set up under Article 20, paragraph 2, of the Convention.

2. The composition of the Chambers shall be determined by the Commission.

3. The Chambers shall be constituted for three years as soon as possible following the election of the President of the Commission in accordance with Rule 6 of these Rules.

4. The Commission may make such special arrangements concerning the constitution of Chambers as it sees fit.

Rule 25

1. Where a member of the Commission elected in respect of the High Contracting Party against which a petition has been lodged is not a member of the Chamber to which that petition has been referred, but wishes to sit on that Chamber in accordance with Article 20, paragraph 2, last sentence, of the Convention, the President of the Chamber shall be so informed.

2. Where members of a Chamber cease to be members of the Commission before the expiration of the period for which the Chamber was constituted, their successors in the Commission shall succeed them as members of the Chamber.

Rule 26

1. A quorum of a Chamber shall be seven members.

2. As a rule, the Chambers meet during the sessions of the Commission.

3. Where circumstances require, the Chamber or, when it is not in session, its President, may decide that the Chamber may meet when the Commission is not in session.

Chapter IV — The Committees

Rule 27

1. There shall be Committees set up under Article 20, paragraph 3, of the Convention.

2. The Committees shall be constituted once a year. The members shall be chosen by the drawing of lots.

Rule 28

1. The Committees shall each be composed of three members. The President of the Commission shall not be a member of a Committee.

2. The members of the Commission who shall sit on the Committees shall be distributed in three lists, following the order of precedence set out in Rule 4 of these Rules. Each Committee shall be composed of one member from each list, chosen in the above order of precedence.

3. The members of the Commission who have not been chosen to sit on Committees shall act as substitute Committee members.

4. If a member is prevented from attending, a substitute member shall sit in that member's place. If none of the substitute members is able to attend, a member appearing on the same list as the member prevented from attending shall sit on the Committee.

Rule 29

Committees meet during the sessions of the Commission.

Title III — Procedure

Chapter I — General Rules

Rule 30

1. The official languages of the Commission shall be English and French.

2. The President may authorise a member to speak in another language.

3. The President may permit the use by a party or a person representing that party of a language other than English or French, either in hearings or documents. Any such document shall be submitted in an original and at least two copies.

4. The Secretary is authorised, in correspondence with an applicant, to employ a language other than English or French.

Rule 31

The High Contracting Parties shall be represented before the Commission by their agents who may have the assistance of advisers.

Rule 32

1. Persons, non-governmental organisations, or groups of individuals, may present and conduct applications under Article 25 of the Convention on their own behalf or through a representative appointed under paragraph 2 of this Rule.

2. Any such applicant may appoint, and be represented in proceedings before the Commission by, a lawyer or any other person, resident in a Convention country, unless the Commission at any stage decides otherwise.

3. Any such applicant or representative shall appear in person before the Commission:

   a. to present the application in a hearing fixed by the Commission; or

   b. for any other purpose, if invited by the Commission.

4. In the other provisions of these Rules the term "applicant" shall, where appropriate, include the applicant's representative.

Rule 33

The Commission shall deal with applications in the order in which they become ready for examination. It may, however, decide to give precedence to a particular application.

Rule 34

1. The Commission may, *proprio motu* or at the request of a party, take any action which it considers expedient or necessary for the proper performance of its duties under the Convention.

2. The Commission may delegate one or more of its members to take any such action in its name, and in particular to hear witnesses or experts, to examine documents or to visit any locality. Such member or members shall duly report to the Commission.

3. In case of urgency when the Commission is not in session, the President of the Commission or, if he is prevented from carrying out his duties, the President of either Chamber, may take any necessary action on behalf of the Commission. As soon as the Commission is again in session, any action which has been taken under this paragraph shall be brought to its attention.

Rule 35

The Commission may, if it considers necessary, order the joinder of two or more applications.

Rule 36

The Commission, or when it is not in session, the President may indicate to the parties any interim measure the adoption of which seems desirable in the interest of the parties or the proper conduct of the proceedings before it.

Chapter II — Hearings

Rule 37

1. Hearings before the Commission shall be held in camera. Unless the Commission decides otherwise, no person shall be admitted, other than:

    a. the persons referred to in Rule 31 or 32;

    b. the individual applicant;

    c. any person being heard by the Commission as a witness;

    d. the persons referred to in Rule 17, paragraph 1.

2. If the applicant is a non-governmental organisation or group of individuals, the Commission shall ensure that those appearing are entitled to represent it.

3. When it considers it in the interest of the proper conduct of a hearing, the Commission may limit the number of the parties' representatives or advisers who may appear.

4. The parties shall inform the Commission at least ten days before the date of the opening of the hearing of the names and functions of the persons who will appear on their behalf at the hearing.

5. The provisions of the present Rule shall apply *mutatis mutandis* to hearings before delegates of the Commission.

Rule 38

1. Any individual applicant, expert or other person whom the Commission decides to hear as a witness, shall be summoned by the Secretary. The summons shall indicate:

    a. the parties to the application;

    b. the facts or issues regarding which the person concerned will be heard;

    c. the arrangements made, in accordance with Rule 42,

paragraph 1 or 2, to reimburse the persons concerned for any expenses incurred by them.

2. Any such persons may, if they have not sufficient knowledge of English or French, be authorised by the President to speak in any other language.

Rule 39

1. After establishing the identity of the witnesses or experts the President or the principal delegate mentioned in Rule 34, paragraph 2, shall request them to take the following oath:

   a. for witnesses: "I swear that I will speak the truth, the whole truth and nothing but the truth."

   b. for experts: "I swear that my statement will be in accordance with my sincere belief."

2. Instead of taking the oath in the terms set out in paragraph 1 of this Rule, the witnesses or experts may make the following declaration:

   a. for witnesses: "I solemnly declare upon my honour and conscience that I will speak the truth, the whole truth and nothing but the truth."

   b. for experts: "I solemnly declare upon my honour and conscience that my statement will be in accordance with my sincere belief."

Rule 40

1. The President, or the principal delegate, shall conduct the hearing or examination of any persons heard. Any member may put questions to the parties or to the persons heard with the leave of the President or the principal delegate.

2. A party may, with the permission of the President or of the principal delegate, also put questions to any person heard.

Rule 41

1. The Secretary shall be responsible for the production of verbatim records of hearings before the Commission.

2. The parties or, where appropriate, their representatives shall receive a draft verbatim record of their submissions in order that they may propose corrections to the Secretary within a time-limit laid down by the President. After necessary corrections, if any, the text shall constitute certified matters of record.

Rule 42

1. The expenses incurred by any person who is heard by the Commission as a witness at the request of a party shall be borne either by that party or by the Council of Europe, as the Commission may decide. Where it is decided that the expenses shall be borne by the Council of Europe, the amount shall be fixed by the President of the Commission.

2. The expenses incurred by any such person whom the Commission hears *proprio motu* shall be fixed by the President and be borne by the Council of Europe.

3. Where the Commission decides to obtain written expert opinions, the costs, as agreed by the President, shall be borne by the Council of Europe.

4. Where the Commission decides to obtain written evidence, any costs incurred by the party who submits it shall be borne either by that party or by the Council of Europe, as the Commission may decide. Where it is decided that the costs shall be borne by the Council of Europe, the amount shall be agreed by the President of the Commission.

Chapter III — Institution of Proceedings

Rule 43

1. Any application made under Articles 24 or 25 of the Convention shall be submitted in writing and shall be signed by the applicant or by the applicant's representative.

2. Where an application is submitted by a non-governmental organisation or by a group of individuals, it shall be signed by those persons competent to represent such organisation or group. The Commission shall determine any question as to whether the persons who have signed an application are competent to do so.

3. Where applicants are represented in accordance with Rule 32 of these Rules, a power of attorney or written authorisation shall be supplied by their representative or representatives.

Rule 44

1. Any application under Article 25 of the Convention shall be made on the application form provided by the Secretariat, unless the President decides otherwise. It shall set out:

    a. the name, age, occupation and address of the applicant;

    b. the name, occupation and address of the representative, if any;

    c. the name of the High Contracting Party against which the application is made;

    d. the object of the application and the provision of the Convention alleged to have been violated;

    e. a statement of the facts and arguments;

    f. any relevant documents and in particular the decisions, whether judicial or not, relating to the object of the application.

2. Applicants shall furthermore:

    a. provide information enabling it to be shown that the conditions laid down in Article 26 of the Convention have been satisfied;

b. indicate whether they have submitted their complaints to any other procedure of international investigation or settlement;

c. indicate in which of the official languages they wish to receive the Commission's decisions;

d. indicate whether they do or do not object to their identity being disclosed to the public;

e. declare that they will respect the confidentiality of the proceedings before the Commission.

3. Failure to comply with the requirements set out under paragraphs 1 and 2 above may result in the application not being registered and examined by the Commission.

4. The date of introduction of the application shall in general be considered to be the date of the first communication from the applicant setting out, even summarily, the object of the application. The Commission may nevertheless for good cause decide that a different date be considered to be the date of introduction.

5. Applicants shall keep the Commission informed of any change of their address and of all circumstances relevant to the application.

Chapter IV — Proceedings on admissibility

Rule 45

1. Where, pursuant to Article 24 of the Convention, an application is brought before the Commission by a High Contracting Party, the President of the Commission shall give notice of such application to the High Contracting Party against which the claim is made and shall invite it to submit to the Commission its observations in writing on the admissibility of such application. The observations so obtained shall be communicated to the High Contracting Party which brought the application and it may submit written observations in reply.

2. The Commission shall designate one or more of its members to submit a report on admissibility. Rule 47, paragraph 3, is, by analogy, applicable to this report.

3. Before deciding upon the admissibility of the application the Commission may invite the parties to submit further observations, either in writing or at a hearing.

Rule 46

In any case of urgency, the Secretary to the Commission may, without prejudice to the taking of any other procedural steps, inform a High Contracting Party concerned in an application, by any available means, of the introduction of the application and of a summary of its objects.

Rule 47

1. Any application submitted pursuant to Article 25 of the Convention shall be referred to a member of the Commission who, as rapporteur, shall examine the application and submit a report to the Commission on its admissibility and a proposal on the procedure to be adopted.

2. Rapporteurs, in their examination of the application:

   a. may request relevant information on matters connected with the application, from the applicant or the High Contracting Party concerned;

   b. shall communicate any information so obtained from the High Contracting Party to the applicant for comments;

   c. shall decide whether to refer the application to a Committee.

3. The report of the rapporteur on the admissibility of the application shall contain:

   a. a statement of the relevant facts, including any information or comments obtained under paragraph 2 of this Rule;

   b. if necessary, an indication of the issues arising under the Convention in the application;

   c. a proposal on admissibility and on any other action to be taken, as the case may require.

Rule 48

1. The Commission shall consider the report of the rapporteur and may declare at once that the application is inadmissible or to be struck off its list.

2. Alternatively, the Commission may:

   a. request relevant information on matters connected with the application from the applicant or the High Contracting Party concerned. Any information so obtained from the High Contracting Party shall be communicated to the applicant for comments;

   b. give notice of the application to the High Contracting Party against which it is brought and invite that Party to present to the Commission written observations on the application. Any observations so obtained shall be communicated to the applicant for any written observations in reply.

Rule 49

1. An application shall be referred to a Chamber unless it has been referred to a Committee under Rule 47, paragraph 2 c, or its examination by a Chamber is excluded under Article 20, paragraph 2, of the Convention.

2. Applications shall normally be referred to the Chamber which includes the member of the Commission elected in respect of the High Contracting Party against which the application has been made.

3. If there is a reasoned request from a party that the application should be referred to the Plenary Commission, that request shall be considered by the Plenary Commission.

4. The members of the Commission shall be informed of the decisions of the Chambers.

Rule 50

Before deciding upon the admissibility of the application, the Commission may invite the parties:

   a. to submit further observations in writing;

b. to submit further observations orally at a hearing on issues of admissibility and at the same time, if the Commission so decides, on the merits of the application.

Rule 51

Time-limits shall be fixed by the rapporteur for any information or comments requested under Rule 47, paragraph 2, and by the Commission for any information, observations or comments requested under Rule 48, paragraph 2 and under Rule 50.

Rule 52

1. The decision of the Commission shall be communicated by the Secretary of the Commission to the applicant and to the High Contracting Party or Parties concerned. However, in the case provided for in paragraph 1 of Rule 48 or where information has been obtained from the applicant only, the decision shall be communicated to the High Contracting Party or Parties concerned only at their request and provided that the Commission does not decide otherwise.

2. The decision of the Commission shall state whether it was taken unanimously or by majority and shall be accompanied or followed by reasons.

Chapter V — Procedure after the admission of an application

Rule 53

1. After deciding to admit an application, the Commission shall decide on the procedure to be followed:

a. for the examination of the application under Article 28, paragraph 1 a, of the Convention;

b. with a view to securing a friendly settlement under Article 28, paragraph 1 b, of the Convention.

2. In order to accomplish its tasks under Article 28, paragraph 1 a, of the Convention, the Commission may invite the parties to submit further evidence and observations.

3. The Commission shall decide in each case whether observations should be submitted in writing or orally at a hearing.

4. The President shall lay down the time-limits within which the parties shall submit evidence and written observations.

Rule 54

1. The Commission shall appoint one or more of its members as rapporteur.

2. The rapporteur may at any stage of the examination of an application under Article 25 of the Convention invite the parties to submit further written evidence and observations.

3. The rapporteur shall:

    a. draft such memoranda as may be required by the Commission for its consideration of the case before it;

    b. draft a Report for the Commission in accordance with Rule 57, Rule 60 or Rule 62, as the case may be.

Rule 55

The Commission may, when it sees fit, deliberate with a view to reaching a provisional opinion on the merits of the case.

Rule 56

Where the Commission decides to reject an application under Article 29 of the Convention, its decision shall be accompanied by reasons. The Secretary shall communicate the decision to the parties.

Chapter VI — The Report of the Commission

Rule 57

1. The Report provided for in Article 28, paragraph 2, of the Convention shall contain:

a. a description of the parties, their representatives and advisers;

b. a statement of the facts;

c. the terms of the settlement reached.

2. The Report shall also contain the names of the President and members participating and shall be signed by the President and the Secretary.

3. The Report shall be sent to the High Contracting Party or Parties concerned, to the Committee of Ministers and to the Secretary General of the Council of Europe for publication. It shall also be sent to the applicant.

Rule 58

1. When the Commission has found that no friendly settlement in accordance with Article 28, paragraph 1 b, of the Convention can be reached, it shall consider a draft Report drawn up by the Rapporteur on the basis of any provisional opinion reached by the Commission in its deliberations under Rule 55.

2. Where the Commission has been divided in its provisional opinion, the draft Report shall include alternative opinions, if the Commission so decides.

Rule 59

1. When the Commission considers the draft Report referred to in Rule 58, it shall adopt in the first place the parts of the Report in which it establishes the facts.

2. It shall then deliberate and vote on whether the facts found disclose any violation by the State concerned of its obligations under the Convention.

3. Only those members who have participated in the deliberations and votes provided for in this Rule shall be entitled to express their separate opinion in the Report.

Rule 60

1. The Report provided for in Article 31 of the Convention shall contain:

a. a description of the parties, their representatives and advisers;

b. a statement of the proceedings followed before the Commission;

c. a statement of the facts established;

d. the complaints declared admissible;

e. the opinion of the Commission, with an indication of the number of members forming the majority, as to whether or not the facts found disclose any breach by the State concerned of its obligations under the Convention;

f. the reasons upon which that opinion is based;

g. any separate opinion of a member of the Commission.

2. The Report shall contain the names of the President and the members participating in the deliberations and vote provided for in Rule 59, paragraph 2. It shall be signed by the President and by the Secretary.

3. It shall be sent, together with any proposal under Article 31, paragraph 3, of the Convention, to the Committee of Ministers and to the High Contracting Party or Parties concerned.

Rule 61

1. After the adoption of the Report drawn up under Article 31 of the Convention the Commission shall decide in plenary session whether or not to bring the case before the European Court of Human Rights under Article 48 a of the Convention.

2. Where the Commission decides to bring the case before the Court, it shall file its request with the Registry of the Court within three months after the transmission of the Report to the Committee of

Ministers. It shall also inform the Committee of Ministers and the parties to the application.

3. Where the Commission decides not to bring the case before the Court, it shall so inform the Court, the Committee of Ministers and the parties to the application.

Rule 62

1. The Report provided for in Article 30, paragraph 2, of the Convention shall contain:

   a. a description of the parties, their representatives and advisers;

   b. a statement of the facts;

   c. a brief account of the proceedings;

   d. the terms of the decision striking out the application together with the reasons therefor.

2. The Report shall contain the names of the President and members who participated in the decision striking out the application. It shall be signed by the President and by the Secretary.

3. It shall be communicated to the Committee of Ministers of the Council of Europe for information and to the parties. The Commission may publish it.

Title IV — Relations of the Commission with the Court

Rule 63

1. The Commission shall assist the European Court of Human Rights in any case brought before the Court. When a case is referred to the Court the Commission shall appoint, at a plenary session, one or more delegates to take part in the consideration of the case before the Court. These delegates may be assisted by any person appointed by the Commission. In discharging their functions they shall act in accordance with such directives as they may receive from the Commission.

2. Until delegates have been appointed, the President may, if consulted by the Court, express views upon the procedure to be followed before the Court.

Rule 64

1. When, in pursuance of Article 48 a of the Convention, the Commission decides to bring a case before the Court, it shall draw up a request indicating in particular:

    a. the parties to the proceedings before the Commission;

    b. the date on which the Commission adopted its Report;

    c. the date on which the Report was transmitted to the Committee of Ministers;

    d. the object of the request;

    e. the names and addresses of its delegates.

2. The Secretary of the Commission shall transmit to the Registry of the Court forty copies of the request referred to in paragraph 1 of this Rule.

Rule 65

When, in pursuance of Article 48 b, c or d of the Convention, a High Contracting Party brings a case before the Court, the Secretary of the Commission shall communicate to the Registry of the Court as soon as possible:

    a. the names and addresses of the Commission's delegates;

    b. any other information which the Commission may consider appropriate.

Rule 66

The Secretary to the Commission shall, as soon as the request referred to in Rule 64, paragraph 2, above, has been transmitted or the communication mentioned in Rule 33, paragraph 1 c, of the Rules of

Court, has been received, file with the Registry of the Court an adequate number of copies of the Commission's Report.

Rule 67

The Commission shall communicate to the Court, at its request, any memorial, evidence, document or information concerning the case, with the exception of documents relating to the attempt to secure a friendly settlement in accordance with Article 28, paragraph 1 b, of the Convention. The communication of those documents shall be subject in each case to a decision of the Commission.

Final title

Rule 68

1. Any Rule may be amended upon motion made after notice when such motion is carried at a plenary session of the Commission by a majority of all the members of the Commission. Notice of such a motion shall be delivered in writing to the Secretary of the Commission at least one month before the session where it is to be discussed. On receipt of such notice of motion the Secretary shall be required to inform all members of the Commission at the earliest possible moment.

2. Any Rule may be suspended upon motion made without notice, provided that this decision is taken unanimously. The suspension of a Rule shall in this case be limited in its operation to the particular purpose for which such suspension has been sought.

Addendum to the Rules of Procedure — Legal Aid

Rule 1

The Commission may, either at the request of an applicant lodging an application under Article 25 of the Convention or *proprio motu*, grant free legal aid to that applicant in connection with the representation of the case:

a. where observations in writing on the admissibility of that application have been received from the High Contracting Party concerned in pursuance of Rule 48, paragraph 2 b, or where the time-limit for their submission has expired, or

b. where the application has been declared admissible.

Rule 2

Free legal aid shall only be granted where the Commission is satisfied:

a. that it is essential for the proper discharge of the Commission's duties;

b. that the applicant has not sufficient means to meet all or part of the costs involved.

Rule 3

1. In order to determine whether or not applicants have sufficient means to meet all or part of the costs involved, the Commission shall require them to complete a form of declaration stating their income, capital assets and any financial commitments in respect of dependents, or any other financial obligations. Such declaration shall be certified by the appropriate domestic authority or authorities.

2. Before making a grant of free legal aid, the Commission shall request the High Contracting Party concerned to submit its comments in writing.

3. The Commission shall, after receiving the information mentioned in paragraphs 1 and 2 above, decide whether or not to grant free legal aid and shall inform the parties accordingly.

4. The President shall fix the time-limits within which the parties shall be requested to supply the information referred to in this Rule.

Rule 4

1. Fees shall be payable only to a barrister-at-law, solicitor or professor of law or professionally qualified person of similar status. Fees

may, where appropriate, be paid to more than one such lawyer as defined above.

2. Legal aid may be granted to cover not only lawyers' fees but also travelling and subsistence expenses and other necessary out-of-pocket expenses incurred by the applicant or appointed lawyer.

Rule 5

1. On the Commission deciding to grant legal aid, the Secretary shall, by agreement with the appointed lawyer, fix the rate of fees to be paid.

2. The Secretary shall as soon as possible notify the Secretary General of the Council of Europe of the rate of fees so agreed.

Rule 6

The Commission may, at any time, if it finds that the conditions set out in Rule 2 above are no longer satisfied, revoke its grant of free legal aid to an applicant, in whole or in part, and shall at once notify the parties thereof.

Rule 7

In case of urgency when the Commission is not in session, the President of the Commission or the President of either Chamber may exercise the powers conferred on the Commission by this Addendum. As soon as the Commission is again in session, any action which has been taken under this paragraph shall be brought to its attention.

National authorities competent to certify the indigence of applicants for the purposes of Rule 3 of the Legal Aid Addendum to the Commission's Rules of Procedure[1]

Austria

The mayor of the locality where the applicant has his or her legal or actual residence.

Belgium

The direct taxation department of the district in which the applicant lives issues him with a certificate of income or, with his authorisation, express and in writing, issues such to another person or administrative department.

The request, accompanied by such authorisation, may be addressed either to the local direct taxation department or to the *Administration centrale des contributions directes,* 45 rue Belliard, B - 1040 Brussels.

Denmark

The local tax authority.

Finland

The local social welfare authority.

France

The local tax authority for the applicant's place of residence.

---

1 The list has been completed by the Commission Secretariat on the basis of information available on 1 December 1992.

Germany

None. The applicant submits a prescribed form, duly completed and with supporting documents, which the Commission submits to the Federal Ministry of Justice.

Greece

a. A certificate from the mayor or president of the district in which the applicant lives giving details of his family situation, his employment and his assets; and

b. a certificate from the tax authority showing the applicant has made a tax return for the previous three years with the results thereof.

Iceland

The *Rikisskattstjóri* (Director of Internal Revenue), Skúlagotu 57, IS-Reykjavik.

Ireland

The Chief Inspector, Department of Social Welfare, 101/104 Marlboro Street, IRL-Dublin I.

Italy

a. Certification, by the responsible section of the tax authorities, of a declaration of means prepared by the applicant; or

b. certificate of indigence issued by the mayor of the municipality in which the applicant lives.

Luxembourg

On production of a certificate stating the amount of tax paid the previous year the College of Mayors and Aldermen of the municipality in which the applicant lives issues a certificate of indigence.

Malta

Dr. Joseph Mifsud, LL.D., The Law Courts, Valletta, Malta.

Netherlands

The local government *(gemeentebestuur)* in accordance with Article 11 of the Legal Aid Act *(Wet rechtsbijstand on- en minvermogenden)*

Norway

The local tax authority *(ligningskontor)* of the district in which the applicant lives.

Portugal

The local government *(junta de frequesia)* for the district in which the applicant lives.

Spain

The district office of the Finance Minister *(Delegación de Hacienda)* for the district in which the applicant lives.

Sweden

The local tax authority *(lokala skattemyndigheten)* certifies the means of persons requesting free legal aid.

Switzerland

The local tax authority for the applicant's place of residence.

Turkey

   a. The mayor of the municipality in which the applicant lives; or

   b. The elders' council for the village or district in which the applicant lives (Article 468 of the Code of civil procedure).

United Kingdom

a. England and Wales: DHSS, Legal Aid Assessment Office, No. 3 The Pavilions, Ashton on Ribble, Preston PR2 2PA

b. Scotland: The Scottish Legal Aid Board, 44 Drumsheugh Gardens, Edinburgh EH3 7SW

B. Second Protocol to the General Agreement on Privileges and Immunities of the Council of Europe

(Provisions in respect of the members of the European Commission of Human Rights)

Paris, 15 December 1956

Entry into force: 15 December 1956,
in accordance with Article 6

The governments signatory hereto, being members of the Council of Europe,

Considering that, under the terms of Article 59 of the Convention for the Protection of Human Rights and Fundamental Freedoms, signed at Rome on 4th November 1950, the members of the European Commission of Human Rights (hereinafter referred to as "the Commission") are entitled, during the discharge of their functions, to the privileges and immunities provided for in Article 40 of the Statute of the Council of Europe and in the Agreements made thereunder;

Considering that it is necessary to specify and define the said privileges and immunities in a Protocol to the General Agreement on Privileges and Immunities of the Council of Europe, signed at Paris on 2nd September 1949,

Have agreed as follows:

Article 1

The members of the Commission shall, while exercising their functions and during their journeys to and from their place of meeting, enjoy the following privileges and immunities:

   a. immunity from personal arrest or detention and from seizure of their personal baggage, and, in respect of words spoken or written and all acts done by them in their official capacity, immunity from legal process of every kind;

   b. inviolability for all papers and documents;

c. exemption in respect of themselves and their spouses from immigration restrictions or aliens registration in the State which they are visiting or through which they are passing in the exercise of their functions.

Article 2

1. No administration or other restrictions shall be imposed on the free movement of members of the Commission to and from the place of meeting of the Commission.

2. Members of the Commission shall, in the matter of customs and exchange control, be accorded:

a. by their own government, the same facilities as those accorded to senior officials travelling abroad on temporary official duty;

b. by the governments of other members, the same facilities as those accorded to representatives of foreign governments on temporary official duty.

Article 3

In order to secure for the members of the Commission complete freedom of speech and complete independence in the discharge of their duties, the immunity from legal process in respect of words spoken or written and all acts done by them in discharging their duties shall continue to be accorded, notwithstanding that the persons concerned are no longer engaged in the discharge of such duties.

Article 4

Privileges and immunities are accorded to the members of the Commission, not for the personal benefit of the individual themselves, but in order to safeguard the independent exercise of their functions. The Commission alone shall be competent to waive the immunity of its members; it has not only the right, but it is under a duty, to waive the immunity of one of its members in any case where, in its opinion, the immunity would impede the course of justice, and where it can be waived without prejudice to the purpose for which the immunity is accorded.

Article 5

This Protocol shall be open to the signature of the members of the Council of Europe who may become Parties to it either by:

  a. signature without reservation in respect of ratification; or by

  b. signature with reservation in respect of ratification followed by ratification.

Instruments of ratification shall be deposited with the Secretary General of the Council of Europe.

Article 6

1. This Protocol shall enter into force as soon as three members of the Council of Europe shall, in accordance with Article 5, have signed it without reservation in respect of ratification or shall have ratified it.

2. As regards any member subsequently signing it without reservation in respect of ratification, or ratifying it, this Protocol shall enter into force at the date of signature or deposit of the instrument of ratification.

Article 7

The Secretary General of the Council of Europe shall notify members of the Council of the date of entry into force of this Protocol and shall give the names of any members who have signed it without reservation in respect of ratification or who have ratified it.

In witness whereof the undersigned, being duly authorised to that effect, have signed the present Protocol.

Done at Paris, this 15th day of December 1956, in English and in French, both texts being equally authoritative, in a single copy which shall remain deposited in the archives of the Council of Europe. The Secretary General shall send certified copies to each of the signatory governments.

Signatures and ratifications[1]

Opening for signature: Paris, 15/12/56

Entry into force: 15/12/56

Member States	Date of signature	Date of ratification	Entry into force
Austria	13/11/58[2]	13/11/58[2]	13/11/58
Belgium	15/12/56	07/09/61	07/09/61
Bulgaria			
Cyprus	16/12/61	30/11/67	30/11/67
Czech Republic			
Denmark	15/12/56[2]	15/12/56[2]	15/12/56
Estonia			
Finland	16/11/89	11/12/89	11/12/89
France	15/12/56	10/03/78	10/03/78
Germany	15/12/56	07/07/60	07/07/60 D
Greece	15/12/56	02/02/61	02/02/61
Hungary	09/02/93		
Iceland	15/12/56[2]	15/12/56[2]	15/12/56
Ireland	21/09/67	21/09/67	21/09/67
Italy	15/12/56	04/06/58	04/06/58
Liechtenstein	16/05/79	11/12/79	11/12/79
Lithuania			
Luxembourg	15/12/56	08/01/60	08/01/60
Malta	12/12/66	06/05/69	06/05/69
Netherlands	29/04/57[2]	29/04/57[2]	29/04/57 T
Norway	15/12/56[2]	15/12/56[2]	15/12/56
Poland	16/03/93	22/04/93	22/04/93

Member States	Date of signature	Date of ratification	Entry into force
Portugal	27/04/78	06/07/82	06/07/82
Romania			
San Marino	01/03/89	22/03/89	22/03/89
Slovakia			
Slovenia			
Spain	23/07/87	23/06/89	23/06/89
Sweden	15/12/56[2]	15/12/56[2]	15/12/56
Switzerland	15/04/64	29/11/65	29/11/65
Turkey	25/09/57	07/01/60	07/01/60
United Kingdom	15/12/56	08/07/58	08/07/58

1   Treaty open for signature by the member States.

2   Signature without reservation as to ratification

T: Territorial Declaration.

Declarations

Federal Republic of Germany

Declaration contained in a letter from the Permanent Representative of the Federal Republic of Germany, dated 20 August 1960, registered at the Secretariat General on 23 August 1960 (Or. Fr.)

The Second Protocol to the General Agreement on Privileges and Immunities of the Council of Europe is also applicable to the "Land Berlin" with effect from 7 July 1960.

Netherlands

Declaration made at the time of signature, on 29 April 1957 (Or. Fr.)

At the time of signing the Second Protocol to the General Agreement on Privileges and Immunities of the Council of Europe, opened to signature on 15 December 1956 at Paris, I declare on behalf of the government of the Kingdom of the Netherlands that my signature shall be valid only for the parts of the Kingdom to which apply or shall apply the Convention for the Protection of Human Rights and Fundamental Freedoms signed at Rome on 4 November 1950 and the Protocol signed at Paris on 20 March 1952.

Declaration contained in a letter from the Permanent Representative of the Netherlands, dated 24 December 1985, registered at the Secretariat General on 3 January 1986 (Or. Engl.)

The island of Aruba, which is at present still part of the Netherlands Antilles, will obtain internal autonomy as a country within the Kingdom of the Netherlands as of 1 January 1986. Consequently the Kingdom will from then on no longer consist of two countries, namely the Netherlands (the Kingdom in Europe) and the Netherlands Antilles (situated in the Caribbean region), but will consist of three countries, namely the said two countries and the country Aruba.

As the changes being made on 1 January 1986 concern a shift only in the internal constitutional relations within the Kingdom of the Netherlands, and as the Kingdom as such will remain the subject under international law with which treaties are concluded, the said changes will have no consequences in international law regarding to treaties concluded by the Kingdom which already apply to the Netherlands Antilles, including Aruba. These treaties will remain in force for Aruba in its new capacity of country within the Kingdom. Therefore these treaties will as of 1 January 1986, as concerns the Kingdom of the Netherlands, apply to the Netherlands Antilles (without Aruba) and Aruba.

Consequently the treaties referred to in the annex, to which the Kingdom of the Netherlands is a Party and which apply to the Netherlands Antilles, will as of 1 January 1986 as concerns the Kingdom of the Netherlands apply to the Netherlands Antilles and Aruba.

C. Fifth Protocol to the General Agreement on Privileges and Immunities of the Council of Europe

(This Protocol applies at once to the Commission and to the Court: see text on p. 306)

D. Composition of the European Commission of Human Rights (January 1994)

Order of precedence		End of mandate
Prof. Carl Aage Nørgaard, President	(Danish)	17.05.1996
Prof. Stefan Trechsel, President of Second Chamber	(Swiss)	17.05.1999
Mr Albert Weitzel, President of First Chamber	(Luxemburger)	17.05.1999
Prof. Felix Ermacora	(Austrian)	17.05.1996
Prof. Edwin Busuttil	(Maltese)	17.05.1984[1]
Prof. Gaukur Jöründsson	(Iceland)	17.05.1999
Prof. A. Seref Gözübüyük	(Turkish)	17.05.1999
Prof. Jean-Claude Soyer	(French)	17.05.1999
Prof. Henry G. Schermers	(Dutch)	17.05.1996
Mr Hans Danelius	(Swedish)	17.05.1999
Mrs Gro Hillestad Thune	(Norwegian)	17.05.1996
Sir Basil Hall	(British)	17.05.1996
Mr Luis Fernando Martínez Ruíz	(Spanish)	17.05.1996
Prof. Christos L. Rozakis	(Greek)	17.05.1999
Mrs Jane Liddy	(Irish)	17.05.1999
Mr Loukis Loucaides	(Cypriot)	17.05.1996
Mr Jean-Claude Geus	(Belgian)	17.05.1996
Prof. Matti Paavo Pellonpää	(Finnish)	17.05.1996
Mr Benedikt Marxer	(Liechtensteiner)	17.05.1996
Mr Giordano Bruno Reffi	(San Marinese)	17.05.1996
Mr Marek A. Nowicki	(Polish)	17.05.1999
Mr Ireneu Cabral Barreto	(Portuguese)	17.05.1996
Prof. Benedetto Conforti	(Italian)	17.05.1999

---

1. In accordance with the provision of Article 22, para. 6, first sentence, Mr Busuttil still sits as full member of the Commission, although his term of office has formally expired.

European Court
of Human Rights

European Court of Human Rights

A. Rules of Court "A"

Adopted on 27 January 1994

Entry into force: 1 February 1994

The European Court of Human Rights,

Having regard to the Convention for the Protection of Human Rights and Fundamental Freedoms and the Protocols thereto,

Makes the present Rules:

Rule 1

(Definitions)

For the purposes of these Rules unless the context otherwise requires:

    a. the term "Convention" means the Convention for the Protection of Human Rights and Fundamental Freedoms and the Protocols thereto;

    b. the expression "Protocol No. 2" means Protocol No. 2 to the Convention conferring upon the European Court of Human Rights competence to give advisory opinions;

c. the expression "plenary Court" means the European Court of Human Rights sitting in plenary session;

d.[1] the term "Chamber" means any Chamber constituted in pursuance of Article 43 of the Convention; the term "Grand Chamber" means the Chamber provided for under Rule 51;

e.[1] the term "Court" means either the plenary Court, the Grand Chambers or the Chambers;

f. the expression *"ad hoc judge"* means any person, other than an elected judge, chosen by a Contracting Party in pursuance of Article 43 of the Convention to sit as a member of a Chamber;

g. the term "judge" or "judges" means the judges elected by the Consultative Assembly of the Council of Europe or *ad hoc* judges;

h. the term "Parties" means those Contracting Parties which are the applicant and respondent Parties;

i. the term "Commission" means the European Commission of Human Rights;

j. the expression "Delegates of the Commission" means the member or members of the Commission delegated by it to take part in the consideration of a case before the Court;

k.[2] the term "applicant" means:

– in Title I and in Rules 50, 53, 54 and 55 of the present Rules, the person, non-governmental organisation or group of individuals who lodged a complaint with the Commission under Article 25 of the Convention;

– in Title II with the exception of Rules 50, 53, 54 and 55, such a person, organisation or group when he or it expressed the desire, in accordance with Rule 33, to take part in the proceedings pending before the Court;

---

1 As amended by the Court on 27 January 1994.

2 As amended by the Court on 26 January 1989 and 23 May 1991.

l. the expression "report of the Commission" means the report provided for in Article 31 of the Convention;

m. the expression "Committee of Ministers" means the Committee of Ministers of the Council of Europe.

Title I — Organisation and working of the Court

Chapter I — Judges

Rule 2

(Calculation of term of office)

1. The duration of the term of office of an elected judge shall be calculated as from his election. However, when a judge is re-elected on the expiry of his term of office or is elected to replace a judge whose term of office has expired or is about to expire, the duration of his term of office shall, in either case, be calculated as from the date of such expiry.

2. In accordance with Article 40, paragraph 5, of the Convention, a judge elected to replace a judge whose term of office has not expired shall hold office for the remainder of his predecessor's term.

3. In accordance with Article 40, paragraph 6, of the Convention, an elected judge shall hold office until his successor has taken the oath or made the declaration provided for in Rule 3. Thereafter he shall continue to deal with any case in connection with which hearings or, failing that, deliberations have begun before him.

Rule 3

(Oath or solemn declaration)

1. Before taking up his duties, each elected judge shall, at the first sitting of the plenary Court at which he is present after his election or, in case of need, before the President, take the following oath or make the following solemn declaration:

"I swear" — or "I solemnly declare" — "that I will exercise my functions as a judge honourably, independently and impartially and that I will keep secret all deliberations."

2. This act shall be recorded in minutes.

Rule 4

(Obstacle to the exercise of the functions of judge)

A judge may not exercise his functions while he is a member of a Government or while he holds a post or exercises a profession which is incompatible with his independence and impartiality. In case of need the plenary Court shall decide.

Rule 5

(Precedence)

1. Elected judges shall take precedence after the President and the Vice-President according to the date of their election; in the event of re-election, even if it is not an immediate re-election, the length of time during which the judge concerned previously exercised his functions as a judge shall be taken into account.

2. Judges elected on the same date shall take precedence according to age.

3. Ad hoc judges shall take precedence after the elected judges according to age.

Rule 6

(Resignation)

Resignation of a judge shall be notified to the President who shall transmit it to the Secretary General of the Council of Europe. Subject to the provisions of Rule 2, paragraph 3, resignation shall constitute vacation of office.

Chapter II — Presidency of the Court

Rule 7

(Election of the President and Vice-President)

1. The Court shall elect its President and Vice-President for a period of three years, provided that such period shall not exceed the duration of their term of office as judges. They may be re-elected.

2. The President and Vice-President shall continue to exercise their functions until the election of their respective successors.

3. If the President or Vice-President ceases to be a member of the Court or resigns his office before its normal expiry, the plenary Court shall elect a successor for the remainder of the term of that office.

4. The elections referred to in this Rule shall be by secret ballot; only the elected judges who are present shall take part. If no judge receives an absolute majority of the elected judges present, a ballot shall take place between the two judges who have received most votes. In the case of equal voting, preference shall be given to the judge having precedence in accordance with Rule 5.

Rule 8

(Functions of the President)

The President shall direct the work and administration of the Court and shall preside at its sessions. He shall represent the Court and, in particular, be responsible for its relations with the authorities of the Council of Europe.

Rule 9

(Functions of the Vice-President)

The Vice-President shall take the place of the President if the latter is unable to carry out his functions or if the office of President is vacant.

Rule 10

(Replacement of the President and Vice-President)

If the President and Vice-President are at the same time unable to carry out their functions or if their offices are at the same time vacant, the office of President shall be assumed by another elected judge in accordance with the order of precedence provided for in Rule 5.

Chapter III — The registry

Rule 11

(Election of the Registrar)

1. The plenary Court shall elect its Registrar after the President has in this respect consulted the Secretary General of the Council of Europe. The candidates must possess the legal knowledge and the experience necessary to carry out the functions attaching to the post and must have an adequate working knowledge of the two official languages of the Court.

2. The Registrar shall be elected for a term of seven years. He may be re-elected.

3. The elections referred to in this Rule shall be by secret ballot; only the elected judges who are present shall take part. If no candidate receives an absolute majority of the elected judges present, a ballot shall take place between the two candidates who have received most votes. In the case of equal voting, preference shall be given to the older candidate.

4. Before taking up his functions, the Registrar shall take the following oath or make the following solemn declaration before the plenary Court or, if it is not in session, before the President:

> "I swear" — or "I solemnly declare" — "that I will exercise loyally, discreetly and conscientiously the functions conferred upon me as Registrar of the European Court of Human Rights."

This act shall be recorded in minutes.

Rule 12

(Election of the Deputy Registrar)

1. The plenary Court shall also elect a Deputy Registrar according to the conditions and in the manner and for the term prescribed in Rule 11. It shall first consult the Registrar.

2. Before taking up his functions, the Deputy Registrar shall take an oath or make a solemn declaration before the plenary Court or, if it is not in session, before the President, in similar terms to those prescribed in respect of the Registrar. This act shall be recorded in minutes.

Rule 13

(Other staff, equipment and facilities)

The President, or the Registrar on his behalf, shall request the Secretary General of the Council of Europe to provide the Registrar with the staff, permanent or temporary, equipment and facilities necessary for the Court.

The officials of the registry, other than the Registrar and the Deputy Registrar, shall be appointed by the Secretary General, with the agreement of the President or of the Registrar acting on the President's instructions.

Rule 14

(Functions of the Registrar)

1. The Registrar shall assist the Court in the performance of its functions. He shall be responsible for the organisation and activities of the registry under the authority of the President.

2. The Registrar shall have the custody of the archives of the Court and shall be the channel for all communications and notifications made by, or addressed to, the Court in connection with the cases brought or to be brought before it.

3. The Registrar shall ensure that the dates of despatch and receipt of any communication or notification relating to the above-mentioned cases may be easily verified. Communications or notifications addressed to the Agents of the Parties, to the Delegates of the Commission or to the representative, if any, of the applicant shall be considered as having been addressed to the Parties, to the Commission or to the applicant, as the case may be. The date of receipt shall be noted on each document received by the Registrar who shall transmit to the sender a receipt bearing this date and the number under which the document has been registered.

4. The Registrar shall, subject to the discretion attaching to his functions, reply to requests for information concerning the work of the Court, in particular from the press. He shall announce the date and time fixed for the hearings in open court and shall be responsible for making immediately available to the public all judgments delivered by the Court.

5. General instructions drawn up by the Registrar and sanctioned by the President shall provide for the working of the registry.

Chapter IV — The working of the Court

Rule 15[1]

(Seat of the Court)

The seat of the Court shall be at the seat of the Council of Europe at Strasbourg. The Court may, however, if it considers it expedient, exercise its functions elsewhere in the territories of the Member States of the Council of Europe.

Rule 16

(Sessions of the plenary Court)

The plenary sessions of the Court shall be convened by the President whenever the exercise of its functions under the Convention and

---

1 As amended by the Court on 27 May 1993.

under these Rules so requires. The President shall convene a plenary session if at least one-third of the members of the Court so request, and in any event once a year to consider administrative matters.

Rule 17

(Quorum)

1.[1] The quorum of the plenary Court shall be two-thirds of the judges.

2. If there is no quorum, the President shall adjourn the sitting.

Rule 18

(Public character of the hearings)

The hearings shall be public unless the Court shall in exceptional circumstances decide otherwise.

Rule 19

(Deliberations)

1. The Court shall deliberate in private. Its deliberations shall remain secret.

2. Only the judges shall take part in the deliberations. The Registrar or his substitute, as well as such other officials of the registry and interpreters whose assistance is deemed necessary, shall be present. No other person may be admitted except by special decision of the Court.

3. Each judge present at such deliberations shall state his opinion and the reasons therefor.

4. Any question which is to be voted upon shall be formulated in precise terms in the two official languages and the text shall, if a judge so requests, be distributed before the vote is taken.

---

1 As amended by the Court on 27 January 1994.

5. The minutes of the private sittings of the Court for deliberations shall remain secret; they shall be limited to a record of the subject of the discussions, the votes taken, the names of those voting for and against a motion and any statements expressly made for insertion in the minutes.

Rule 20

(Votes)

1. The decisions of the Court shall be taken by the majority of judges present.

2. The votes shall be cast in the inverse order to the order of precedence provided for in Rule 5.

3. If the voting is equal, the President shall have a second and casting vote.

Chapter V — The Chambers

Rule 21

(Composition of the Court when constituted in a Chamber)

1.[1] When a case is brought before the Court either by the Commission or by a Contracting State having the right to do so under Article 48 of the Convention, the Court shall be constituted in a Chamber of nine judges.

2. On the reference of a case to the Court, the Registrar shall notify all the judges, including the newly-elected judges, that such a Chamber is to be constituted. If any judge, upon receiving such notification, believes that for one of the reasons set out in Rule 24 he will be unable to sit, he shall so inform the Registrar. The President shall then draw up the list of judges available to constitute the Chamber.

3.[2] There shall sit as *ex officio* members of the Chamber:

---

1 As amended by the Court on 23 May 1990.

2 As amended by the Court on 27 May 1993.

a. in accordance with Article 43 of the Convention, every judge who has the nationality of a Party;

b. the President of the Court, or, failing him, the Vice-President, provided that they do not sit by virtue of the preceding sub-paragraph.

4. The other judges named on the list provided for in paragraph 2 shall be called upon to complete the Chamber, as members or as substitutes, in the order determined by a drawing of lots effected by the President of the Court in the presence of the Registrar.

5.[1] The President of the Chamber shall be the judge sitting by virtue of paragraph 3.b or, failing one, a judge appointed under paragraph 4 as a member of the Chamber, in accordance with the order of precedence provided for in Rule 5.

If the President of the Chamber is unable to sit or withdraws, he shall be replaced by the Vice-President or, if the same applies to him, by a judge appointed under paragraph 4 as a member of the Chamber, in accordance with the said order of precedence. However, where he is unable to sit or withdraws less than twenty-four hours before the opening of, or during or after, the hearing, his place shall be taken, in accordance with the said order of precedence, by one of the judges called upon to be present or present at the hearing.

6. If the President of the Court finds that two cases concern the same Party or Parties and raise similar issues, he may refer the second case to the Chamber already constituted, or in the course of constitution, for the consideration of the first case or, if there is none, proceed to the constitution of one Chamber to consider both cases.

Rule 22

(Substitute judges)

1. The substitute judges shall be called upon, in the order determined by the drawing of lots, to replace the judges appointed as members of the Chamber by virtue of Rule 21, paragraph 4.

---

1 As amended by the Court on 27 May 1993.

2. Judges who have been so replaced shall cease to be members of the Chamber.

3. The substitute judges shall be supplied with the documents relating to the proceedings. The President may convoke one or more of them, according to the above order of precedence, to attend the hearings and deliberations.

Rule 23

(Ad hoc judges)

1.[1] If the Court does not include a judge elected in respect of a Party or if the judge called upon to sit in that capacity is unable to sit or withdraws, the President of the Court shall invite that Party to inform him within thirty days whether it wishes to appoint to sit as judge either another elected judge or, as an *ad hoc* judge, any other person possessing the qualifications required under Article 39, paragraph 3, of the Convention and, if so, to state at the same time the name of the person so appointed. The same rule shall apply if the person so appointed is unable to sit or withdraws.

2. The Party concerned shall be presumed to have waived such right of appointment if it does not reply within thirty days.

3. An *ad hoc* judge shall, at the opening of the first sitting fixed for the consideration of the case after he has been appointed, take the oath or make the solemn declaration provided for in Rule 3. This act shall be recorded in minutes.

Rule 24

(Inability to sit, withdrawal or exemption)

1. Any judge who is prevented from taking part in sittings for which he has been convoked shall, as soon as possible, give notice thereof to the President of the Chamber or to the Registrar.

2. A judge may not take part in the consideration of any case in which he has a personal interest or has previously acted either as the

---

1 As amended by the Court on 27 May 1993.

agent, advocate or adviser of a Party or of a person having an interest in the case, or as member of a tribunal or commission of enquiry, or in any other capacity.

3. If a judge withdraws for one of the said reasons, or for some special reason, he shall inform the President who shall exempt him from sitting.

4. If the President considers that a reason exists for a judge to withdraw, he shall consult with the judge concerned; in the event of disagreement, the Court shall decide.

5. Any judge who has been called upon to sit on one or more recent cases may, at his own request, be exempted by the President from sitting on a new case.

Rule 25

(Common interest)

1.[1] If several Parties have a common interest, the President of the Court may invite them to agree to appoint a single elected judge or *ad hoc* judge in accordance with Article 43 of the Convention. If the Parties are unable to agree, the President shall choose by lot, from among the persons proposed as judges by these Parties, the judge called upon to sit *ex officio*. The names of the other judges and substitute judges shall then be chosen by lot by the President from among the judges who have not been elected in respect of a Party.

2. In the event of dispute as to the existence of a common interest, the plenary Court shall decide.

---

1 As amended by the Court on 23 May 1991 and 27 May 1993.

Title II — Procedure

Chapter I — General Rules

Rule 26[1]

(Possibility of particular derogations)

The provisions of this Title shall not prevent the Court from derogating from them for the consideration of a particular case after having consulted the Party or Parties, the Delegates of the Commission and the applicant.

Rule 27

(Official languages)

1. The official languages of the Court shall be English and French.

2. A Party may, not later than the consultation provided for in Rule 38, apply to the President for leave to use another language at the oral hearings. If such leave is granted by the President, the Party concerned shall be responsible for the interpretation into English or French of the oral arguments or statements made by its Agent, advocates or advisers and shall, to the extent which the President may determine in each case, bear the other extra expenses involved in the use of a non-official language.

3. The President may grant the applicant, as well as any person assisting the Delegates under Rule 29, paragraph 1, leave to use a non-official language. In that event, the Registrar shall make the necessary arrangements for the translation or interpretation into English and French of their comments or statements.

4. Any witness, expert or other person appearing before the Court may use his own language if he does not have sufficient knowledge of either of the two official languages. The Registrar shall, in that event, make the necessary arrangements for the interpretation into

---

1 As amended by the Court on 27 May 1993.

English and French of the statements of the witness, expert or other person concerned.

5. All judgments shall be given in English and in French; unless the Court decides otherwise, both texts shall be authentic.

Rule 28

(Representation of the Parties)

The Parties shall be represented by Agents who may have the assistance of advocates or advisers.

Rule 29

(Relations between the Court and the Commission and release of the report of the Commission)

1. The Commission shall delegate one or more of its members to take part in the consideration of a case before the Court. The Delegates may be assisted by other persons.

2. The Court shall, whether a case is referred to it by a Contracting Party or by the Commission, take into consideration the report of the latter.

3. Unless the President decides otherwise, the said report shall be made available to the public through the Registrar as soon as possible after the case has been brought before the Court.

Rule 30

(Representation of the applicant)

1. The applicant shall be represented by an advocate authorised to practise in any of the Contracting States and resident in the territory of one of them, or by any other person approved by the President. The President may, however, give leave to the applicant to present his own case, subject, if need be, to his being assisted by an advocate or other person as aforesaid.

2. Unless the President decides otherwise, the advocate or other person representing or assisting the applicant, or the applicant

himself if he seeks leave to present his own case, must have an adequate knowledge of one of the Court's official languages.

Rule 31

(Communications, notifications and summonses addressed to persons other than the Agents of the Parties or the Delegates of the Commission)

1. If, for any communication, notification or summons addressed to persons other than the Agents of the Parties or the Delegates of the Commission, the Court considers it necessary to have the assistance of the Government of the State on whose territory such communication, notification or summons is to have effect, the President shall apply directly to that Government in order to obtain the necessary facilities.

2. The same rule shall apply when the Court desires to make or arrange for the making of an investigation on the spot in order to establish the facts or to procure evidence or when it orders the appearance of a person resident in, or having to cross, that territory.

Chapter II — Institution of proceedings

Rule 32

(Filing of the application or request)

1. Any Contracting Party which intends to bring a case before the Court under Article 48 of the Convention shall file with the registry an application, in forty copies, indicating:

    a. the parties to the proceedings before the Commission;

    b. the date on which the Commission adopted its report;

    c. the date on which the report was transmitted to the Committee of Ministers;

    d. the object of the application;

    e. the name and address of the person appointed as Agent.

2. If the Commission intends to bring a case before the Court under Article 48 of the Convention, it shall file with the registry a request, in forty copies, signed by its President and containing the particulars indicated in sub-paragraphs a, b, c and d of paragraph 1 of this Rule together with the names and addresses of the Delegates of the Commission.

Rule 33

(Communication of the application or request)

1. On receipt of an application or request, the Registrar shall transmit a copy thereof:

a.[1] to all the members of the Court, and also, as the case may be,

b. to any Contracting Party mentioned in Article 48 of the Convention,

c. to the Commission,

d. to the person, non-governmental organisation or group of individuals who lodged the complaint with the Commission under Article 25 of the Convention.

He shall also inform the Committee of Ministers, through the Secretary General of the Council of Europe, of the filing of the application or request.

2. The communications provided for in sub-paragraphs a, b and d of paragraph 1 shall include a copy of the report of the Commission.

3. When making the communications provided for in sub-paragraphs b, c and d of paragraph 1, the Registrar shall invite:

a. the Contracting Party against which the complaint has been lodged before the Commission to notify him within two weeks of the name and address of its Agent;

b. any other Contracting Party which appears to have the right, under Article 48 of the Convention, to bring a case before the Court

---

1 As amended by the Court on 27 May 1993.

and which has not availed itself of that right, to inform him within four weeks whether it wishes to take part in the proceedings and, if so, to notify him at the same time of the name and address of its Agent;

c. the Commission to notify him as soon as possible of the names and addresses of its Delegates;

d. the person, non-governmental organisation or group of individuals who lodged the complaint with the Commission under Article 25 of the Convention to notify him within two weeks

– whether he or it wishes to take part in the proceedings pending before the Court;

– if so, of the name and address of the person appointed by him or it in accordance with Rule 30.

Rule 34[1]

(Question whether a Contracting Party has the right to bring a case before the Court)

In the event of a dispute as to whether a Contracting Party has the right under Article 48 to bring a case before the Court, the President shall submit that question for decision to the Grand Chamber provided for in paragraph 2 of Rule 51 of these Rules, without prejudice to the possible application of paragraph 5 of Rule 51.

Rule 35

(Notice of the composition of the Chamber)

As soon as a Chamber has been constituted for the consideration of a case, the Registrar shall communicate its composition to the judges, to the Agents of the Parties, to the Commission and to the applicant.

---

1 As amended by the Court on 27 January 1994.

Rule 36[1]

(Interim measures)

1. Before the constitution of a Chamber, the President of the Court may, at the request of a Party, of the Commission, of the applicant or of any other person concerned, or *proprio motu,* indicate to any Party and, where appropriate, the applicant, any interim measure which it is advisable for them to adopt. The Chamber when constituted or, if the Chamber is not in session, its President shall have the same power.

Notice of these measures shall be immediately given to the Committee of Ministers.

2. Where the Commission, pursuant to Rule 36 of its Rules of Procedure, has indicated an interim measure as desirable, its adoption or maintenance shall remain recommended to the Parties and, where appropriate, the applicant after the case has been brought before the Court, unless and until the President or the Chamber otherwise decides or until paragraph 1 of this Rule is applied.

Chapter III — Examination of cases

Rule 37 [2]

(Written procedure)

1. The proceedings before the Court shall, as a general rule, comprise as their first stage a written procedure in which memorials are filed by the Parties, the applicant and, if it so wishes, the Commission.

As soon as possible after the reference of a case to the Court, the President shall consult the Agents of the Parties, the applicant and the Delegates of the Commission, or, if the latter have not yet been appointed, the President of the Commission, as to the organisation

---

1 As amended by the Court on 26 January 1989.

2 As amended by the Court on 26 January 1989, 23 May 1991 and 27 May 1993.

of the proceedings; unless, with their agreement, he directs that a written procedure is to be dispensed with, he shall lay down the time-limits for the filing of the memorials.

No memorial or other document may be filed except within such time-limit (if any) or with the authorisation of the President or at his or the Chamber's request.

2. The President may, in the interests of the proper administration of justice, invite or grant leave to any Contracting State which is not a Party to the proceedings to submit written comments within a time-limit and on issues which he shall specify. He may extend such an invitation or grant such leave to any person concerned other than the applicant.

3. Where two cases have been referred to the same Chamber under Rule 21, paragraph 6, the President of the Chamber may, in the interests of the proper administration of justice and after consulting the Agents of the Parties, the Delegates of the Commission and the applicants, order that the proceedings in both cases be conducted simultaneously, without prejudice to the decision of the Chamber on the joinder of the cases.

4. Memorials, comments and documents annexed thereto shall be filed with the registry; they shall be filed in forty copies when they are submitted by a Party, by another State or by the Commission. The Registrar shall transmit copies thereof to the judges, to the Agents of the Parties, to the Delegates of the Commission and to the applicant, as the case may be.

Rule 38[1]

(Fixing of the date of the hearing)

The President of the Chamber shall, after consulting the Agents of the Parties, the Delegates of the Commission and the applicant, fix the date of the hearing. The Registrar shall notify them of the decision taken in this respect.

---

1 As amended by the Court on 27 May 1993.

Rule 39[1]

(Conduct of hearings)

The President of the Chamber shall direct hearings. He shall prescribe the order in which the Agents, advocates or advisers of the Parties, the Delegates of the Commission, any person assisting the Delegates in accordance with Rule 29, paragraph 1, and the applicant shall be called upon to speak.

Rule 40[2]

(Failure to appear at hearings)

Where, without showing sufficient cause, a Party or the applicant fails to appear, the Chamber may, provided that it is satisfied that such a course is consistent with the proper administration of justice, proceed with the hearing.

Rule 41

(Measures for taking evidence)

1. The Chamber may, at the request of a Party, of the Delegates of the Commission, of the applicant or of a third party invited or granted leave to submit written comments under Rule 37, paragraph 2, or *proprio motu,* obtain any evidence which it considers capable of providing clarification on the facts of the case. The Chamber may, *inter alia,* decide to hear as a witness or expert or in any other capacity any person whose evidence or statements seem likely to assist it in the carrying out of its task.

When the Chamber is not in session, the President of the Chamber may exercise, by way of preparatory measure, the powers set forth in the immediately foregoing sub-paragraph, without prejudice to the decision of the Chamber on the relevance of the evidence so taken or sought.

---

1 As amended by the Court on 27 May 1993.
2 Inserted by the Court on 26 January 1989. As a result, the subsequent Rules were renumbered and certain cross-references amended. As amended by the Court on 27 May 1993.

2. The Chamber may ask any person or institution of its choice to obtain information, express an opinion or make a report, upon any specific point.

3. Where a report drawn up in accordance with the preceding paragraphs has been prepared at the request of a Party, the costs relating thereto shall be borne by that Party unless the Chamber decides otherwise. In other cases, the Chamber shall decide whether such costs are to be borne by the Council of Europe, or awarded against an applicant, or a third party, at whose request the report was prepared. In all cases, the costs shall be taxed by the President.

4. The Chamber may, at any time during the proceedings, depute one or more of its members to conduct an enquiry, carry out an investigation on the spot or take evidence in some other manner.

Rule 42

(Convocation of witnesses, experts and other persons; costs of their appearance)

1. Witnesses, experts or other persons whom the Chamber or the President of the Chamber decides to hear shall be summoned by the Registrar. If they appear at the request of a Party, the costs of their appearance shall be borne by that Party unless the Chamber decides otherwise. In other cases, the Chamber shall decide whether such costs are to be borne by the Council of Europe or awarded against an applicant, or a third party within the meaning of Rule 41, paragraph 1, at whose request the person summoned appeared. In all cases, the costs shall, if need be, be taxed by the President.

2. The summons shall indicate:

– the case in connection with which it has been issued;

– the object of the enquiry, expert opinion or other measures ordered by the Chamber or the President of the Chamber;

– any provisions for the payment of the sum due to the person summoned.

Rule 43

(Oath or solemn declaration by witnesses and experts)

1. After the establishment of his identity and before giving evidence, every witness shall take the following oath or make the following solemn declaration:

> "I swear" — or "I solemnly declare upon my honour and conscience" — "that I will speak the truth, the whole truth and nothing but the truth."

This act shall be recorded in minutes.

2. After the establishment of his identity and before carrying out his task, every expert shall take the following oath or make the following solemn declaration:

> "I swear" — or "I solemnly declare" — "that I will discharge my duty as expert honourably and conscientiously."

This act shall be recorded in minutes.

This oath may be taken or this declaration made before the President of the Chamber, or before a judge or any public authority nominated by the President.

Rule 44[1]

(Objection to a witness or expert; hearing of a person for the purpose of information)

The Chamber shall decide in the event of any dispute arising from an objection to a witness or expert. It may hear for the purpose of information a person who cannot be heard as a witness.

Rule 45[1]

(Questions put during hearings)

1. The President or any judge may put questions to the Agents, advocates or advisers of the Parties, to the witnesses and experts, to

---

1 As amended by the Court on 27 May 1993.

the Delegates of the Commission, to the applicant and to any other persons appearing before the Chamber.

2. The witnesses, experts and other persons referred to in Rule 41, paragraph 1, may, subject to the control of the President, be examined by the Agents, advocates or advisers of the Parties, by the Delegates of the Commission, by any person assisting the Delegates in accordance with Rule 29, paragraph 1, and by the applicant. In the event of an objection as to the relevance of a question put, the Chamber shall decide.

Rule 46

(Failure to appear or false evidence)

When, without good reason, a witness or any other person who has been duly summoned fails to appear or refuses to give evidence, the Registrar shall, on being so required by the President, inform that Contracting Party to whose jurisdiction such witness or other person is subject. The same provisions shall apply when a witness or expert has, in the opinion of the Chamber, violated the oath or solemn declaration provided for in Rule 43.

Rule 47

(Verbatim record of hearings)

1. The Registrar shall be responsible for the making of a verbatim record of each hearing. The verbatim record shall include:

   a. the composition of the Chamber at the hearing;

   b. a list of those appearing before the Court, that is to say, Agents, advocates and advisers of the Parties, Delegates of the Commission and persons assisting them, applicants, Contracting States and other persons referred to in Rule 37, paragraph 2;

c.[1] the surnames, forenames, description and address of each witness, expert or other person heard;

d. the text of statements made, questions put and replies given;

e. the text of any decision delivered by the Chamber during the hearing.

2. The Agents, advocates and advisers of the Parties, the Delegates of the Commission, the applicant and the witnesses, experts and other persons mentioned in Rules 29, paragraph 1, and 41, paragraph 1, shall receive the verbatim record of their arguments, statements or evidence, in order that they may, subject to the control of the Registrar or the President of the Chamber, make corrections, but in no case may such corrections affect the sense and bearing of what was said. The Registrar, in accordance with the instructions of the President, shall fix the time-limits granted for this purpose.

3.[2] The verbatim record, once so corrected, shall be signed by the President and the Registrar and shall then constitute certified matters of record.

Rule 48

(Preliminary objections)

1. A Party wishing to raise a preliminary objection must file a statement setting out the objection and the grounds therefor not later than the time when that Party informs the President of its intention not to submit a memorial or, alternatively, not later than the expiry of the time-limit laid down under Rule 37, paragraph 1, for the filing of its first memorial.

2. Unless the Chamber decides otherwise, the filing of a preliminary objection shall not have the effect of suspending the proceedings on the merits. In all cases, the Chamber shall, after following the procedure provided for under Chapter III herein, give its decision on the objection or join the objection to the merits.

---

1 As amended by the Court on 27 May 1993.

2 As amended by the Court on 26 January 1989.

Rule 49

(Striking out of the list)

1. When the Party which has brought the case before the Court notifies the Registrar of its intention not to proceed with the case and when the other Parties agree to such discontinuance, the Chamber shall, after consulting the Commission and the applicant, decide whether or not it is appropriate to approve the discontinuance and accordingly to strike the case out of its list.

2.[1] When the Chamber is informed of a friendly settlement, arrangement or other fact of a kind to provide a solution of the matter, it may, after consulting, if necessary, the Parties, the Delegates of the Commission and the applicant, strike the case out of the list.

The same shall apply where the circumstances warrant the conclusion that the applicant does not intend to pursue his complaints or if, for any other reason, further examination of the case is not justified.

3. The striking out of a case shall be effected by means of a judgment which the President shall forward to the Committee of Ministers in order to allow them to supervise, in accordance with Article 54 of the Convention, the execution of any undertakings which may have been attached to the discontinuance or solution of the matter.

4. The Chamber may, having regard to the responsibilities of the Court under Article 19 of the Convention, decide that, notwithstanding the notice of discontinuance, friendly settlement, arrangement or other fact referred to in paragraphs 1 and 2 of this Rule, it should proceed with the consideration of the case.

Rule 50

(Question of the application of Article 50 of the Convention)

1.[2] Any claims which the applicant may wish to make under Article 50 of the Convention shall, unless the President otherwise directs,

---

1 As amended by the Court on 27 May 1993.

2 As amended by the Court on 26 January 1989.

be set out in his memorial or, if he does not submit a memorial, in a special document filed at least one month before the date fixed pursuant to Rule 38 for the hearing.

2. The Chamber may, at any time during the proceedings, invite any Party, the Commission and the applicant to submit comments on this question.

Rule 51[1]

(Relinquishment of jurisdiction by the Chamber in favour of the Grand Chamber; and by the Grand Chamber in favour of the plenary Court)

1. Where a case pending before a Chamber raises one or more serious questions affecting the interpretation of the Convention, the Chamber may, at any time during the proceedings, relinquish jurisdiction in favour of a Grand Chamber. Relinquishment of jurisdiction shall be obligatory where the resolution of such a question or questions might have a result inconsistent with a judgment previously delivered by the Court. Reasons need not be given for the decision to relinquish jurisdiction.

2. The Grand Chamber shall comprise nineteen judges and be composed as follows:

   a. the President and the Vice-President(s) of the Court;

   b. the other members of the Chamber which has relinquished jurisdiction;

   c. additional judges appointed by means of a separate drawing of lots by the President of the Court in the presence of the Registrar immediately after the Chamber has relinquished jurisdiction.

3. The quorum of the Grand Chamber shall be seventeen judges.

4. The Grand Chamber, when the case has been referred to it, may either retain jurisdiction over the whole case or, after deciding the said question or questions, order that the case be referred back to

---

1 As amended by the Court on 27 October 1993.

the Chamber, which shall, in regard to the remaining part of the case, recover its original jurisdiction.

5.[1] The Grand Chamber may exceptionally, when the issues raised are particularly serious or involve a significant change of existing case-law, relinquish jurisdiction in favour of the plenary Court, which for this purpose shall comprise all the judges.

When a case is referred to the plenary Court, any *ad hoc* judge who is a member of the Grand Chamber shall sit as a judge on the plenary Court.

The plenary Court, when the case has been referred to it, may either retain jurisdiction over the whole case or, after deciding the said question or questions, order that the case be referred back to the Grand Chamber, which shall, in regard to the remaining part of the case, recover its jurisdiction.

6. Any provisions governing the Chambers shall apply, *mutatis mutandis*, to proceedings before the Grand Chamber and the plenary Court.

Chapter IV — Judgments

Rule 52

(Procedure by default)

Where a Party fails to appear or to present its case, the Chamber shall, subject to the provisions of Rule 49, give a decision in the case.

Rule 53

(Contents of the judgment)

1. The judgment shall contain:

    a. the names of the President and the judges constituting the

---

1 As amended by the Court on 27 January 1994.

Chamber, and also the names of the Registrar and, where appropriate, the Deputy Registrar;

b. the dates on which it was adopted and delivered;

c. a description of the Party or Parties;

d. the names of the Agents, advocates or advisers of the Party or Parties;

e. the names of the Delegates of the Commission and of the persons assisting them;

f. the name of the applicant;

g. an account of the procedure followed;

h. the final submissions of the Party or Parties and, if any, of the Delegates of the Commission and of the applicant;

i. the facts of the case;

j. the reasons in point of law;

k. the operative provisions of the judgment;

l. the decision, if any, in respect of costs;

m. the number of judges constituting the majority;

n. where appropriate, a statement as to which of the two texts, English or French, is authentic.

2. Any judge who has taken part in the consideration of the case shall be entitled to annex to the judgment either a separate opinion, concurring with or dissenting from that judgment, or a bare statement of dissent.

Rule 54

(Judgment on the application of Article 50 of the Convention)

1.[1] Where the Chamber finds that there is a breach of the Convention, it shall give in the same judgment a decision on the application

---

1 As amended by the Court on 26 January 1989 and 27 May 1993.

of Article 50 of the Convention if that question, after being raised in accordance with Rule 50, is ready for decision; if the question is not ready for decision, the Chamber shall reserve it in whole or in part and shall fix the further procedure. If, on the other hand, this question has not been raised in accordance with Rule 50, the Chamber may lay down a time-limit for the applicant to submit any claims for just satisfaction that he may have.

2. For the purposes of ruling on the application of Article 50 of the Convention, the Chamber shall, as far as possible, be composed of those judges who sat to consider the merits of the case. Those judges who have ceased to be members of the Court shall be recalled in order to deal with the question in accordance with Article 40, paragraph 6, of the Convention; however, in the event of death, inability to sit, withdrawal or exemption from sitting, the judge concerned shall be replaced in the same manner as was applied for his appointment to the Chamber.

3.[1] When the judgment finding a breach has been delivered under Rule 51 and does not contain a ruling on the application of Article 50 of the Convention, the plenary Court or the Grand Chamber may decide, without prejudice to the provisions of paragraph 1 above, to refer the question back to the Chamber.

4. If the Court is informed that an agreement has been reached between the injured party and the Party liable, it shall verify the equitable nature of such agreement and, where it finds the agreement to be equitable, strike the case out of the list by means of a judgment. Rule 49, paragraph 3, shall apply in such circumstances.

Rule 55

(Signature, delivery and notification of the judgment)

1. The judgment shall be signed by the President and by the Registrar.

2. The judgment shall be read out by the President, or by another judge delegated by him, at a public hearing in one of the two official

---

1 As amended by the Court on 27 January 1994.

languages. It shall not be necessary for the other judges to be present. The Agents of the Parties, the Delegates of the Commission and the applicant shall be informed in due time of the date and time of delivery of the judgment.

However, in respect of a judgment striking a case out of the list or relating to the application of Article 50 of the Convention, the President may direct that the notification provided for under paragraph 4 of this Rule shall count as delivery.

3. The judgment shall be transmitted by the President to the Committee of Ministers.

4. The original copy, duly signed and sealed, shall be placed in the archives of the Court. The Registrar shall send certified copies to the Party or Parties, to the Commission, to the applicant, to the Secretary General of the Council of Europe, to the Contracting States and persons referred to in Rule 37, paragraph 2, and to any other person directly concerned.

Rule 56

(Publication of judgments and other documents)

1.[1] The Registrar shall be responsible for the publication of:

– judgments of the Court;

– documents relating to the proceedings, including the report of the Commission but excluding any document which the President considers unnecessary or inadvisable to publish;

– verbatim records of public hearings;

– any document which the President considers useful to publish.

Publication shall take place in the two official languages in the case of judgments, applications or requests instituting proceedings and the Commission's reports; the other documents shall be published in the official language in which they occur in the proceedings.

---

1 As amended by the Court on 26 January 1989.

2. Documents deposited with the Registrar and not published shall be accessible to the public unless otherwise decided by the President either on his own initiative or at the request of a Party, of the Commission, of the applicant or of any other person concerned.

Rule 57

(Request for interpretation of a judgment)

1. A Party or the Commission may request the interpretation of a judgment within a period of three years following the delivery of that judgment.

2. The request shall state precisely the point or points in the operative provisions of the judgment on which interpretation is required. It shall be filed with the registry in forty copies.

3. The Registrar shall communicate the request, as appropriate, to any other Party, to the Commission and to the applicant, and shall invite them to submit any written comments within a time-limit laid down by the President of the Chamber. The President of the Chamber shall also fix the date of the hearing should the Chamber decide to hold one.

Written comments shall be filed with the registry; they shall be filed in forty copies when they are submitted by a Party or by the Commission.

4. The request for interpretation shall be considered by the Chamber which gave the judgment and which shall, as far as possible, be composed of the same judges. Those judges who have ceased to be members of the Court shall be recalled in order to deal with the case in accordance with Article 40, paragraph 6, of the Convention; however, in the event of death, inability to sit, withdrawal or exemption from sitting, the judge concerned shall be replaced in the same manner as was applied for his appointment to the Chamber.

5. The Chamber shall decide by means of a judgment.

Rule 58

(Request for revision of a judgment)

1. A Party or the Commission may, in the event of the discovery of a fact which might by its nature have a decisive influence and which, when a judgment was delivered, was unknown both to the Court and to that Party or the Commission, request the Court, within a period of six months after that Party or the Commission, as the case may be, acquired knowledge of such fact, to revise that judgment.

2. The request shall mention the judgment of which the revision is requested and shall contain the information necessary to show that the conditions laid down in paragraph 1 have been complied with. It shall be accompanied by the original or a copy of all supporting documents. The request and supporting documents shall be filed with the registry in forty copies.

3. The Registrar shall communicate the request, as appropriate, to any other Party, to the Commission and to the applicant, and shall invite them to submit any written comments within a time-limit laid down by the President. The President shall also fix the date of the hearing should the Chamber decide to hold one.

Written comments shall be filed with the registry; they shall be filed in forty copies if they are submitted by a Party or by the Commission.

4. The request for revision shall be considered by a Chamber constituted in accordance with Article 43 of the Convention, which shall decide whether the request is admissible or not under paragraph 1 of this Rule. In the affirmative, the Chamber shall refer the request to the Chamber which gave the original judgment or, if in the circumstances that is not reasonably possible, it shall retain the request and examine the merits thereof.

5. The Chamber shall decide by means of a judgment.

Chapter V — Advisory opinions
Rule 59

In proceedings in regard to advisory opinions the Court shall, in addition to the provisions of Protocol No. 2, apply the provisions which follow. It shall also apply the other provisions of these Rules to the extent to which it considers this to be appropriate.

Rule 60

The request for an advisory opinion shall be filed with the registry in forty copies. It shall state fully and precisely the question on which the opinion of the Court is sought, and also:

a. the date on which the Committee of Ministers adopted the decision referred to in Article 1, paragraph 3, of Protocol No. 2;

b. the names and addresses of the person or persons appointed by the Committee of Ministers to give the Court any explanations which it may require.

The request shall be accompanied by all documents likely to elucidate the question.

Rule 61

1.[1] On receipt of a request, the Registrar shall transmit a copy thereof to all the members of the Court and to the Commission.

2. He shall inform the Contracting Parties that the Court is prepared to receive their written comments. The President may decide that, by reason of the nature of the question, a similar invitation is to be sent to the Commission.

Rule 62

1. The President shall lay down the time-limits for the filing of written comments or other documents.

2.[1] Written comments or other documents shall be filed with the registry in sixty copies. The Registrar shall transmit copies thereof to all the members of the Court, to the Committee of Ministers, to each of the Contracting Parties and to the Commission.

---

1 As amended by the Court on 27 May 1993.

Rule 63

After the closure of the written procedure, the President shall decide whether the Contracting Parties or the Commission which have submitted written comments are to be given an opportunity to develop them at an oral hearing held for the purpose.

Rule 64

If the Court considers that the request for an advisory opinion is not within its consultative competence as defined in Article 1 of Protocol No. 2, it shall so declare in a reasoned decision.

Rule 65

1. Advisory opinions shall be given by majority vote of the plenary Court. They shall mention the number of judges constituting the majority.

2. Any judge may, if he so desires, attach to the opinion of the Court either a separate opinion, concurring with or dissenting from the advisory opinion, or a bare statement of dissent.

Rule 66

The advisory opinion shall be read out by the President, or by another judge delegated by him, at a public hearing in one of the two official languages, prior notice having been given to the Committee of Ministers, to each of the Contracting Parties and to the Commission.

Rule 67

The opinion, as well as any decision given under Rule 64, shall be signed by the President and by the Registrar. The original copy, duly signed and sealed, shall be placed in the archives of the Court. The Registrar shall send certified copies to the Committee of Ministers, to the Contracting Parties, to the Commission and to the Secretary General of the Council of Europe.

Rule 68[1]

(Final clause)

The present Rules shall enter into force on 1 January 1983. They shall, however, apply only to cases brought before the Court after that date.

Addendum [2] — Rules on legal aid to applicants

The European Court of Human Rights,

Having regard to the Convention for the Protection of Human Rights and Fundamental Freedoms and the Protocols thereto;

Having regard to the Rules of Court,

Adopts the present addendum to the Rules of Court:

Rule 1

(Definitions)

1. For the purposes of the present addendum:

   a. the term "applicant" is to be understood as meaning the person, non-governmental organisation or group of individuals who, after lodging a complaint with the Commission under Article 25 of the Convention, has expressed the desire, in accordance with Rule 33 of the Rules of Court, to take part in the proceedings before the Court;

   b. the term "President" is to be understood as meaning the President of the Court until the constitution of the Chamber or in the event of relinquishment of jurisdiction under Rule 51 of the Rules of Court, and the President of the Chamber in all other instances.

---

1 The amendments adopted on 26 January 1989, 23 May 1990, 23 May 1991, 27 May 1993, 27 October 1993 and 27 January 1994 entered into force, respectively, on 1 April 1989, 1 January 1990, 31 May 1991, 1 July 1993 and 27 January 1994, as regards cases brought before the Court after those dates.

2 To Rules of Court "A".

2. Subject to the foregoing, the terms used herein shall, unless the context otherwise requires, have the same meaning as they have in the Rules of Court.

Rule 2

(Requests for information regarding legal aid before the Commission)

1. Unless the information is already available to him, the Registrar shall enquire whether or not the applicant applied for, and, if so, whether or not he was granted, legal aid in connection with the representation of his case before the Commission pursuant to the addendum to the Rules of Procedure of the Commission.

2. At the same time the Registrar may, on the instructions of the President, ask the Commission to produce to the Court the file relating to the grant or refusal, if any, of legal aid to the applicant.

Rule 3

(Continuation in force of a grant made by the Commission)

1. Subject to the provisions of Rule 5 herein, where the applicant has been granted legal aid in connection with the representation of his case before the Commission, that grant shall continue in force for the purposes of his representation before the Court.

2. The President may, however, instruct the Registrar to obtain from the applicant information evidencing that the conditions laid down in Rule 4, paragraph 2, herein are fulfilled. The Registrar shall bring any information so obtained to the attention of the Agents of the Parties and the Delegates of the Commission, in order to give them the opportunity to verify its correctness.

Rule 4

(Grant of legal aid by the President)

1. Where the applicant did not receive a grant of legal aid in connection with the representation of his case before the Commission or

had such a grant revoked, the President may at any time, at the request of the applicant, grant free legal aid to the applicant for the purposes of his representation before the Court.

2. Legal aid may be so granted only where the President is satisfied that:

a. the applicant lacks sufficient means to meet all or part of the costs involved; and

b. such a course is necessary for the proper conduct of the case before the Court.

3. In order to determine whether or not the applicant lacks the sufficient means, the Registrar shall ask him to complete a form of declaration stating his income, capital assets and any financial commitments in respect of dependants, or any other financial obligations. Such declaration shall be certified by the appropriate domestic authority or authorities. This certified declaration may be replaced by a certificate of indigence delivered by the appropriate domestic authority or authorities as listed in the appendix to this addendum.

4. Before the President makes a grant of legal aid, the Registrar shall request the Agents of the Parties and the Delegates of the Commission to submit their comments in writing.

5. After receiving the information mentioned in paragraphs 3 and 4 and, if appropriate, Rule 2, paragraph 2, above, the President shall decide whether or not legal aid is to be granted and to what extent. The Registrar shall notify the applicant, the Agents of the Parties and the Delegates of the Commission accordingly.

6. The Registrar, on the instructions of the President, shall fix the time-limits within which the information referred to in this Rule is to be supplied.

Rule 5

(Revocation or variation of a grant)

The President may, if he is satisfied that the conditions stated in Rule 4, paragraph 2, are no longer fulfilled, at any time revoke or vary, in whole or in part, a grant of legal aid made or continued in force under the present addendum. The Registrar shall at once notify the applicant, the Agents of the Parties and the Delegates of the Commission accordingly.

Rule 6

(Fees and expenses payable)

1. Fees shall be payable only to the advocates or other persons appointed in accordance with Rule 30 of the Rules of Court.

2. Legal aid may be granted to cover not only fees for representation but also travelling and subsistence expenses and other necessary out-of-pocket expenses incurred by the applicants or by their representatives.

3. After consulting the representatives, the Registrar shall, on the instructions of the President, fix the amount of fees to be paid. The Registrar shall also in each case decide what particular expenses referred to above at paragraph 2 are to be covered by the grant of legal aid.

Rule 7

(Derogation from procedural requirements)

In case of urgency, the President may sanction a derogation from the procedural requirements of this addendum provided that the derogation in question is essential for the proper conduct of the case before the Court.

Rule 8

(Entry into force and transitional arrangements)

This addendum shall come into force at a date[1] to be fixed by the

---

1 1 November 1983.

President of the Court. Pending such entry into force, the grant of legal aid to an applicant in connection with the representation of his case before the Court shall continue to be governed by the addendum to the Rules of Procedure of the Commission.

Appendix — National authorities competent to deliver a certificate of indigence

The declaration of means referred to in Rule 4, paragraph 3, of the addendum to the Rules of Court A (Rules on legal aid to applicants) may be replaced by a certificate of indigence delivered by the appropriate domestic authority or authorities. The competent domestic authorities are as follows:

Austria

The mayor of the locality where the applicant has his or her legal or actual residence.

Belgium

The direct taxation department of the district in which the applicant lives issues him with a certificate of income or, with his authorisation, express and in writing, issues such to another person or administrative department.

The request, accompanied by such authorisation, may be addressed either to the local direct taxation department or to the Administration centrale des contributions directes, 45, rue Belliard, B-1040 Bruxelles.

Cyprus

The Social Welfare Services, Ministry of Labour and Social Insurance.

Czech Republic

The social welfare authority in the municipality of the applicant's place of domicile.

Denmark

The local tax authority.

Finland

The social welfare authority in the municipality of the applicant's place of domicile.

France

The mayor of the municipality in which the applicant lives.

Germany

None. The applicant submits a prescribed form, duly completed and with supporting documents, which is forwarded to the Federal Ministry of Justice.

Greece

a. A certificate from the mayor or president of the district in which the applicant lives giving details of his family situation, his employment and his assets; and

b. A certificate from the tax authority showing that the applicant has made a tax return for the previous three years with the results thereof.

Hungary

None. In court proceedings, the applicant, the tax authorities, and the applicant's employer complete a prescribed form and attach supporting documents, if any. The applicant then submits this group of documents to the proceeding court.

Iceland

The *Rikisskattstjóri* (Director of Internal Revenue), Skúlagotu 57, IS-Reykjavik.

Ireland

The Chief Inspector, Department of Social Welfare, 101/104 Marlboro Street, IRL-Dublin 1.

Italy

a. Certification, by a responsible section of the tax authorities, of a declaration of means prepared by the applicant; or

b. Certificate of indigence issued by the mayor of the municipality in which the applicant lives.

Liechtenstein

The Court of Justice (*Fürstliches Landgericht*).

Luxembourg

On production of a certificate stating the amount of tax paid the previous year, the College of Mayor and Aldermen of the municipality in which the applicant lives issues a certificate of indigence.

Netherlands

The local government (*gemeentebestuur*) in accordance with Article 11 of the Legal Aid Act (*Wet Rechtsbijstand on- en minvermogenden*).

Norway

The local tax authority (*ligningskontor*) of the district in which the applicant lives.

Portugal

The local government (*junta de frequesia*) for the district in which the applicant lives.

San Marino

The certificate of indigence is issued by the office of the Secretary of State for Internal Affairs following a declaration made by the San Marinese tax office.

Spain

The district office of the Finance Minister (*Delegación de Hacienda*) for the district in which the applicant lives.

Sweden

The local tax authority (*lokala skattemyndigheten*) certifies the means of persons requesting free legal aid.

Switzerland

The local tax authority for the applicant's place of residence.

Turkey

    a. The mayor of the municipality in which the applicant lives; or

    b. The elders' council for the village or district in which the applicant lives (Article 468 of the Code of Civil Procedure).

United Kingdom

a. *England and Wales*

DHSS, Legal Aid Assessment Office, No. 3 The Pavilions, Ashton on Ribble, Preston PR2 2PA;

b. *Scotland*

The Scottish Legal Aid Board, 44 Drumsheugh Gardens, Edinburgh EH3 7SW.

The relevant information concerning four States — Bulgaria, Malta, Poland and Slovakia — has not yet been communicated to the registry of the Court.

B. Rules of Court "B"

Adopted on 27 January 1994 and applicable to cases concerning States bound by Protocol No. 9 to the Convention.

Scheduled to come into force as specified under Rule 70.

The European Court of Human Rights,

Having regard to the Convention for the Protection of Human Rights and Fundamental Freedoms and the Protocols thereto,

Having regard to the Rules of Court that entered into force on 1 January 1983 ("Rules of Court A"), which apply to cases concerning States not bound by Protocol No. 9 to the said Convention,

Makes the present Rules ("Rules of Court B"), which apply to cases concerning States bound by Protocol No. 9:

Rule 1

(Definitions)

For the purposes of these Rules unless the context otherwise requires:

a. the term "Convention" means the Convention for the Protection of Human Rights and Fundamental Freedoms and the Protocols thereto;

b. the expression "Protocol No. 2" means Protocol No. 2 to the Convention conferring upon the European Court of Human Rights competence to give advisory opinions;

c. the expression "plenary Court" means the European Court of Human Rights sitting in plenary session;

d.[1] the term "Chamber" means any Chamber constituted in pursuance of Article 43 of the Convention; the term "Grand Chamber" means the Chamber provided for under Rule 53;

e.[1] the term "Court" means either the plenary Court, the Grand Chambers or the Chambers;

---

1 As amended by the Court on 27 January 1994.

f. the expression "Screening Panel" means the Panel provided for in Article 48, paragraph 2, of the Convention;

g. the expression "*ad hoc* judge" means any person, other than an elected judge, chosen by a Contracting Party in pursuance of Article 43 or Article 48, paragraph 2, of the Convention to sit as a member of a Chamber or of a Screening Panel;

h. the term "judge" or "judges" means the judges elected by the Consultative Assembly of the Council of Europe or *ad hoc* judges;

i. the term "parties" means:

– the applicant or respondent Contracting Parties;

– the private party (the person, non-governmental organisation or group of individuals) who lodged a complaint with the European Commission of Human Rights under Article 25 and whose case has been referred to the Court;

j. the term "Commission" means the European Commission of Human Rights;

k. the expression "Delegates of the Commission" means the member or members of the Commission delegated by it to take part in the consideration of a case before the Court;

l. the expression "report of the Commission" means the report provided for in Article 31 of the Convention;

m. the expression "Committee of Ministers" means the Committee of Ministers of the Council of Europe.

Title I — Organisation and working of the Court

Chapter I — Judges

Rule 2

(Calculation of term of office)

1. The duration of the term of office of an elected judge shall be calculated as from his election. However, when a judge is re-elected on

the expiry of his term of office or is elected to replace a judge whose term of office has expired or is about to expire, the duration of his term of office shall, in either case, be calculated as from the date of such expiry.

2. In accordance with Article 40, paragraph 5, of the Convention, a judge elected to replace a judge whose term of office has not expired shall hold office for the remainder of his predecessor's term.

3. In accordance with Article 40, paragraph 6, of the Convention, an elected judge shall hold office until his successor has taken the oath or made the declaration provided for in Rule 3. Thereafter he shall continue to deal with any case in connection with which hearings or, failing that, deliberations have begun before him.

Rule 3

(Oath or solemn declaration)

1. Before taking up his duties, each elected judge shall, at the first sitting of the plenary Court at which he is present after his election or, in case of need, before the President, take the following oath or make the following solemn declaration:

> "I swear" — or "I solemnly declare" — "that I will exercise my functions as a judge honourably, independently and impartially and that I will keep secret all deliberations."

2. This act shall be recorded in minutes.

Rule 4

(Obstacle to the exercise of the functions of judge)

A judge may not exercise his functions while he is a member of a Government or while he holds a post or exercises a profession which is incompatible with his independence and impartiality. In case of need the plenary Court shall decide.

Rule 5

(Precedence)

1. Elected judges shall take precedence after the President and the Vice-President according to the date of their election; in the event of re-election, even if it is not an immediate re-election, the length of time during which the judge concerned previously exercised his functions as a judge shall be taken into account.

2. Judges elected on the same date shall take precedence according to age.

3. *Ad hoc* judges shall take precedence after the elected judges according to age.

Rule 6

(Resignation)

Resignation of a judge shall be notified to the President who shall transmit it to the Secretary General of the Council of Europe. Subject to the provisions of Rule 2, paragraph 3, resignation shall constitute vacation of office.

Chapter II — Presidency of the Court

Rule 7

(Election of the President and Vice-President)

1. The Court shall elect its President and Vice-President for a period of three years, provided that such period shall not exceed the duration of their term of office as judges. They may be re-elected.

2. The President and Vice-President shall continue to exercise their functions until the election of their respective successors.

3. If the President or Vice-President ceases to be a member of the Court or resigns his office before its normal expiry, the plenary Court shall elect a successor for the remainder of the term of that office.

4. The elections referred to in this Rule shall be by secret ballot; only the elected judges who are present shall take part. If no judge receives an absolute majority of the elected judges present, a ballot shall take place between the two judges who have received most votes. In the case of equal voting, preference shall be given to the judge having precedence in accordance with Rule 5.

Rule 8

(Functions of the President)

The President shall direct the work and administration of the Court and shall preside at its sessions. He shall represent the Court and, in particular, be responsible for its relations with the authorities of the Council of Europe.

Rule 9

(Functions of the Vice-President)

The Vice-President shall take the place of the President if the latter is unable to carry out his functions or if the office of President is vacant.

Rule 10

(Replacement of the President and Vice-President)

If the President and Vice-President are at the same time unable to carry out their functions or if their offices are at the same time vacant, the office of President shall be assumed by another elected judge in accordance with the order of precedence provided for in Rule 5.

Chapter III — The registry

Rule 11

(Election of the Registrar)

1. The plenary Court shall elect its Registrar after the President has in this respect consulted the Secretary General of the Council of

Europe. The candidates must possess the legal knowledge and the experience necessary to carry out the functions attaching to the post and must have an adequate working knowledge of the two official languages of the Court.

2. The Registrar shall be elected for a term of seven years. He may be re-elected.

3. The elections referred to in this Rule shall be by secret ballot; only the elected judges who are present shall take part. If no candidate receives an absolute majority of the elected judges present, a ballot shall take place between the two candidates who have received most votes. In the case of equal voting, preference shall be given to the older candidate.

4. Before taking up his functions, the Registrar shall take the following oath or make the following solemn declaration before the plenary Court or, if it is not in session, before the President:

> "I swear" — or "I solemnly declare" — "that I will exercise loyally, discreetly and conscientiously the functions conferred upon me as Registrar of the European Court of Human Rights."

This act shall be recorded in minutes.

Rule 12

(Election of the Deputy Registrar)

1. The plenary Court shall also elect a Deputy Registrar according to the conditions and in the manner and for the term prescribed in Rule 11. It shall first consult the Registrar.

2. Before taking up his functions, the Deputy Registrar shall take an oath or make a solemn declaration before the plenary Court or, if it is not in session, before the President, in similar terms to those prescribed in respect of the Registrar. This act shall be recorded in minutes.

Rule 13

(Other staff, equipment and facilities)

The President, or the Registrar on his behalf, shall request the Secretary General of the Council of Europe to provide the Registrar with the staff, permanent or temporary, equipment and facilities necessary for the Court.

The officials of the registry, other than the Registrar and the Deputy Registrar, shall be appointed by the Secretary General, with the agreement of the President or of the Registrar acting on the President's instructions.

Rule 14

(Functions of the Registrar)

1. The Registrar shall assist the Court in the performance of its functions. He shall be responsible for the organisation and activities of the registry under the authority of the President.

2. The Registrar shall have the custody of the archives of the Court and shall be the channel for all communications and notifications made by, or addressed to, the Court in connection with the cases brought or to be brought before it.

3. Communications or notifications addressed to the Agents or advocates of the parties and to the Delegates of the Commission shall be considered as having been addressed to the parties or to the Commission, as the case may be.

4. The Registrar shall, subject to the discretion attaching to his functions, reply to requests for information concerning the work of the Court, in particular from the press. He shall announce the date and time fixed for the hearings in open court and shall be responsible for making immediately available to the public all judgments delivered by the Court.

5. General instructions drawn up by the Registrar and sanctioned by the President shall provide for the working of the registry.

Chapter IV — The working of the Court

Rule 15

(Seat of the Court)

The seat of the Court shall be at the seat of the Council of Europe at Strasbourg. The Court may, however, if it considers it expedient, exercise its functions elsewhere in the territories of the Member States of the Council of Europe.

Rule 16

(Sessions of the plenary Court)

The plenary sessions of the Court shall be convened by the President whenever the exercise of its functions under the Convention and under these Rules so requires. The President shall convene a plenary session if at least one third of the members of the Court so request, and in any event once a year to consider administrative matters.

Rule 17

(Quorum)

1.[1] The quorum of the plenary Court shall be two-thirds of the judges.

2. If there is no quorum, the President shall adjourn the sitting.

Rule 18

(Public character of the hearings)

The hearings shall be public unless the Court shall in exceptional circumstances decide otherwise.

Rule 19

(Deliberations)

1. The Court and the Screening Panels shall deliberate in private. Their deliberations shall remain secret.

---

1 As amended by the Court on 27 January 1994.

2. Only the judges shall take part in the deliberations. The Registrar or his substitute, as well as such other officials of the registry and interpreters whose assistance is deemed necessary, shall be present. No other person may be admitted except by special decision of the Court.

3. Each judge present at such deliberations shall state his opinion and the reasons therefor.

4. Any question which is to be voted upon shall be formulated in precise terms in the two official languages and the text shall, if a judge so requests, be distributed before the vote is taken.

5. The minutes of the private sittings of the Court for deliberations shall remain secret; they shall be limited to a record of the subject of the discussions, the votes taken, the names of those voting for and against a motion and any statements expressly made for insertion in the minutes.

Rule 20

(Votes)

1. The decisions of the Court shall be taken by the majority of judges present.

2. The votes shall be cast in the inverse order to the order of precedence provided for in Rule 5.

3. If the voting is equal, the President shall have a second and casting vote.

Chapter V — The Chambers

Rule 21

(Composition of the Court when constituted in a Chamber)

1. For the consideration of any case referred to it under one or more of the sub-paragraphs of Article 48, paragraph 1, of the Convention, the Court shall be constituted in a Chamber of nine judges.

2. On the reference of a case to the Court, the Registrar shall notify all the judges, including the newly-elected judges, that such a Chamber is to be constituted. If any judge, upon receiving such notification, believes that for one of the reasons set out in Rule 24 he will be unable to sit, he shall so inform the Registrar. The President shall then draw up the list of judges available to constitute the Chamber.

3. There shall sit as *ex officio* members of the Chamber:

   a. every judge elected in respect of an applicant or respondent Contracting Party or, failing him, a person appointed pursuant to Rule 23, paragraph 1;

   b. the President of the Court, or, failing him, the Vice-President, provided that they do not sit by virtue of the preceding sub-paragraph.

4. The other judges named on the list provided for in paragraph 2 shall be called upon to complete the Chamber, as members or as substitutes, in the order determined by a drawing of lots effected by the President of the Court in the presence of the Registrar.

5. The President of the Chamber shall be the judge sitting by virtue of paragraph 3.b or, failing one, a judge appointed under paragraph 4 as a member of the Chamber, in accordance with the order of precedence provided for in Rule 5.

If the President of the Chamber is unable to sit or withdraws, he shall be replaced by the Vice-President or, if the same applies to him, by a judge appointed under paragraph 4 as a member of the Chamber, in accordance with the said order of precedence. However, where he is unable to sit or withdraws less than twenty-four hours before the opening of, or during or after, the hearing, his place shall be taken, in accordance with the said order of precedence, by one of the judges called upon to be present or present at the hearing.

6. If the President of the Court finds that two cases concern the same Contracting Party or Parties and raise similar issues, he may refer the

second case to the Chamber already constituted, or in the course of constitution, for the consideration of the first case or, if there is none, proceed to the constitution of one Chamber to consider both cases.

Rule 22

(Substitute judges)

1. The substitute judges shall be called upon, in the order determined by the drawing of lots, to replace the judges appointed as members of the Chamber by virtue of Rule 21, paragraph 4.

2. Judges who have been so replaced shall cease to be members of the Chamber.

3. The substitute judges shall be supplied with the documents relating to the proceedings. The President may convoke one or more of them, according to the above order of precedence, to attend the hearings and deliberations.

Rule 23

(*Ad hoc* judges)

1. If the Court does not include a judge elected in respect of a Contracting Party or if the judge called upon to sit in that capacity is unable to sit or withdraws, the President of the Court shall invite that Party to inform him within thirty days whether it wishes to appoint to sit as judge either another elected judge or, as an *ad hoc* judge, any other person possessing the qualifications required under Article 39, paragraph 3, of the Convention and, if so, to state at the same time the name of the person so appointed. The same rule shall apply if the person so appointed is unable to sit or withdraws.

2. The Contracting Party concerned shall be presumed to have waived such right of appointment if it does not reply within thirty days.

3. An *ad hoc* judge shall, at the opening of the first sitting fixed for the consideration of the case after he has been appointed, take the oath or make the solemn declaration provided for in Rule 3. This act shall be recorded in minutes.

Rule 24

(Inability to sit, withdrawal or exemption)

1. Any judge who is prevented from taking part in sittings for which he has been convoked shall, as soon as possible, give notice thereof to the President of the Chamber or to the Registrar.

2. A judge may not take part in the consideration of any case in which he has a personal interest or has previously acted either as the Agent, advocate or adviser of a party or of a person having an interest in the case, or as member of a tribunal or commission of enquiry, or in any other capacity.

3. If a judge withdraws for one of the said reasons, or for some special reason, he shall inform the President who shall exempt him from sitting.

4. If the President considers that a reason exists for a judge to withdraw, he shall consult with the judge concerned; in the event of disagreement, the Court shall decide.

5. Any judge who has been called upon to sit on one or more recent cases may, at his own request, be exempted by the President from sitting on a new case.

Rule 25

(Common interest)

1. If several applicant or respondent Contracting Parties have a common interest, the President of the Court may invite them to agree to appoint a single elected judge or *ad hoc* judge in accordance with Article 43 of the Convention. If the Parties are unable to agree, the President shall choose by lot, from among the persons proposed as judges by these Parties, the judge called upon to sit *ex officio*. The names of the other judges and substitute judges shall then be chosen by lot by the President from among the judges who have not been elected in respect of an applicant or respondent Contracting Party.

2. In the event of dispute as to the existence of a common interest, the plenary Court shall decide.

Chapter VI — The Screening Panels

Rule 26

(Composition of the Screening Panels)

1. Any case referred to the Court by virtue solely of Article 48, paragraph 1.e, of the Convention shall first be submitted to a Screening Panel.

2. There shall sit as an *ex officio* member of the Panel:

   a.   any judge elected in respect of a respondent Contracting Party;

   b.   failing him, that is to say in one of the instances specified in Rule 23, paragraph 1, a person appointed under that same provision.

3. The other two members shall be the first two judges designated by the drawing of lots provided for in Rule 21, paragraph 4. If one of these judges is unable to sit or withdraws, he shall be replaced by one of the remaining members of the Chamber in accordance with the order determined by the aforementioned drawing of lots.

4. The Chairman of the Panel shall be one of the judges appointed under paragraph 3 above, in accordance with the order of precedence provided for in Rule 5.

5. In the event of Rule 21, paragraph 6, being applied, the Panel already constituted, or in the course of constitution, for the consideration of the first case shall also consider the second case.

Title II — Procedure

Chapter I — General Rules

Rule 27

(Possibility of particular derogations)

The provisions of this Title shall not prevent the Court from derogating from them for the consideration of a particular case after having consulted the parties and the Delegates of the Commission.

Rule 28

(Official languages)

1. The official languages of the Court shall be English and French.

2. An applicant or respondent Contracting Party may, not later than the consultation provided for in Rule 40, apply to the President of the Chamber for leave to use another language at the hearing. If such leave is granted by the President, the Party concerned shall be responsible for the interpretation into English or French of the oral arguments or statements made by its Agent, advocates or advisers and shall, to the extent which the President may determine in each case, bear the other extra expenses involved in the use of a non-official language.

3. The President may grant the private party, as well as any person assisting the Delegates under Rule 30, paragraph 1, leave to use a non-official language. In that event, the Registrar shall make the necessary arrangements for the translation or interpretation into English and French of their comments or statements.

4. Any witness, expert or other person appearing before the Court may use his own language if he does not have sufficient knowledge of either of the two official languages. The Registrar shall, in that event, make the necessary arrangements for the interpretation into English and French of the statements of the witness, expert or other person concerned.

5. All judgments shall be given in English and in French; unless the Court decides otherwise, both texts shall be authentic.

Rule 29

(Representation of the applicant or respondent Contracting Parties)

The applicant or respondent Contracting Parties shall be represented by Agents who may have the assistance of advocates or advisers.

Rule 30

(Relations between the Court and the Commission and release of the report of the Commission)

1. The Commission shall delegate one or more of its members to take part in the consideration of a case before the Court. The Delegates may be assisted by other persons.

2. In every case referred to it, the Court shall take into consideration the report of the Commission.

3. Unless the President decides otherwise, the said report shall be made available to the public through the Registrar:

    a. in cases referred to the Court by virtue solely of Article 48, paragraph 1.e, of the Convention, as soon as possible after the Screening Panel has decided not to decline consideration of the case pursuant to paragraph 2 of the same Article;

    b. in other cases, as soon as possible after the reference of the case to the Court.

Rule 31

(Representation of private parties)

1. Any private party shall be represented by an advocate authorised to practise in any of the Contracting States and resident on the territory of one of them, or by any other person approved by the President. A private party may however present his own case before the Screening Panel and, if the President gives leave to do so, in the

ensuing proceedings, subject, if need be, to his being assisted by an advocate or other person as aforesaid.

2. Unless the President decides otherwise, the advocate or other person representing or assisting the private party, or the latter himself if he presents his own case or seeks leave to do so, must have an adequate knowledge of one of the Court's official languages.

Rule 32

(Communications, notifications and summonses addressed to persons other than the Agents or advocates of the parties or the Delegates of the Commission)

1. If, for any communication, notification or summons addressed to persons other than the Agents or advocates of the parties or the Delegates of the Commission, the Court considers it necessary to have the assistance of the Government of the State on whose territory such communication, notification or summons is to have effect, the President shall apply directly to that Government in order to obtain the necessary facilities.

2. The same rule shall apply when the Court desires to make or arrange for the making of an investigation on the spot in order to establish the facts or to procure evidence or when it orders the appearance of a person resident in, or having to cross, that territory.

Chapter II — Institution of proceedings

Rule 33

(Cases referred to the Court by a Contracting Party or by the Commission)

1. Any Contracting Party which intends to refer a case to the Court under Article 48, paragraph 1.b, c or d of the Convention shall file with the registry an application, in forty copies, indicating:

    a. the parties to the proceedings before the Commission;

    b. the date on which the Commission adopted its report;

c. the date on which the report was transmitted to the Committee of Ministers;

d. the object of the application;

e. the name and address of the person appointed as Agent.

2. If the Commission intends to refer a case to the Court under Article 48, paragraph 1.a, of the Convention, it shall file with the registry a request, in forty copies, signed by its President and containing the particulars indicated in sub-paragraphs a, b, c and d of paragraph 1 of this Rule together with the names and addresses of the Delegates of the Commission.

Rule 34

(Cases referred to the Court by a private party)

1. If a private party intends to refer a case to the Court under Article 48, paragraph 1.e, of the Convention, he shall file with the registry an application containing the particulars indicated in sub-paragraphs a, b and c of Rule 33, paragraph 1, and specifying:

a. the object of the application, and in particular the serious question affecting the interpretation or application of the Convention which, in his opinion, the case raises or the other reasons for which, in his opinion, the case warrants consideration by the Court;

b. the name and address of any person appointed by him pursuant to Rule 31.

2. On receipt of such application, the Registrar shall notify accordingly:

a. all members of the Court;

b. any Contracting Party mentioned in Article 48 of the Convention;

c. the Commission;

d. the Committee of Ministers.

3. As soon as it becomes established that the case has been referred to the Court by virtue solely of Article 48, paragraph 1.e, of the Convention, the Screening Panel shall proceed to examine the application; it shall do so solely on the basis of the existing case-file.

4. If the case does not raise a serious question affecting the interpretation or application of the Convention and does not for any other reason warrant consideration by the Court, the Panel may, by a unanimous vote, decide to decline consideration of the case.

In that event, the Panel shall deliver a briefly reasoned decision signed by the President and the Registrar. The original copy thereof shall be placed in the archives of the Court. The Registrar shall send certified copies to the private party, to the respondent Contracting Party, to the Commission and to the Committee of Ministers. This notification shall count as delivery.

Rule 35

(Communication of the application or request)

1. If a case has been referred to the Court by a Contracting Party or the Commission, the Registrar shall transmit a copy of the application or request:

   a. to all members of the Court and, as appropriate,

   b. to any Contracting Party mentioned in Article 48 of the Convention,

   c. to the Commission,

   d. to the private party.

The communications provided for in sub-paragraphs a, b and d above shall be accompanied by a copy of the report of the Commission. The Registrar shall in addition inform the Committee of Ministers of the filing of the application or request.

2. If a case has been referred to the Court by virtue solely of Article 48, paragraph 1.e, of the Convention and thereafter the Screening Panel has decided not to decline consideration of the case, the Registrar shall immediately transmit a copy of the application:

a. to the respondent Contracting Party, together with a copy of the report of the Commission;

b. to the Commission.

The Registrar shall in addition inform the parties, the Commission and the Committee of Ministers of the decision of the Screening Panel.

3. When making the communications provided for in sub-paragraphs b to d of paragraph 1 and in paragraph 2, the Registrar shall invite, as appropriate:

a. the respondent Contracting Party in the proceedings before the Commission to notify him within two weeks of the name and address of its Agent;

b. any other Contracting Party which appears to have the right, under Article 48 of the Convention, to bring a case before the Court and which has not availed itself of that right, to inform him, within four weeks, whether it wishes to take part in the proceedings and, if so, to notify him at the same time of the name and address of its Agent;

c. the Commission to notify him as soon as possible of the names and addresses of its Delegates;

d. the private party to notify him within two weeks of the name and address of any person whom he may wish to appoint pursuant to Rule 31.

Rule 36[1]

(Question whether a Contracting Party has the right to bring a case before the Court)

In the event of a dispute as to whether a Contracting Party has the right under Article 48 to bring a case before the Court, the President shall submit that question for decision to the Grand Chamber pro-

---

1 As amended by the Court on 27 January 1994.

vided for in paragraph 2 of Rule 53 of these Rules, without prejudice
to the possible application of paragraph 5 of Rule 53.

Rule 37

(Notice of the composition of the Chamber)

As soon as a Chamber has been constituted for the consideration of
a case, the Registrar shall communicate its composition to the judges,
to the Agents and advocates of the parties and to the Commission.

Rule 38

(Interim measures)

1. Before the constitution of a Chamber, the President of the Court
may, at the request of a party, of the Commission or of any other
person concerned, or *proprio motu*, indicate to any Contracting
Party and, where appropriate, the private party, any interim measure which it is advisable for them to adopt. The Chamber when constituted or, if the Chamber is not in session, its President shall have
the same power.

Notice of these measures shall be immediately given to the Committee of Ministers.

2. Where the Commission, pursuant to Rule 36 of its Rules of Procedure, has indicated an interim measure as desirable, its adoption
or maintenance shall remain recommended to the Contracting Parties and, where appropriate, the private party after the case has been
brought before the Court, unless and until the President or the
Chamber otherwise decides or until paragraph 1 of this Rule is
applied.

Chapter III — Examination of cases

Rule 39

(Written procedure)

1. The proceedings before the Court shall, as a general rule, comprise as their first stage a written procedure in which memorials are
filed by the parties and, if it so wishes, the Commission.

As soon as possible after the reference of a case to the Court, the President shall consult the Agents and advocates of the parties and the Delegates of the Commission, or, if the latter have not yet been appointed, the President of the Commission, as to the organisation of the proceedings; unless, with their agreement, he directs that a written procedure is to be dispensed with, he shall lay down the time-limits for the filing of the memorials.

No memorial or other document may be filed except within such time-limit (if any) or with the authorisation of the President or at his or the Chamber's request.

2. The President may, in the interests of the proper administration of justice, invite or grant leave to any Contracting State which is not a Party to the proceedings to submit written comments within a time-limit and on issues which he shall specify. He may extend such an invitation or grant such leave to any person concerned other than the private party.

3. Where two cases have been referred to the same Chamber under Rule 21, paragraph 6, the President of the Chamber may, in the interests of the proper administration of justice and after consulting the Agents and advocates of the parties and the Delegates of the Commission, order that the proceedings in both cases be conducted simultaneously, without prejudice to the decision of the Chamber on the joinder of the cases.

4. Memorials, comments and documents annexed thereto shall be filed with the registry; they shall be filed in forty copies when they are submitted by an applicant or respondent Contracting Party, by another State or by the Commission. The Registrar shall transmit copies thereof to the judges, to the Agents and advocates of the parties and to the Delegates of the Commission, as the case may be.

Rule 40
(Fixing of the date of the hearing)

The President of the Chamber shall, after consulting the Agents and advocates of the parties and the Delegates of the Commission, fix the date of the hearing. The Registrar shall notify them of the decision taken in this respect.

Rule 41

(Conduct of hearings)

The President of the Chamber shall direct hearings. He shall prescribe the order in which the Agents, advocates or advisers of the parties, the Delegates of the Commission and any person assisting the Delegates in accordance with Rule 30, paragraph 1, shall be called upon to speak.

Rule 42

(Failure to appear at hearings)

Where, without showing sufficient cause, a party fails to appear, the Chamber may, provided that it is satisfied that such a course is consistent with the proper administration of justice, proceed with the hearing.

Rule 43

(Measures for taking evidence)

1. The Chamber may, at the request of a party, of the Delegates of the Commission or of a third party invited or granted leave to submit written comments under Rule 39, paragraph 2, or *proprio motu*, obtain any evidence which it considers capable of providing clarification on the facts of the case. The Chamber may, *inter alia*, decide to hear as a witness or expert or in any other capacity any person whose evidence or statements seem likely to assist it in the carrying out of its task.

When the Chamber is not in session, the President of the Chamber may exercise, by way of preparatory measure, the powers set forth in the immediately foregoing sub-paragraph, without prejudice to the decision of the Chamber on the relevance of the evidence so taken or sought.

2. The Chamber may ask any person or institution of its choice to obtain information, express an opinion or make a report, upon any specific point.

3. Where a report drawn up in accordance with the preceding paragraphs has been prepared at the request of an applicant or respondent Contracting Party, the costs relating thereto shall be borne by that Party unless the Chamber decides otherwise. In other cases, the Chamber shall decide whether such costs are to be borne by the Council of Europe, or awarded against a private party, or a third party, at whose request the report was prepared. In all cases, the costs shall be taxed by the President.

4. The Chamber may, at any time during the proceedings, depute one or more of its members to conduct an enquiry, carry out an investigation on the spot or take evidence in some other manner.

Rule 44

(Convocation of witnesses, experts and other persons; costs of their appearance)

1. Witnesses, experts or other persons whom the Chamber or the President of the Chamber decides to hear shall be summoned by the Registrar. If they appear at the request of an applicant or respondent Contracting Party, the costs of their appearance shall be borne by that Party unless the Chamber decides otherwise. In other cases, the Chamber shall decide whether such costs are to be borne by the Council of Europe or awarded against a private party, or a third party within the meaning of Rule 43, paragraph 1, at whose request the person summoned appeared. In all cases, the costs shall, if need be, be taxed by the President.

2. The summons shall indicate:

– the case in connection with which it has been issued;

– the object of the enquiry, expert opinion or other measure ordered by the Chamber or the President of the Chamber;

– any provisions for the payment of the sum due to the person summoned.

Rule 45

(Oath or solemn declaration by witnesses and experts)

1. After the establishment of his identity and before giving evidence, every witness shall take the following oath or make the following solemn declaration:

> "I swear" — or "I solemnly declare upon my honour and conscience" — "that I will speak the truth, the whole truth and nothing but the truth."

This act shall be recorded in minutes.

2. After the establishment of his identity and before carrying out his task, every expert shall take the following oath or make the following solemn declaration:

> "I swear" — or "I solemnly declare" — "that I will discharge my duty as expert honourably and conscientiously."

This act shall be recorded in minutes.

This oath may be taken or this declaration made before the President of the Chamber, or before a judge or any public authority nominated by the President.

Rule 46

(Objection to a witness or expert; hearing of a person for the purpose of information)

The Chamber shall decide in the event of any dispute arising from an objection to a witness or expert. It may hear for the purpose of information a person who cannot be heard as a witness.

Rule 47

(Questions put during hearings)

1. The President or any judge may put questions to the Agents, advocates or advisers of the parties, to the witnesses and experts, to

the Delegates of the Commission and to any other persons appearing before the Chamber.

2. The witnesses, experts and other persons referred to in Rule 43, paragraph 1, may, subject to the control of the President, be examined by the Agents, advocates or advisers of the parties, by the Delegates of the Commission and by any person assisting the Delegates in accordance with Rule 30, paragraph 1. In the event of an objection as to the relevance of a question put, the Chamber shall decide.

Rule 48

(Failure to appear or false evidence)

When, without good reason, a witness or any other person who has been duly summoned fails to appear or refuses to give evidence, the Registrar shall, on being so required by the President, inform that Contracting Party to whose jurisdiction such witness or other person is subject. The same provisions shall apply when a witness or expert has, in the opinion of the Chamber, violated the oath or solemn declaration provided for in Rule 45.

Rule 49

(Verbatim record of hearings)

1. The Registrar shall be responsible for the making of a verbatim record of each hearing. The verbatim record shall include:

   a. the composition of the Chamber at the hearing;

   b. a list of those appearing before the Court, that is to say, Agents, advocates and advisers of the parties, Delegates of the Commission and persons assisting them, Contracting States and other persons referred to in Rule 39, paragraph 2;

   c. the surnames, forenames, description and address of each witness, expert or other person heard;

d. the text of statements made, questions put and replies given;

e. the text of any decision delivered by the Chamber during the hearing.

2. The Agents, advocates and advisers of the parties, the Delegates of the Commission and the witnesses, experts and other persons mentioned in Rules 30, paragraph 1, and 43, paragraph 1, shall receive the verbatim record of their arguments, statements or evidence, in order that they may, subject to the control of the Registrar or the President of the Chamber, make corrections, but in no case may such corrections affect the sense and bearing of what was said. The Registrar, in accordance with the instructions of the President, shall fix the time-limits granted for this purpose.

3. The verbatim record, once so corrected, shall be signed by the President and the Registrar and shall then constitute certified matters of record.

Rule 50

(Preliminary objections)

1. A party wishing to raise a preliminary objection must file a statement setting out the objection and the grounds therefor not later than the time when that party informs the President of its intention not to submit a memorial or, alternatively, not later than the expiry of the time-limit laid down under Rule 39, paragraph 1, for the filing of its first memorial.

2. Unless the Chamber decides otherwise, the filing of a preliminary objection shall not have the effect of suspending the proceedings on the merits. In all cases, the Chamber shall, after following the procedure provided for under Chapter III herein, give its decision on the objection or join the objection to the merits.

Rule 51

(Striking out of the list)

1. When a party which has brought the case before the Court notifies the Registrar of its intention not to proceed with the case and

when the other party or parties agree to such discontinuance, the Chamber shall, after consulting the Commission, decide whether or not it is appropriate to approve the discontinuance and accordingly to strike the case out of its list.

2. When the Chamber is informed of a friendly settlement, arrangement or other fact of a kind to provide a solution of the matter, it may, after consulting, if necessary, the parties and the Delegates of the Commission, strike the case out of the list.

The same shall apply where the circumstances warrant the conclusion that a party who filed an application by virtue of Article 48, paragraph 1.e, of the Convention does not intend to pursue the application or if, for any other reason, further examination of the case is not justified.

3. The striking out of a case shall be effected by means of a judgment which the President shall forward to the Committee of Ministers in order to allow them to supervise, in accordance with Article 54 of the Convention, the execution of any undertakings which may have been attached to the discontinuance or solution of the matter.

4. The Chamber may, having regard to the responsibilities of the Court under Article 19 of the Convention, decide that, notwithstanding the notice of discontinuance, friendly settlement, arrangement or other fact referred to in paragraphs 1 and 2 of this Rule, it should proceed with the consideration of the case.

Rule 52

(Question of the application of Article 50 of the Convention)

1. Any claims which the private party may wish to make under Article 50 of the Convention shall, unless the President otherwise directs, be set out in his memorial or, if he does not submit a memorial, in a special document filed at least one month before the date fixed pursuant to Rule 40 for the hearing.

2. The Chamber may, at any time during the proceedings, invite any party and the Commission to submit comments on this question.

Rule 53[1]

(Relinquishment of jurisdiction by the Chamber in favour of the Grand Chamber; and by the Grand Chamber in favour of the plenary Court)

1. Where a case pending before a Chamber raises one or more serious questions affecting the interpretation of the Convention, the Chamber may, at any time during the proceedings, relinquish jurisdiction in favour of a Grand Chamber. Relinquishment of jurisdiction shall be obligatory where the resolution of such a question or questions might have a result inconsistent with a judgment previously delivered by the Court. Reasons need not be given for the decision to relinquish jurisdiction.

2. The Grand Chamber, shall comprise nineteen judges and be composed as follows:

   a. the President and Vice-President(s) of the Court;

   b. the other members of the Chamber which has relinquished jurisdiction;

   c. additional judges appointed by means of a separate drawing of lots by the President of the Court in the presence of the Registrar immediately after the Chamber has relinquished jurisdiction.

3. The quorum of the Grand Chamber shall be seventeen judges.

4. The Grand Chamber, when the case has been referred to it, may either retain jurisdiction over the whole case, or after deciding the said question or questions, order that the case be referred back to the Chamber, which shall, in regard to the remaining part of the case, recover its original jurisdiction.

5.[2] The Grand Chamber may exceptionally, when the issues raised are particularly serious or involve a significant change of existing case-law, relinquish jurisdiction in favour of the plenary Court, which for this purpose shall comprise all the judges.

---

1 As amended by the Court on 27 October 1993.

2 As amended by the Court on 27 January 1994.

When a case is referred to the plenary Court, any *ad hoc* judge who is a member of the Grand Chamber shall sit as a judge on the plenary Court.

The plenary Court, when the case has been referred to it, may either retain jurisdiction over the whole case or, after deciding the said question or questions, order that the case be referred back to the Grand Chamber, which shall, in regard to the remaining part of the case, recover its jurisdiction.

6. Any provisions governing the Chambers shall apply, *mutatis mutandis*, to proceedings before the Grand Chamber and the plenary Court.

Chapter IV — Judgments

Rule 54

(Procedure by default)

Where a party fails to appear or to present its case, the Chamber shall, subject to the provisions of Rule 51, give a decision in the case.

Rule 55

(Contents of the judgment)

1. The judgment shall contain:

    a. the names of the President and the judges constituting the Chamber, and also the names of the Registrar and, where appropriate, the Deputy Registrar;

    b. the dates on which it was adopted and delivered;

    c. a description of the party or parties;

    d. the names of the Agents, advocates or advisers of the party or parties;

    e. the names of the Delegates of the Commission and of the persons assisting them;

f.　an account of the procedure followed;

g.　the final submissions of the party or parties and, if any, of the Delegates of the Commission;

h.　the facts of the case;

i.　the reasons in point of law;

j.　the operative provisions of the judgment;

k.　the decision, if any, in respect of costs;

l.　the number of judges constituting the majority;

m.　where appropriate, a statement as to which of the two texts, English or French, is authentic.

2. Any judge who has taken part in the consideration of the case shall be entitled to annex to the judgment either a separate opinion, concurring with or dissenting from that judgment, or a bare statement of dissent.

Rule 56

(Judgment on the application of Article 50 of the Convention)

1. Where the Chamber finds that there is a breach of the Convention, it shall give in the same judgment a decision on the application of Article 50 of the Convention if that question, after being raised in accordance with Rule 52, is ready for decision; if the question is not ready for decision, the Chamber shall reserve it in whole or in part and shall fix the further procedure. If, on the other hand, this question has not been raised in accordance with Rule 52, the Chamber may lay down a time-limit for the private party to submit any claims for just satisfaction that he may have.

2. For the purposes of ruling on the application of Article 50 of the Convention, the Chamber shall, as far as possible, be composed of those judges who sat to consider the merits of the case. Those judges who have ceased to be members of the Court shall be recalled in order to deal with the question in accordance with Article 40, paragraph 6, of the Convention; however, in the event of death,

inability to sit, withdrawal or exemption from sitting, the judge concerned shall be replaced in the same manner as was applied for his appointment to the Chamber.

3.[1] When the judgment finding a breach has been delivered under Rule 53 and does not contain a ruling on the application of Article 50 of the Convention, the plenary Court or the Grand Chamber may decide, without prejudice to the provisions of paragraph 1 above, to refer the question back to the Chamber.

4. If the Court is informed that an agreement has been reached between the injured party and Contracting Party liable, it shall verify the equitable nature of such agreement and, where it finds the agreement to be equitable, strike the case out of the list by means of a judgment. Rule 51, paragraph 3, shall apply in such circumstances.

Rule 57

(Signature, delivery and notification of the judgment)

1. The judgment shall be signed by the President and by the Registrar.

2. The judgment shall be read out by the President, or by another judge delegated by him, at a public hearing in one of the two official languages. It shall not be necessary for the other judges to be present. The Agents and advocates of the parties and the Delegates of the Commission shall be informed in due time of the date and time of delivery of the judgment.

However, in respect of a judgment striking a case out of the list or relating to the application of Article 50 of the Convention, the President may direct that the notification provided for under paragraph 4 of this Rule shall count as delivery.

3. The judgment shall be transmitted by the President to the Committee of Ministers.

---

1 As amended by the Court on 27 January 1994.

4. The original copy, duly signed and sealed, shall be placed in the archives of the Court. The Registrar shall send certified copies to the parties, to the Commission, to the Secretary General of the Council of Europe, to the Contracting States and persons referred to in Rule 39, paragraph 2, and to any other person directly concerned.

Rule 58

(Publication of judgments and other documents)

1. The Registrar shall be responsible for the publication of:

– judgments of the Court;

– documents relating to the proceedings, including the report of the Commission but excluding any document which the President considers unnecessary or inadvisable to publish;

– verbatim records of public hearings;

– any document which the President considers useful to publish.

Publication shall take place in the two official languages in the case of judgments, applications or requests instituting proceedings and the Commission's reports; the other documents shall be published in the official language in which they occur in the proceedings.

2. Documents deposited with the Registrar and not published shall be accessible to the public unless otherwise decided by the President either on his own initiative or at the request of a party, of the Commission or of any other person concerned.

Rule 59

(Request for interpretation of a judgment)

1. A party or the Commission may request the interpretation of a judgment within a period of three years following the delivery of that judgment.

2. The request shall state precisely the point or points in the operative provisions of the judgment on which interpretation is required.

It shall be filed with the registry in forty copies when it has been submitted by a Contracting Party.

3. When the request has been submitted by a private party, a Screening Panel may decide, by a unanimous vote, to reject it on the ground that there is no reason to warrant its consideration by the Court. The Panel shall in principle be composed of the judges who delivered the decision provided for in Rule 35, paragraph 2; if and in so far as that is not reasonably possible in the circumstances, Rule 26 shall apply *mutatis mutandis*.

4. When the request has been submitted by a Contracting Party or by the Commission, the Registrar shall communicate it, as appropriate, to any other party and to the Commission and shall invite them to submit any written comments within a time-limit laid down by the President of the Chamber. The President of the Chamber shall also fix the date of the hearing should the Chamber decide to hold one.

Written comments shall be filed with the registry; they shall be filed in forty copies when they are submitted by a Contracting Party or by the Commission.

5. If the Screening Panel does not reject the request or if it has been submitted by a Contracting Party or by the Commission, it shall be considered by the Chamber which gave the judgment and which shall, as far as possible, be composed of the same judges. Those judges who have ceased to be members of the Court shall be recalled in order to deal with the case in accordance with Article 40, paragraph 6, of the Convention; however, in the event of death, inability to sit, withdrawal or exemption from sitting, the judge concerned shall be replaced in the same manner as was applied for his appointment to the Chamber.

6. The Chamber shall decide by means of a judgment.

Rule 60

(Request for revision of a judgment)

1. A party or the Commission may, in the event of the discovery of a fact which might by its nature have a decisive influence and which,

when a judgment was delivered, was unknown both to the Court and to that party or the Commission, request the Court, within a period of six months after that party or the Commission, as the case may be, acquired knowledge of such fact, to revise that judgment.

2. The request shall mention the judgment of which the revision is requested and shall contain the information necessary to show that the conditions laid down in paragraph 1 have been complied with. It shall be accompanied by the original or a copy of all supporting documents. The request and supporting documents shall be filed with the registry; they shall be filed in forty copies when they have been submitted by a Contracting Party.

3. When the request has been submitted by a private party, it shall be considered by a Screening Panel composed as provided in Rule 59, paragraph 4. The Panel shall, in the event of declaring the request admissible under paragraph 1 of this Rule, refer the request to the Chamber which gave the original judgment or, if in the circumstances that is not reasonably possible, to a Chamber constituted in accordance with Article 43 of the Convention.

4. When the request has been submitted by a Contracting Party or by the Commission, the Registrar shall communicate it, as appropriate, to any other party and to the Commission, and shall invite them to submit any written comments within a time-limit laid down by the President. The President shall also fix the date of the hearing should the Chamber decide to hold one.

Written comments shall be filed with the registry; they shall be filed in forty copies if they are submitted by a Contracting Party or by the Commission.

5. In the cases provided for in the preceding paragraph, the request shall be considered by a Chamber constituted in accordance with Article 43 of the Convention. This Chamber shall, in the event of its declaring the request admissible under paragraph 1 of this Rule, refer the request to the Chamber which gave the original judgment or, if in the circumstances that is not reasonably possible, it shall retain the request and consider the merits thereof.

6. The Chamber shall decide by means of a judgment.

Chapter V — Advisory opinions

Rule 61

In proceedings in regard to advisory opinions the Court shall, in addition to the provisions of Protocol No. 2, apply the provisions which follow. It shall also apply the other provisions of these Rules to the extent to which it considers this to be appropriate.

Rule 62

The request for an advisory opinion shall be filed with the registry in forty copies. It shall state fully and precisely the question on which the opinion of the Court is sought, and also:

   a. the date on which the Committee of Ministers adopted the decision referred to in Article 1, paragraph 3, of Protocol No. 2;

   b. the names and addresses of the person or persons appointed by the Committee of Ministers to give the Court any explanations which it may require.

The request shall be accompanied by all documents likely to elucidate the question.

Rule 63

1. On receipt of a request, the Registrar shall transmit a copy thereof to all members of the Court and to the Commission.

2. He shall inform the Contracting Parties that the Court is prepared to receive their written comments. The President may decide that, by reason of the nature of the question, a similar invitation is to be sent to the Commission.

Rule 64

1. The President shall lay down the time-limits for the filing of written comments or other documents.

2. Written comments or other documents shall be filed with the registry in sixty copies. The Registrar shall transmit copies thereof to all

the members of the Court, to the Committee of Ministers, to each of the Contracting Parties and to the Commission.

Rule 65

After the closure of the written procedure, the President shall decide whether the Contracting Parties or the Commission which have submitted written comments are to be given an opportunity to develop them at an oral hearing held for the purpose.

Rule 66

If the Court considers that the request for an advisory opinion is not within its consultative competence as defined in Article 1 of Protocol No. 2, it shall so declare in a reasoned decision.

Rule 67

1. Advisory opinions shall be given by majority vote of the plenary Court. They shall mention the number of judges constituting the majority.

2. Any judge may, if he so desires, attach to the opinion of the Court either a separate opinion, concurring with or dissenting from the advisory opinion, or a bare statement of dissent.

Rule 68

The advisory opinion shall be read out by the President, or by another judge delegated by him, at a public hearing in one of the two official languages, prior notice having been given to the Committee of Ministers, to each of the Contracting Parties and to the Commission.

Rule 69

The opinion, as well as any decision given under Rule 66, shall be signed by the President and by the Registrar. The original copy, duly signed and sealed, shall be placed in the archives of the Court. The Registrar shall send certified copies to the Committee of Ministers, to the Contracting Parties, to the Commission and to the Secretary General of the Council of Europe.

Rule 70

(Final clause)

The present Rules shall enter into force the day after the entry into force of Protocol No. 9 to the Convention. They shall, however, apply only to cases brought before the Court after that date.

Addendum to Rules "B"[1]

---

1 This addendum will be produced as a separate document.

C. Fourth Protocol to the General Agreement on Privileges and Immunities of the Council of Europe

(Provisions concerning the European Court of Human Rights)

Paris, 16 December 1961

Entry into force: 16 December 1961,
in accordance with Article 10

The governments signatory hereto, being members of the Council of Europe,

Considering that, under the terms of Article 59 of the Convention for the Protection of Human Rights and Fundamental Freedoms, signed at Rome on 4th November 1950 (hereinafter referred to as "the Convention"), the members of the European Court of Human Rights (hereinafter referred to as "the Court") are entitled, during the discharge of their functions, to the privileges and immunities provided for in Article 40 of the Statute of the Council of Europe and in the Agreements made thereunder;

Considering that it is necessary to specify and define the said privileges and immunities in a Protocol to the General Agreement on Privileges and Immunities of the Council of Europe, signed at Paris on 2nd September 1949;

Have agreed as follows:

Article 1

For the purposes of this Protocol, the term "judges" means judges elected in accordance with Article 39 of the Convention as well as any *ad hoc* judge appointed by a State party concerned in pursuance of Article 43 of the Convention.

Article 2

The judges shall, while exercising their functions and during journeys made in the exercise of their functions, enjoy the following privileges and immunities:

a. immunity from personal arrest or detention and from seizure of their personal baggage, and, in respect of words spoken or written and all acts done by them in their official capacity, immunity from legal process of every kind;

b. exemption in respect of themselves and their spouses as regards any restrictions on their freedoms of movement on exit from and return to their country of residence, and entry into and exit from the country in which they exercise their functions; and from aliens' registration in the country which they are visiting or through which are passing in the exercise of their functions.

Article 3

In the course of journeys undertaken in the exercise of their functions, the judges shall, in the matter of customs and exchange control, be accorded:

a. by their own government the same facilities as those accorded to senior government officials travelling abroad on temporary official duty;

b. by the governments of other members, the same facilities as those accorded to heads of diplomatic missions.

Article 4

1. Documents and papers of the Court, judges and Registry, in so far as they relate to the business of the Court, shall be inviolable.

2. The official correspondence and other official communication of the Court, its members and the Registry may not be held up or subjected to censorship.

Article 5

In order to secure for the judges complete freedom of speech and complete independence in the discharge of their duties, the immunity from legal process in respect of words spoken or written and all acts done by them in discharging their duties shall continue to be accorded, notwithstanding that the persons concerned are no longer engaged in the discharge of such duties.

Article 6

Privileges and immunities are accorded to judges not for the personal benefit of the individuals themselves but in order to safeguard the independent exercise of their functions. The Court alone, sitting in plenary session, shall be competent to waive the immunity of judges; it has not only the right, but is under a duty, to waive the immunity of a judge in any case where, in its opinion, the immunity would impede the course of justice, and where it can be waived without prejudice to the purpose for which the immunity is accorded.

Article 7

1. The provisions of Article 2 to 5 of this Protocol shall apply to the Registrar of the Court and to the Deputy Registrar when he is acting as the Registrar, without prejudice to any privileges and immunities to which they may be entitled under Article 18 of the General Agreement on Privileges and Immunities of the Council of Europe.

2. The provisions of Article 18 of the General Agreement on Privileges and Immunities of the Council of Europe shall apply to the Deputy Registrar of the Court in respect of his services as such when he is not acting as Registrar.

3. The privileges and immunities referred to in paragraphs 1 and 2 of this Article are accorded to the Registrar and Deputy Registrar, not for the personal benefit of the individuals themselves but to facilitate the discharge of their duties. The Court alone, sitting in plenary session, shall be competent to waive the immunity of its Registrar and Deputy Registrar; it has not only the right, but is under a duty, to waive such immunity in any case where, in its opinion, the immunity would impede the course of justice, and where it can be waived without prejudice to the purpose for which the immunity is accorded.

Article 8

1. Any State may, at the time of its signature without reservation in respect of ratification, of its ratification or at any time thereafter, declare, by notification addressed to the Secretary General of the Council of Europe, that the present Protocol shall extend to all or any of the territories for whose international relations it is responsible and where, according to Article 63 of the Convention for the Protection of Human Rights and Fundamental Freedoms, the said Convention applies.

2. The Protocol shall extend to the territory or territories named in the notification as from the thirtieth day after the receipt of this notification by the Secretary General of the Council of Europe.

Article 9

This Protocol shall be open to the signature of the members of the Council of Europe who may become Parties to it either by:

    a. signature without reservation in respect of ratification, or by

    b. signature with reservation in respect of ratification followed by ratification.

Instruments of ratification shall be deposited with the Secretary General of the Council of Europe.

Article 10

1. This Protocol shall enter into force as soon as three members of the Council of Europe shall, in accordance with Article 9, have signed it without reservation in respect of ratification or shall have ratified it.

2. As regards any members subsequently signing it without reservation in respect of ratification, or ratifying it, this Protocol shall enter into force at the date of signature or deposit of the instrument of ratification.

Article 11

The Secretary General of the Council of Europe shall notify members of the Council of:

a. the names of signatories and the deposit of any instrument of ratification;

b. the date of entry into force of this Protocol.

In witness whereof the undersigned, being duly authorised to that effect, have signed the present Protocol.

Done at Paris, this 16th day of December, 1961, in English and in French, both texts being equally authoritative, in a single copy which shall remain deposited in the archives of the Council of Europe. The Secretary General shall send certified copies to each of the signatory governments.

Signatures and ratifications[1]

Opening for signature: Paris, 16/12/61

Entry into force: 16/12/61

Member States	Date of signature	Date of ratification	Entry into force
Austria	16/12/61[2]	16/12/61[2]	16/12/61
Belgium	16/12/61	04/06/64	04/06/64
Bulgaria			
Cyprus	16/12/61	30/11/67	30/11/67
Czech Republic			
Denmark	16/12/61[2]	16/12/61[2]	16/12/61
Estonia			
Finland	16/11/89	11/12/89	11/12/89
France	16/12/61	10/03/78	10/03/78 D
Germany	16/12/61	10/12/63	10/12/63 D
Greece	16/12/61	24/05/65	24/05/65
Hungary	09/02/93		

Member States	Date of signature	Date of ratification	Entry into force
Iceland			
Ireland	21/09/67	21/09/67	21/09/67
Italy	16/12/61	20/09/66	20/09/66
Liechtenstein	16/05/79	11/12/79	11/12/79
Lithuania			
Luxembourg	16/12/61	05/11/63	05/11/63
Malta	12/12/66	06/05/69	06/05/69
Netherlands	16/12/61[2]	16/12/61[2]	16/12/61 T
Norway	16/12/61[2]	16/12/61[2]	16/12/61
Poland	16/03/93	22/04/93	22/04/93
Portugal	27/04/78	06/07/82	06/07/82
Romania			
San Marino	01/03/89	22/03/89	22/03/89
Slovakia			
Slovenia			
Spain	23/07/87	23/06/89	23/06/89
Sweden	16/12/61	18/09/62	18/09/62
Switzerland	15/04/64	29/11/65	29/11/65
Turkey	01/06/62[2]	01/06/62[2]	01/03/65 D
United Kingdom	16/12/61	24/02/71	24/02/71 T

1   Treaty open for signature by the member States.

2   Signature without reservation as to ratification.

D: Declarations.

T: Territorial Declarations.

Declarations and reservations

France

[Reservation[1] made at the time of signature, on 16 February 1961(Or. Fr.)

At the time of signature, the government of the French Republic declares that it will not apply the provisions of Article 3 b.]

Declaration contained in a letter from the Ministry of Foreign Affairs, dated 16 February 1962, registered at the Secretariat General on 19 February 1962 (Or. Fr.)

The French government declares that, in application of Article 3 b, it will accord to the Judges during meetings of the Court, such facilities in the matter of customs and exchange control as may be necessary to the unimpeded exercise of their duties.

Federal Republic of Germany

Declaration contained in a letter from the Permanent Representative of the Federal Republic of Germany, dated 29 January 1964, registered at the Secretariat General on 30 January 1964 (Or. Germ/Fr.)

The Fourth Protocol to the General Agreement on Privileges and Immunities of the Council of Europe of 16 December 1961 shall also apply to the Land Berlin with effect from 10 December 1963, i.e. the date on which it entered into force for the Federal Republic of Germany.

---

1 Reservation withdrawn by letter from the Ministry for Foreign Affairs, dated 16 February 1962, registered at the Secretariat General on 19 February 1962.

Netherlands

Declaration made at the time of signature, on 16 December 1961 (Or. Fr.)

.... for the Kingdom in Europe.

Declaration contained in a letter from the Permanent Representative of the Netherlands, dated 25 July 1962, registered at the Secretariat General on 26 July 1962 (Or. Fr.)

The government of the Netherlands declares that the Fourth Protocol to the General Agreement on Privileges and Immunities of the Council of Europe signed at Paris on 16 December 1961 shall apply to the Dutch West Indies.

Declaration contained in a letter from the Permanent Representative of the Netherlands, dated 24 December 1985, registered at the Secretariat General on 3 January 1986 (Or. Engl.)

The island of Aruba, which is at present still part of the Netherlands Antilles, will obtain internal autonomy as a country within the Kingdom of the Netherlands as of 1 January 1986. Consequently the Kingdom will from then on no longer consist of two countries, namely the Netherlands (the Kingdom in Europe) and the Netherlands Antilles (situated in the Caribbean region), but will consist of three countries, namely the said two countries and the country Aruba.

As the changes being made on 1 January 1986 concern a shift only in the internal constitutional relations within the Kingdom of the Netherlands, and as the Kingdom as such will remain the subject under international law with which treaties are concluded, the said changes will have no consequences in international law regarding to treaties concluded by the Kingdom which already apply to the Netherlands Antilles, including Aruba. These treaties will remain in force for Aruba in its new capacity of country within the Kingdom. Therefore these treaties will as of 1 January 1986, as concerns the Kingdom of the Netherlands, apply to the Netherlands Antilles (without Aruba) and Aruba.

Consequently the treaties referred to in the annex, to which the Kingdom of the Netherlands is a Party and which apply to the Netherlands Antilles, will as of 1 January 1986 as concerns the Kingdom of the Netherlands apply to the Netherlands Antilles and Aruba.

Turkey

Declaration made at the time of signature, on 1 June 1962 (Or. Fr.)

The Fourth Protocol, owing to the provisions of the Constitution of the Republic of Turkey and in derogation from paragraph 2 of Article 10 of the said Protocol, will enter into force at the time of its publication in the Official Gazette; the Secretary General of the Council of Europe will be notified of the date, so that it may be communicated to the other member States.[1]

United Kingdom

Declaration contained in a letter from the Permanent Representative of the United Kingdom, dated 19 October 1971, registered at the Secretariat General on 20 October 1971 (Or. Engl.)

In accordance with Article 8 of the Fourth Protocol I have the honour to declare on behalf of the United Kingdom of Great Britain and Northern Ireland that the provisions of this Protocol shall hereby extend to the following territories: the Bailiwick of Jersey, the Bailiwick of Guernsey and the Isle of Man.

---

1 The Fourth Protocol was published in the Official Gazette on 1 March 1965.

D. Fifth Protocol to the General Agreement on Privileges and Immunities of the Council of Europe

(Provisions concerning the European Commission and the European Court of Human Rights)

Strasbourg, 18 June 1990

Entry into force: 1 November 1991,
in accordance with Article 4

The member States of the Council of Europe, signatories hereto,

Considering that, under the terms of Article 59 of the Convention for the Protection of Human Rights and Fundamental Freedoms (hereinafter referred to as "the Convention"), signed at Rome on 4 November 1950, the members of the European Commission of Human Rights (hereinafter referred to as "the Commission") and of the European Court of Human Rights (hereinafter referred to as "the Court") are entitled, during the discharge of their functions, to the privileges and immunities provided for in Article 40 of the Statute of the Council of Europe and in the Agreements made thereunder;

Recalling that the said privileges and immunities have been specified and defined in the Second and Fourth Protocols, signed at Paris on 15 December 1956 and 16 December 1961 respectively, to the General Agreement on Privileges and Immunities of the Council of Europe, signed at Paris on 2 September 1949;

Considering that it is necessary, in the light of changes in the operation of the Convention's control machinery, to supplement the above-mentioned General Agreement by another Protocol,

Have agreed as follows:

Article 1

1. Members of the Commission and members of the Court shall be exempt from taxation on salaries, emoluments and allowances paid to them by the Council of Europe.

2. The term "members of the Commission and members of the Court" includes members who, after having been replaced, continue to deal with cases which they already have under consideration as well as any *ad hoc* judge appointed in pursuance of the provisions of the Convention.

Article 2

1. This Protocol shall be open for signature by the member States of the Council of Europe, which may express their consent to be bound by:

a. signature without reservation as to ratification, acceptance or approval, or

b. signature subject to ratification, acceptance or approval, followed by ratification, acceptance or approval.

2. No member State of the Council of Europe shall sign without reservation as to ratification, ratify, accept or approve this Protocol unless it has already ratified, or simultaneously ratifies, the General Agreement on Privileges and Immunities of the Council of Europe.

3. Instruments of ratification, acceptance or approval shall be deposited with the Secretary General of the Council of Europe.

Article 3

1. This Protocol shall enter into force on the first day of the month following the expiration of a period of three months after the date on which three member States of the Council of Europe have expressed their consent to be bound by the Protocol in accordance with the provisions of Article 2.

2. In respect of any member State which subsequently expresses its consent to be bound by it, the Protocol shall enter into force on the first day of the month following the expiration of a period of three months after the date of signature or of the deposit of the instrument of ratification, acceptance or approval.

Article 4

Pending the entry into force of this Protocol in accordance with paragraphs 1 and 2 of Article 3, the Signatories agree to apply the Protocol provisionally from the date of signature, so far as it is possible to do so under their respective constitutional systems.

Article 5

The Secretary General of the Council of Europe shall notify the member States of the Council of:

a. any signature;

b. the deposit of any instrument of ratification, acceptance or approval;

c. any date of entry into force of this Protocol in accordance with Article 3;

d. any other act, notification or communication relating to this Protocol.

In witness whereof the undersigned, being duly authorised thereto, have signed this Protocol.

Done at Strasbourg, this 18th day of June 1990, in English and French, both texts being equally authentic, in a single copy which shall be deposited in the archives of the Council of Europe. The Secretary General of the Council of Europe shall transmit certified copies to each member State of the Council of Europe.

Signatures and ratifications[1]

Opening for signature: Strasbourg, 18/06/90

Entry into force: 01/11/91

Member States	Date of signature	Date of ratification	Entry into force
Austria	26/03/92[2]	26/03/92[2]	01/07/92
Belgium			
Bulgaria			
Cyprus			
Czech Republic			
Denmark	18/06/90[2]	18/06/90[2]	01/11/91
Estonia			
Finland	18/06/90	23/11/90	01/11/91
France			
Germany	16/12/92		
Greece	27/02/91	15/06/93	01/10/93
Hungary	09/02/93		
Iceland			
Ireland	26/03/91	22/03/93	01/07/93
Italy	24/01/91		
Liechtenstein			
Lithuania			
Luxembourg	26/11/90		
Malta			
Netherlands			
Norway			
Poland	16/03/93	22/04/93	01/08/93
Portugal			
Romania			
San Marino			
Slovakia			
Slovenia			
Spain			
Sweden			

Member States	Date of signature	Date of ratification	Entry into force
Switzerland	15/12/93[2]	15/12/93[2]	01/04/94
Turkey	30/09/91		
United Kingdom	18/06/90	19/07/91	01/11/91

1　Treaty open for signature by the member States.

2　Signature without reservation as to ratification.

E. Composition of the European Court of Human Rights (January 1994)[1]

In order of precedence		End of mandate
Mr Rolv Ryssdal, President	(Norwegian)	20.01.1995
Mr Rudolf Bernhardt, Vice-President	(German)	20.01.2001
Mr Thór Vilhjálmsson	(Icelandic)	20.01.1998
Mr Feyyaz Gölcüklü	(Turkish)	20.01.1995
Mr Franz Matscher	(Austrian)	20.01.1995
Mr Louis-Edmond Pettiti	(French)	20.01.1998
Mr Brian Walsh	(Irish)	20.01.1998
Mr Ronald MacDonald	(Canadian)[2]	20.01.1998
Mr Carlo Russo	(Italian)	20.01.2001
Mr Alphonse Spielmann	(Luxemburger)	20.01.1995
Mr Jan De Meyer	(Belgian)	20.01.1995
Mr Nicolas Valticos	(Greek)	20.01.2001
Mr Sibrand Karel Martens	(Dutch)	20.01.1995
Mrs Elisabeth Palm	(Swedish)	20.01.2001
Mr Isi Foighel	(Danish)	20.01.1998
Mr Raimo Pekkanen	(Finnish)	20.01.1998
Mr Andreas Nicolas Loizou	(Cypriot)	20.01.1998
Mr José Maria Morenilla	(Spanish)	20.01.1995
Mr Federico Bigi	(San Marinese)	20.01.2001
Sir John Freeland	(British)	20.01.2001
Mr András Baka	(Hungarian)	20.01.2001
Mr Manuel Antonio Lopes Rocha	(Portuguese)	20.01.1995
Mr Luzius Wildhaber	(Swiss)	20.01.1998
Mr Giuseppe Mifsud Bonnici	(Maltese)	20.01.2001
Mr Bohumil Repik	(Slovak)	20.01.2001
Mr Jerzy Makarczyk	(Polish)	20.01.2001
Mr Dimitar Gotchev	(Bulgarian)	20.01.2001
Mr Peter Jambrek	(Slovenian)	20.01.2001
Mr Karel Jungwiert	(Czech)	20.01.2001
Mr Marc-André Eissen, Registrar	(French)	00.06.1994
Mr Herbert Petzold, Deputy Registrar	(German)	00.09.1996

---

1 The judges in respect of Estonia and Lithuania have not yet been elected.

2 Elected as the judge in respect of Liechtenstein.

Rules adopted by the Committee of Ministers for the application of Articles 32 and 54 of the European Convention on Human Rights

Rules for the application of Article 32

Text approved by the Committee of Ministers at the 181st meeting of the Ministers' Deputies in June 1969[1] and amended at the 215th (November 1972), 245th (May 1975), 307th (September 1979), 409th (June 1987), 449th (December 1990) and 451st (January 1991) meetings and at the special meeting of the Ministers' Deputies on 19 December 1991.

A. Rules of Substance

Rule 1

When exercising its functions under Article 32 of the Convention, the Committee of Ministers is entitled to discuss the substance of any case on which the Commission has submitted a report, for exam-

---

1 The text approved at the 181st meeting of the Ministers' Deputies contained a restatement of the rules previously adopted at the 68th (January 1959), 94th (January 1961), 99th (May 1961), 140th (April 1965) and 164th (October 1967) meetings.

ple by considering written or oral statements of the parties and hearing of witnesses (see Rule 4).

Rule 2

The representative of any member state on the Committee of Ministers shall be fully qualified to take part in exercising the functions and powers set forth in Article 32 of the Convention, even if that state has not yet ratified the Convention.

Rule 3

Each representative on the Committee of Ministers has an instrinsic right to make submissions and deposit documents. Consequently, the representative on the Committee of Ministers of a government which was not a party to the proceedings before the Commission, may play a full part in the proceedings before the Committee of Ministers.[1]

Rule 4

While the Committee of Ministers must have all the necessary powers to reach a decision on a report of the Commission, nevertheless, it may not itself wish to undertake the task of taking evidence, etc., should the need arise. The procedure to be followed in such a case will be decided *ad hoc.*[2]

Rule 5[3]

Rule 6

The Committee of Ministers considers that the Commission is not entitled to make proposals under Article 31, paragraph 3, of the Convention in cases where it considers that there has not been a violation of the Convention.

---

1 See Appendix, paragraph 1.

2 See Appendix, paragraph 2.

3 Rule 5 was deleted by the Ministers' Deputies on 19 December 1991.

Rule 6 bis

Prior to taking a decision under Article 32, paragraph 1, of the Convention, the Committee of Ministers may be informed of a friendly settlement, arrangement or other fact of a kind to provide a solution of the matter. In that event, it may decide to discontinue its examination of the case, after satisfying itself that the solution envisaged is based on respect for human rights as defined in the Convention.

B. Procedural Rules

Rule 7

If the chairmanship of the Committee of Ministers is held by the representative of a state which is party to a dispute referred to the Committee of Ministers, that representative shall step down from the chair during the discussion of the Commission's report.

Rule 8

The Chairman of the Committee shall obtain the opinion of the representatives of the State Party or States Parties to the dispute in regard to the procedure to be followed, and the Committee shall specify, if necessary, in what order and within what time-limits any written submissions or other documents are to be deposited.[1]

Rule 9

1. During the examination of the case and before taking the decision mentioned in Article 32, paragraph 1, of the Convention, the Committee of Ministers may, if it deems advisable, request the Commission for information on particular points in the report which it has transmitted to the Committee.

2. After taking a decision under Article 32, paragraph 1, to the effect that there has been a violation of the Convention, the Committee of Ministers may request the Commission to make proposals concern-

---

1 This Rule applies not only to inter-state disputes but also when the Committee of Ministers is considering the report of the Commission on an individual application.

ing in particular the appropriateness, nature and extent of just satisfaction for the injured party.

Rule 9 bis

When a vote is taken in accordance with Article 32, paragraph 1, and the majority required to decide whether there has been a violation of the Convention has not been attained, a second and final vote shall be taken at one of the three following meetings of the Committee of Ministers.

Rule 9 ter

1. The Commission's report shall be published when the Committee of Ministers has completed consideration of the case under Article 32, paragraph 1.

2. The Committee of Ministers may, by way of exception and without prejudice to Article 32, paragraph 3, decide not to publish a report of the Commission or a part thereof upon a reasoned request of a Contracting Party or of the Commission.

Rule 10

In the matter of voting, the rules laid down in Article 20 of the Statute should, in general, apply.[1] In particular

  a. the parties to the dispute shall have the right to vote;

  b. decisions taken in pursuance of Rule 6 *bis* require a two-thirds majority of the representatives casting a vote and a majority of the representatives entitled to sit on the Committee;

  c. certain questions of procedure, such as in what order and within what time-limits any written submissions or other documents

---

[1] In the case of a decision by the Committee of Ministers on the question whether there has been a violation of the Convention, paragraph 1 of Article 32 of the Convention already provides that "the Committee of Ministers shall decide by a majority of two-thirds of the members entitled to sit on the Committee whether there has been a violation of the Convention".

are to be deposited, shall be determined by a simple majority of the representatives entitled to sit on the Committee.

Rule 11

The decision taken under Article 32, paragraph 1, will be published in the form of a resolution adopted by a two-thirds majority of the representatives casting a vote and a majority of the representatives entitled to sit on the Committee.

Appendix – Other points discussed by the Committee of Ministers

1. With reference to Rule 3 above, the Committee of Ministers reserved its position on the possibility that the representative of a government which had not been a party to the proceedings before the Commission might make a request to the Committee of Ministers which had not been made before the Commission (for example, a request for damages).

2. In connection with Rule 4, the Committee of Ministers considered that while it must have all the necessary powers to reach a decision on a case submitted to it, nevertheless it is not well-equipped to take evidence, etc. and ought not normally to undertake such tasks. If therefore it should become necessary for the Committee of Ministers to take evidence, etc. when it is considering a case under Article 32, there are the following possibilities:

    a. to conclude a Protocol to the Convention conferring on the Commission the power to undertake such tasks on behalf of the Committee of Ministers;

    b. to invite the Commission to undertake these tasks on its behalf, since the Commission is in its nature better equipped to do so, if the Commission agrees to this procedure;

c. the Committee of Ministers could take evidence, etc. in plenary sessions (possibly with alternate members) or appoint a sub-committee for the purpose;

d. under Article 17 of the Statute, the Committee of Ministers may set up advisory and technical committees for specific purposes.

The Committee of Ministers decided not to adopt the first of these possibilities but to leave the choice open for a decision *ad hoc* should the need arise.

2 *bis*. The Committee of Ministers decided that in every case in which it finds there has been a violation of the Convention, it would consider, taking into account any proposals from the Commission, whether just satisfaction should be afforded to the injured party and, if necessary, indicate measures on this subject to the state concerned.

3. a. The Committee of Ministers decided not to establish a procedure permitting the communication to an applicant of the report of the Commission on his application, or the communication to the Committee of Ministers of the applicant's observations on the report.

b. The communication to an individual applicant of the complete text or extracts from the report of the Commission should take place only as an exceptional measure (for example, where the Committee of Ministers wishes to obtain the observations of the applicant), only on a strictly confidential basis, and only with the consent of the state against which the application was lodged.

c. Since the individual applicant is not a party to the proceedings before the Committee of Ministers under Article 32 of the Convention, he has no right to be heard by the Committee of Ministers or to have any written communication considered by the Committee.

This should be explained by the Secretary General to the applicant when he writes to inform him that the report of the Commission on his case has been transmitted to the Committee of Ministers in accordance with the provisions of Article 31 of the Convention.

d. If communications from the individual applicant intended for the Committee of Ministers are nevertheless received, the Secretary General should acknowledge their receipt and explain to the applicant why they will not form part of the proceedings before the Committee of Ministers and cannot be considered as a document in the case. In appropriate cases, the Secretary General might add that it is possible for the applicant to submit a new application to the Commission if he wishes to invoke important new information.

4. The Committee of Ministers decided not to make provisions in its Rules for participation by delegates of the Commission in its proceedings, since the Commission considered that such participation would be outside its powers as defined in the Convention.[1]

The Committee of Ministers at the 307th meeting of the Ministers' Deputies (September 1979) adopted the following additional Rules:

a. An individual applicant ought normally to be informed of the outcome of the examination of his case before the Committee of Ministers. It would be for the Committee of Ministers to decide in each particular case on the information to be communicated and on the procedure to be followed;

b. a decision to inform an individual applicant about the outcome of his case should be taken, in accordance with Article 21 b of the Statute, by unanimous vote;

c. the Committee of Ministers could indicate in its communication to the applicant if any of the information conveyed to him is to be treated as confidential.

---

1 At the 245th meeting of the Ministers' Deputies (May 1975), the Deputies agreed, unless otherwise decided in a particular case, to transmit to the European Commission of Human Rights, at the end of their discussions on a case referred to the Committee of Ministers in accordance with Article 32 of the European Convention on Human Rights, the texts of every decision appearing in their conclusions, on the understanding that these texts are not made public; they agreed also that this decision cannot be regarded as a precedent with regard to other decisions of the Committee.

Rules for the application of Article 54

Text approved by the Committee of Ministers at the 254th Meeting of the Ministers' Deputies in February 1976.

Rule 1

When a judgment of the Court is transmitted to the Committee of Ministers in accordance with Article 54 of the Convention, the case shall be inscribed on the agenda of the Committee without delay.

Rule 2

a. When, in the judgment transmitted to the Committee of Ministers in accordance with Article 54 of the Convention, the Court decides that there has been a violation of the Convention and/or affords just satisfaction to the injured party under Article 50 of the Convention, the Committee shall invite the state concerned to inform it of the measures which it has taken in consequence of the judgment, having regard to its obligation under Article 53 of the Convention to abide by the judgment.[1]

b. If the state concerned informs the Committee of Ministers that it is not yet in a position to inform it of the measures taken, the case shall be automatically inscribed on the agenda of a meeting of the Committee taking place not more than six months later, unless the Committee of Ministers decides otherwise; the same Rule will be applied on expiration of this and any subsequent period.

Rule 3

The Committee of Ministers shall not regard its functions under Article 54 of the Convention as having been exercised until it has taken

---

1 At the 215th meeting of the Ministers' Deputies (November 1972), it was agreed that the Committee of Ministers is entitled to consider a communication from an individual who claims that he has not received damages in accordance with a decision of the Court under Article 50 of the Convention affording him just satisfaction as an injured party, as well as any further information furnished to it concerning the execution of such a judgment of the Court, and that, consequently, any such communication should be distributed to the Committee of Ministers.

note of the information supplied in accordance with Rule 2 and, when just satisfaction has been afforded, until it has satisfied itself that the state concerned has awarded this just satisfaction to the injured party.

Rule 4

The decision in which the Committee of Ministers declares that its functions under Article 54 of the Convention have been exercised shall take the form of a resolution.

Selected texts
of the Council of Europe
in the field of
human rights

A. Selected texts adopted by the Committee of Ministers

Declaration

Declaration on the freedom of expression and information

Adopted by the Committee of Ministers on 29 April 1982
at its 70th Session

The member States of the Council of Europe,

1. Considering that the principles of genuine democracy, the rule of law and respect for human rights form the basis of their co-operation, and that the freedom of expression and information is a fundamental element of those principles;

2. Considering that this freedom has been proclaimed in national constitutions and international instruments, and in particular in Article 19 of the Universal Declaration of Human Rights and Article 10 of the European Convention on Human Rights;

3. Recalling that through that Convention they have taken steps for the collective enforcement of the freedom of expression and infor-

mation by entrusting the supervision of its application to the organs provided for by the Convention;

4. Considering that the freedom of expression and information is necessary for the social, economic, cultural and political development of every human being, and constitutes a condition for the harmonious progress of social and cultural groups, nations and the international community;

5. Convinced that the continued development of information and communication technology should serve to further the right, regardless of frontiers, to express, to seek, to receive and to impart information and ideas, whatever their source;

6. Convinced that States have the duty to guard against infringements of the freedom of expression and information and should adopt policies designed to foster as much as possible a variety of media and a plurality of information sources, thereby allowing a plurality of ideas and opinions;

7. Noting that, in addition to the statutory measures referred to in paragraph 2 of Article 10 of the European Convention on Human Rights, codes of ethics have been voluntarily established and are applied by professional organisations in the field of the mass media;

8. Aware that a free flow and wide circulation of information of all kinds across frontiers is an important factor for international understanding, for bringing peoples together and for the mutual enrichment of cultures;

I. Reiterate their firm attachment to the principles of freedom of expression and information as a basic element of democratic and pluralist society;

II. Declare that in the field of information and mass media they seek to achieve the following objectives:

a. protection of the right of everyone, regardless of frontiers, to express himself, to seek and receive information and ideas, whatever their source, as well as to impart them under the conditions set out in Article 10 of the European Convention on Human Rights;

b. absence of censorship or any arbitrary controls or constraints on participants in the information process, on media content or on the transmission and dissemination of information;

c. the pursuit of an open information policy in the public sector, including access to information, in order to enhance the individual's understanding of, and his ability to discuss freely political, social, economic and cultural matters;

d. the existence of a wide variety of independent and autonomous media, permitting the reflection of diversity of ideas and opinions;

e. the availability and access on reasonable terms to adequate facilities for the domestic and international transmission and dissemination of information and ideas;

f. the promotion of international co-operation and assistance, through public and private channels, with a view to fostering the free flow of information and improving communication infrastructures and expertise;

III. Resolve to intensify their co-operation in order:

a. to defend the right of everyone to the exercise of the freedom of expression and information;

b. to promote, through teaching and education, the effective exercise of the freedom of expression and information;

c. to promote the free flow of information, thus contributing to international understanding, a better knowledge of convictions and traditions, respect for the diversity of opinions and the mutual enrichment of cultures;

d. to share their experience and knowledge in the media field;

e. to ensure that new information and communication techniques and services, where available, are effectively used to broaden the scope of freedom of expression and information.

Resolutions

Resolution (56) 16
Convention on Human Rights
Interpretation and application of Article 15, paragraph 3

Adopted by the Ministers' Deputies on 26 September 1956

The Committee of Ministers,

Having taken note of the memorandum by the Secretary General dated 16th May 1956 (Doc. SG (56) 1), concerning the application of Article 15, paragraph 3, of the Convention for the Protection of Human Rights and Fundamental Freedoms,

Resolves that any information transmitted to the Secretary General by a Contracting Party in pursuance of Article 15, paragraph 3, of the Convention must be communicated by him as soon as possible to the other Contracting Parties and to the European Commission of Human Rights.

Resolution (70) 17
United Nations Covenant on Civil and Political Rights and the European Convention on Human Rights: procedure for dealing with inter-state complaints

Adopted by the Ministers' Deputies on 15 May 1970

The Committee of Ministers,

Considering that, on 16 December 1966, the General Assembly of the United Nations, by its Resolution 2200 (XXI), adopted the International Covenant on Economic, Social and Cultural Rights, the International Covenant on Civil and Political Rights, and the Optional Protocol to the International Covenant on Civil and Political Rights;

Considering that the Covenant on Civil and Political Rights sets out in its Article 41 an optional procedure under which a State Party may bring to the attention of the UN Human Rights Committee a claim that another State Party is not fulfilling its obligations under the Covenant;

Considering that Article 24 of the European Convention on Human Rights has already established a procedure whereby a Contracting Party may refer to the European Commission of Human Rights any alleged breach of the provisions of that Convention by another Contracting Party;

Considering that there are a certain number of rights which in substance are covered both by the UN Covenant and by the European Convention;

Considering that the procedure instituted by the European Convention provides an effective system for the protection of human rights, including binding decisions by the Court of Human Rights or by the Committee of Ministers;

Recognising the value of the procedure established by the UN Covenant for the protection of rights not included in the European Convention and its protocols;

Considering that Article 44 of the UN Covenant provides that its provisions shall not prevent States Parties from having recourse to other methods of settlement of disputes, and that under Article 62 of the European Convention the Contracting Parties agree that they will not, except by special agreement, submit a dispute arising out of the interpretation or application of the Convention to a means of settlement other than those provided for in the Convention;

Considering, however, that differences of opinion appear to exist as regards the exact scope of the obligation resulting from Article 62;

Considering that Article 33 of the Charter of the United Nations emphasises the importance of regional settlement of inter-state disputes,

Declares that, as long as the problem of interpretation of Article 62 of the European Convention is not resolved, States Parties to the Convention which ratify or accede to the UN Covenant on Civil and Political Rights and make a declaration under Article 41 of the Covenant should normally utilise only the procedure established by the

European Convention in respect of complaints against another Contracting Party to the European Convention relating to an alleged violation of a right which in substance is covered both by the European Convention (or its protocols) and by the UN Covenant on Civil and Political Rights, it being understood that the UN procedure may be invoked in relation to rights not guaranteed in the European Convention (or its protocols) or in relation to States which are not Parties to the European Convention.

Resolution (93) 6
on the control of respect for human rights in European States not yet members of the Council of Europe

Adopted by the Committee of Ministers on 9 March 1993 at the 489th meeting of the Ministers' Deputies

The Committee of Ministers of the Council of Europe,

Acting under the Statute of the Council of Europe signed in London on 5 May 1949;

Having regard to the Convention on the Protection of Human Rights and Fundamental Freedoms of 4 November 1950 and the Protocols thereto;

Considering that it is desirable that all European States become members of the Council of Europe and Parties to the European Convention on Human Rights and the Protocols thereto;

Wishing to make arrangements under which the Council of Europe can contribute to the setting up by European States which are not yet members of the Council of Europe and which so desire, as a transitional measure, within their internal legal system, of a body responsible for the control of respect for human rights that takes into account the substantive provisions of the European Convention on Human Rights;

Considering that the establishment of a transitional human rights control mechanism drawing on the competence and experience of the control organs of the European Convention on Human Rights might promote the process of accession to the Council of Europe;

Having consulted the European Court and Commission of Human Rights which have both indicated their agreement,

Resolves to contribute towards the control of respect for human rights in European non-member States, in accordance with the following principles:

Article 1

At the request of a European non-member State, the Committee of Ministers may, after consultation with the European Court and Commission of Human Rights, appoint specially qualified persons to sit on a court or other body responsible for the control of respect for human rights set up by this State within its internal legal system (hereafter called the "control body").

Article 2

The number of members of the control body set up by the requesting State shall be such that the number of members appointed by virtue of this resolution will be greater than the number of other members.

Article 3

The law applicable by the control body shall include the substantive provisions of the European Convention on Human Rights.

Article 4

Practical arrangements concerning the participation described in Article 1 shall be specified in an agreement concluded by the Secretary General of the Council of Europe with the requesting State on behalf of the Committee of Ministers.

Article 5

The arrangements under this resolution shall cease once the requesting State has become a member of the Council of Europe except as otherwise agreed between the Council of Europe and the State concerned.

Recommendations

Recommendation No. R (80) 2
of the Committee of Ministers concerning the exercise of discretionary powers by administrative authorities

Adopted by the Committee of Ministers on 11 March 1980 at the 316th meeting of the Ministers' Deputies

The Committee of Ministers, under the terms of Article 15.*b* of the Statute of the Council of Europe,

Considering that the aim of the Council of Europe is to achieve greater unity between its members;

Considering that administrative authorities are acting in an increasing number of fields, and, in the process, are frequently called upon to exercise discretionary powers;

Considering it is desirable that common principles be laid down in all member States to promote the protection of the rights, liberties and interests of persons whether physical or legal against arbitrariness or any other improper use of a discretionary power, without at the same time impeding achievement by the administrative authorities of the purpose for which the power has been conferred;

Recalling the general principles governing the protection of the individual in relation to the acts of administrative authorities as set out in Resolution (77) 31;

Considering that it is desirable that the said Resolution be supplemented when applied to acts taken in the exercise of discretionary powers,

Recommends the governments of member States:

a. to be guided in their law and administrative practice by the principles annexed to this recommendation,

b. to inform the Secretary General of the Council of Europe, in due course, of any significant developments relating to the matters referred to in the present recommendation;

Instructs the Secretary General of the Council of Europe to bring the contents of this recommendation to the notice of the Government of Finland.

Appendix to Recommendation No. R (80) 2

Principles applicable to the exercise of discretionary powers by administrative authorities

I. Scope and definitions

The following principles apply to the protection of the rights, liberties and interests of persons with regard to administrative acts taken in the exercise of discretionary powers.

The term "administrative act" means, in accordance with Resolution (77) 31, any individual measure or decision which is taken in the exercise of public authority and which is of such nature as directly to affect the rights, liberties or interests of persons whether physical or legal.

The term "discretionary power" means a power which leaves an administrative authority some degree of latitude as regards the decision to be taken, enabling it to choose from among several legally admissible decisions the one which it finds to be the most appropriate.

In the implementation of these principles the requirements of good and efficient administration, as well as the interests of third parties and major public interests should be duly taken into account. Where these requirements or interests make it necessary to modify or exclude one or more of these principles, either in particular cases or in specific areas of public administration, every endeavour should nevertheless be made to observe the spirit of this recommendation.

II. Basic principles

An administrative authority, when exercising a discretionary power:

1. does not pursue a purpose other than that for which the power has been conferred;

2. observes objectivity and impartiality, taking into account only the factors relevant to the particular case;

3. observes the principle of equality before the law by avoiding unfair discrimination;

4. maintains a proper balance between any adverse effects which its decision may have on the rights, liberties or interests of persons and the purpose which it pursues;

5. takes its decision within a time which is reasonable having regard to the matter at stake;

6. applies any general administrative guidelines in a consistent manner while at the same time taking account of the particular circumstances of each case.

III. Procedure

In addition to the principles of fair administrative procedure governing administrative acts in general as set out in Resolution (77) 31, the following principles apply specifically to the taking of administrative acts in the exercise of a discretionary power.

7. Any general administrative guidelines which govern the exercise of a discretionary power are:

i. made public, or

ii. communicated in an appropriate manner and to the extent that is necessary to the person concerned, at his request, be it before or after the taking of the act concerning him.

8. Where an administrative authority, in exercising a discretionary power, departs from a general administrative guideline in such a manner as to affect adversely the rights, liberties or interests of a person concerned, the latter is informed of the reasons for this decision.

This is done either by stating the reasons in the act or by communicating them, at his request, to the person concerned in writing within a reasonable time.

IV. Control

9. An act taken in the exercise of a discretionary power is subject to control of legality by a court or other independent body.

This control does not exclude the possibility of a preliminary control by an administrative authority empowered to decide both on legality and on the merits.

10. Where no time-limit for the taking of a decision in the exercise of a discretionary power has been set by law and the administrative authority does not take its decision within a reasonable time, its failure to do so may be submitted to control by an authority competent for the purpose.

11. A court or other independent body which controls the exercise of a discretionary power has such powers of obtaining information as are necessary for the exercise of its function.

Recommendation No. R (87) 8
of the Committee of Ministers to member States regarding conscientious objection to compulsory military service[1]

Adopted by the Committee of Ministers on 9 April 1987 at the 406th meeting of the Ministers' Deputies

The Committee of Ministers, under the terms of Article 15.*b* of the Statute of the Council of Europe,

Considering that the aim of the Council of Europe is to achieve a greater unity between its members;

Recalling that respect for human rights and fundamental freedoms is the common heritage of member States of the Council of Europe, as is borne out, in particular, by the European Convention on Human Rights;

Considering that it is desirable to take common action for the further realisation of human rights and fundamental freedoms;

Noting that in the majority of member States of the Council of Europe military service is a basic obligation of citizens;

Considering the problems raised by conscientious objection to compulsory military service;

---

1 When this recommendation was adopted:
– in application of Article 10.2.*c* of the Rules of Procedure for the meetings of the Ministers' Deputies, the Representative of Greece reserved the right of his Government to comply with it or not, and the Representative of Cyprus reserved the right of his Government to comply or not with paragraph 9 of the text;
– in application of Article 10.2.*d* of the Rules of Procedure for the meetings of the Ministers' Deputies, the Representative of Italy recorded his abstention and in an explanatory statement said that his Government was of the opinion that the text as adopted fell short of the suggestions made by the Assembly, and therefore appeared to be deficient;
– in application of Article 10.2.*d* of the Rules of Procedure for the meetings of the Ministers' Deputies, the Representatives of Switzerland and Turkey recorded their abstentions and in explanatory statements said that their Governments would be unable to comply with the text.

Wishing that conscientious objection to compulsory military service be recognised in all the member States of the Council of Europe and governed by common principles;

Noting that, in some member States where conscientious objection to compulsory military service is not yet recognised, specific measures have been taken with a view to improving the situation of the individuals concerned,

Recommends that the governments of member States, insofar as they have not already done so, bring their national law and practice into line with the following principles and rules:

A. *Basic principle*

1. Anyone liable to conscription for military service who, for compelling reasons of conscience, refuses to be involved in the use of arms, shall have the right to be released from the obligation to perform such service, on the conditions set out hereafter. Such persons may be liable to perform alternative service;

B. *Procedure*

2. States may lay down a suitable procedure for the examination of applications for conscientious objector status or accept a declaration giving reasons by the person concerned;

3. With a view to the effective application of the principles and rules of this recommendation, persons liable to conscription shall be informed in advance of their rights. For this purpose, the State shall provide them with all relevant information directly or allow private organisations concerned to furnish that information;

4. Applications for conscientious objector status shall be made in ways and within time-limits to be determined having due regard to the requirement that the procedure for the examination of an application should, as a rule, be completed before the individual concerned is actually enlisted in the forces;

5. The examination of applications shall include all the necessary guarantees for a fair procedure;

6. An applicant shall have the right to appeal against the decision at first instance;

7. The appeal authority shall be separate from the military administration and composed so as to ensure its independence;

8. The law may also provide for the possibility of applying for and obtaining conscientious objector status in cases where the requisite conditions for conscientious objection appear during military service or periods of military training after initial service;

C. Alternative service

9. Alternative service, if any, shall be in principle civilian and in the public interest. Nevertheless, in addition to civilian service, the State may also provide for unarmed military service, assigning to it only those conscientious objectors whose objections are restricted to the personal use of arms;

10. Alternative service shall not be of a punitive nature. Its duration shall, in comparison to that of military service, remain within reasonable limits;

11. Conscientious objectors performing alternative service shall not have less social and financial rights than persons performing military service. Legislative provisions or regulations which relate to the taking into account of military service for employment, career or pension purposes shall apply to alternative service.

Recommendation No. R (92) 10
on the implementation of rights of persons belonging to national minorities

Adopted by the Committee of Ministers on 21 May 1992 at the 476th meeting of the Ministers' Deputies

The Committee of Ministers, under the terms of Article 15.b. of the Statute of the Council of Europe,

Considering that many problems and difficulties exist in Europe today because the rights of persons belonging to national minorities are not fully respected;

Concerned that this situation may lead to increased tension, strife and violence in Europe;

Conscious that States do not always fulfil their obligations and commitments under international instruments, resulting in national minorities being treated badly, and also that States do not make use of existing mechanisms which could resolve some of the disputes;

Aware that if States were to implement their obligations under existing international instruments the difficulties of persons belonging to national minorities would be greatly improved,

Recommends that the governments of member States should, as a matter of urgency, ensure that they implement all their obligations and commitments under international instruments to persons belonging to national minorities and make use of the existing mechanisms which could alleviate the problems of persons belonging to national minorities.

B. List of other recommendations, resolutions and declarations adopted by the Committee of Ministers concerning human rights

Declarations

Declaration on territorial asylum (1977)
Declaration regarding intolerance — a threat to democracy (1981)

Resolutions

Resolution (68) 30
Measures to be taken against incitement to racial, national and religious hatred

Resolution (73) 22
Protection of the privacy of individuals *vis-à-vis* electronic data banks in the private sector

Resolution (74) 26
Right of reply — position of the individual in relation to the press

Resolution (77) 31
Protection of the individual in relation to the acts of administrative authorities

Resolution (78) 41
Teaching of human rights

Resolution (85) 8
Co-operation between the Ombudsmen of member States and between them and the Council of Europe

Recommendations

Recommendation No. R (79) 16
Promotion of human rights research in the member States of the Council of Europe

Recommendation No. R (81) 19
Access to information held by public authorities

Recommendation No. R (83) 2
Legal protection of persons suffering from mental disorder placed as involuntary patients

Recommendation No. R (84) 17
Equality between women and men in the media

Recommendation No. R (85) 2
Legal protection against sex discrimination

Recommendation No. R (85) 7
Teaching and learning about human rights in schools

Recommendation No. R (85) 13
Institution of the Ombudsman

Recommendation No. R (87) 3
European Prison Rules

Recommendation No. R (89) 14
Ethical issues of HIV infection in health care and social settings

Recommendation No. R (90) 3
Medical research on human beings

Recommendation No. R (91) 16
Training of social workers and human rights

Recommendation No. R (93) 1
Effective access to the law and to justice for the very poor

For further information:
Council of Europe, Point i, 67075 Strasbourg Cedex, France
Tel: (33) 88 41 20 33 - Fax: (33) 88 41 27 80/90

Appendix:
Protocol No. 11
to the Convention for the
Protection of Human
Rights and Fundamental
Freedoms restructuring the
control machinery
established thereby

Protocol No. 11
to the European Convention for the Protection of Human Rights and Fundamental Freedoms restructuring the control machinery established thereby[1]

Strasbourg, 11 May 1994[2]

Entry into force: after ratification by all States Parties to the Convention, in accordance with Article 4

The member States of the Council of Europe, signatories to this Protocol to the Convention for the Protection of Human Rights and Fundamental Freedoms, signed at Rome on 4 November 1950 (hereinafter referred to as "the Convention"),

Considering the urgent need to restructure the control machinery established by the Convention in order to maintain and improve the

---

1 Protocol No. 11 establishes a single Court, which will operate on a full-time basis and replace the current control machinery (European Commission and Court of Human Rights).

This restructuring, which has been made necessary by the increase in the number of applications and the expansion of the Council of Europe, aims to reduce the length of proceedings and to maintain the level of human rights protection provided by the Convention.

2 European Treaty Series, No. 155.

efficiency of its protection of human rights and fundamental freedoms, mainly in view of the increase in the number of applications and the growing membership of the Council of Europe;

Considering that it is therefore desirable to amend certain provisions of the Convention with a view, in particular, to replacing the existing European Commission and Court of Human Rights with a new permanent Court;

Having regard to Resolution No. 1 adopted at the European Ministerial Conference on Human Rights, held in Vienna on 19 and 20 March 1985;

Having regard to Recommendation 1194 (1992), adopted by the Parliamentary Assembly of the Council of Europe on 6 October 1992;

Having regard to the decision taken on reform of the Convention control machinery by the Heads of State and Government of the Council of Europe member States in the Vienna Declaration on 9 October 1993,

Have agreed as follows:

Article 1

The existing text of Sections II to IV of the Convention (Articles 19 to 56) and Protocol No. 2 conferring upon the European Court of Human Rights competence to give advisory opinions shall be replaced by the following Section II of the Convention (Articles 19 to 51):

"Section II – European Court of Human Rights

Article 19 – Establishment of the Court

To ensure the observance of the engagements undertaken by the High Contracting Parties in the Convention and the protocols thereto, there shall be set up a European Court of Human Rights, hereinafter referred to as 'the Court'. It shall function on a permanent basis.

Article 20 – Number of judges

The Court shall consist of a number of judges equal to that of the High Contracting Parties.

Article 21 – Criteria for office

1. The judges shall be of high moral character and must either possess the qualifications required for appointment to high judicial office or be jurisconsults of recognised competence.

2. The judges shall sit on the Court in their individual capacity.

3. During their term of office the judges shall not engage in any activity which is incompatible with their independence, impartiality or with the demands of a full-time office; all questions arising from the application of this paragraph shall be decided by the Court.

Article 22 – Election of judges

1. The judges shall be elected by the Parliamentary Assembly with respect to each High Contracting Party by a majority of votes cast from a list of three candidates nominated by the High Contracting Party.

2. The same procedure shall be followed to complete the Court in the event of the accession of new High Contracting Parties and in filling casual vacancies.

Article 23 – Terms of office

1. The judges shall be elected for a period of six years. They may be re-elected. However, the terms of office of one-half of the judges elected at the first election shall expire at the end of three years.

2. The judges whose terms of office are to expire at the end of the initial period of three years shall be chosen by lot by the Secretary General of the Council of Europe immediately after their election.

3. In order to ensure that, as far as possible, the terms of office of one-half of the judges are renewed every three years, the Parliamentary Assembly may decide, before proceeding to any subsequent

election, that the term or terms of office of one or more judges to be elected shall be for a period other than six years but not more than nine and not less than three years.

4. In cases where more than one term of office is involved and where the Parliamentary Assembly applies the preceding paragraph, the allocation of the terms of office shall be effected by a drawing of lots by the Secretary General of the Council of Europe immediately after the election.

5. A judge elected to replace a judge whose term of office has not expired shall hold office for the remainder of his predecessor's term.

6. The terms of office of judges shall expire when they reach the age of 70.

7. The judges shall hold office until replaced. They shall, however, continue to deal with such cases as they already have under consideration.

Article 24 – Dismissal

No judge may be dismissed from his office unless the other judges decide by a majority of two-thirds that he has ceased to fulfil the required conditions.

Article 25 – Registry and legal secretaries

The Court shall have a registry, the functions and organisation of which shall be laid down in the rules of the Court. The Court shall be assisted by legal secretaries.

Article 26 – Plenary Court

The plenary Court shall:

   a. elect its President and one or two Vice-Presidents for a period of three years; they may be re-elected;

   b. set up Chambers, constituted for a fixed period of time;

   c. elect the Presidents of the Chambers of the Court; they may be re-elected;

d. adopt the rules of the Court; and

e. elect the Registrar and one or more Deputy Registrars.

Article 27 – Committees, Chambers and Grand Chamber

1. To consider cases brought before it, the Court shall sit in committees of three judges, in Chambers of seven judges and in a Grand Chamber of seventeen judges. The Court's Chambers shall set up committees for a fixed period of time.

2. There shall sit as an *ex officio* member of the Chamber and the Grand Chamber the judge elected in respect of the State Party concerned or, if there is none or if he is unable to sit, a person of its choice who shall sit in the capacity of judge.

3. The Grand Chamber shall also include the President of the Court, the Vice-Presidents, the Presidents of the Chambers and other judges chosen in accordance with the rules of the Court. When a case is referred to the Grand Chamber under Article 43, no judge from the Chamber which rendered the judgment shall sit in the Grand Chamber, with the exception of the President of the Chamber and the judge who sat in respect of the State Party concerned.

Article 28 – Declarations of inadmissibility by committees

A committee may, by a unanimous vote, declare inadmissible or strike out of its list of cases an individual application submitted under Article 34 where such a decision can be taken without further examination. The decision shall be final.

Article 29 – Decisions by Chambers on admissibility and merits

1. If no decision is taken under Article 28, a Chamber shall decide on the admissibility and merits of individual applications submitted under Article 34.

2. A Chamber shall decide on the admissibility and merits of inter-State applications submitted under Article 33.

3. The decision on admissibility shall be taken separately unless the Court, in exceptional cases, decides otherwise.

Article 30 – Relinquishment of jurisdiction to the Grand Chamber

Where a case pending before a Chamber raises a serious question affecting the interpretation of the Convention or the protocols thereto or where the resolution of a question before it might have a result inconsistent with a judgment previously delivered by the Court, the Chamber may, at any time before it has rendered its judgment, relinquish jurisdiction in favour of the Grand Chamber, unless one of the parties to the case objects.

Article 31 – Powers of the Grand Chamber

The Grand Chamber shall:

a. determine applications submitted either under Article 33 or Article 34 when a Chamber has relinquished jurisdiction under Article 30 or when the case has been referred to it under Article 43; and

b. consider requests for advisory opinions submitted under Article 47.

Article 32 – Jurisdiction of the Court

1. The jurisdiction of the Court shall extend to all matters concerning the interpretation and application of the Convention and the protocols thereto which are referred to it as provided in Articles 33, 34 and 47.

2. In the event of dispute as to whether the Court has jurisdiction, the Court shall decide.

Article 33 – Inter-State cases

Any High Contracting Party may refer to the Court any alleged breach of the provisions of the Convention and the protocols thereto by another High Contracting Party.

Article 34 – Individual applications

The Court may receive applications from any person, non-governmental organisation or group of individuals claiming to be the victim of a violation by one of the High Contracting Parties of the rights set forth in the Convention or the protocols thereto. The High Contracting Parties undertake not to hinder in any way the effective exercise of this right.

Article 35 – Admissibility criteria

1. The Court may only deal with the matter after all domestic remedies have been exhausted, according to the generally recognised rules of international law, and within a period of six months from the date on which the final decision was taken.

2. The Court shall not deal with any individual application submitted under Article 34 that:

   a. is anonymous; or

   b. is substantially the same as a matter that has already been examined by the Court or has already been submitted to another procedure of international investigation or settlement and contains no relevant new information.

3. The Court shall declare inadmissible any individual application submitted under Article 34 which it considers incompatible with the provisions of the Convention or the protocols thereto, manifestly ill-founded, or an abuse of the right of application.

4. The Court shall reject any application which it considers inadmissible under this Article. It may do so at any stage of the proceedings.

Article 36 – Third-party intervention

1. In all cases before a Chamber or the Grand Chamber, a High Contracting Party one of whose nationals is an applicant shall have the right to submit written comments and to take part in hearings.

2. The President of the Court may, in the interest of the proper administration of justice, invite any High Contracting Party which is not a party to the proceedings or any person concerned who is not the applicant to submit written comments or take part in hearings.

Article 37 – Striking out applications

1. The Court may at any stage of the proceedings decide to strike an application out of its list of cases where the circumstances lead to the conclusion that:

   a. the applicant does not intend to pursue his application; or

   b. the matter has been resolved; or

   c. for any other reason established by the Court, it is no longer justified to continue the examination of the application.

However, the Court shall continue the examination of the application if respect for human rights as defined in the Convention and the protocols thereto so requires.

2. The Court may decide to restore an application to its list of cases if it considers that the circumstances justify such a course.

Article 38 – Examination of the case and friendly settlement proceedings

1. If the Court declares the application admissible, it shall:

   a. pursue the examination of the case, together with the representatives of the parties, and if need be, undertake an investigation, for the effective conduct of which the States concerned shall furnish all necessary facilities;

   b. place itself at the disposal of the parties concerned with a view to securing a friendly settlement of the matter on the basis of respect for human rights as defined in the Convention and the protocols thereto.

2. Proceedings conducted under paragraph 1.b shall be confidential.

Article 39 – Finding of a friendly settlement

If a friendly settlement is effected, the Court shall strike the case out of its list by means of a decision which shall be confined to a brief statement of the facts and of the solution reached.

Article 40 – Public hearings and access to documents

1. Hearings shall be public unless the Court in exceptional circumstances decides otherwise.

2. Documents deposited with the Registrar shall be accessible to the public unless the President of the Court decides otherwise.

Article 41 – Just satisfaction

If the Court finds that there has been a violation of the Convention or the protocols thereto, and if the internal law of the High Contracting Party concerned allows only partial reparation to be made, the Court shall, if necessary, afford just satisfaction to the injured party.

Article 42 – Judgments of Chambers

Judgments of Chambers shall become final in accordance with the provisions of Article 44, paragraph 2.

Article 43 – Referral to the Grand Chamber

1. Within a period of three months from the date of the judgment of the Chamber, any party to the case may, in exceptional cases, request that the case be referred to the Grand Chamber.

2. A panel of five judges of the Grand Chamber shall accept the request if the case raises a serious question affecting the interpretation or application of the Convention or the protocols thereto, or a serious issue of general importance.

3. If the panel accepts the request, the Grand Chamber shall decide the case by means of a judgment.

Article 44 – Final judgments

1. The judgment of the Grand Chamber shall be final.

2. The judgment of a Chamber shall become final:

a. when the parties declare that they will not request that the case be referred to the Grand Chamber; or

b. three months after the date of the judgment, if reference of the case to the Grand Chamber has not been requested; or

c. when the panel of the Grand Chamber rejects the request to refer under Article 43.

3. The final judgment shall be published.

Article 45 – Reasons for judgments and decisions

1. Reasons shall be given for judgments as well as for decisions declaring applications admissible or inadmissible.

2. If a judgment does not represent, in whole or in part, the unanimous opinion of the judges, any judge shall be entitled to deliver a separate opinion.

Article 46 – Binding force and execution of judgments

1. The High Contracting Parties undertake to abide by the final judgment of the Court in any case to which they are parties.

2. The final judgment of the Court shall be transmitted to the Committee of Ministers, which shall supervise its execution.

Article 47 – Advisory opinions

1. The Court may, at the request of the Committee of Ministers, give advisory opinions on legal questions concerning the interpretation of the Convention and the protocols thereto.

2. Such opinions shall not deal with any question relating to the content or scope of the rights or freedoms defined in Section I of the Convention and the protocols thereto, or with any other question which the Court or the Committee of Ministers might have to consider in consequence of any such proceedings as could be instituted in accordance with the Convention.

3. Decisions of the Committee of Ministers to request an advisory opinion of the Court shall require a majority vote of the representatives entitled to sit on the Committee.

Article 48 – Advisory jurisdiction of the Court

The Court shall decide whether a request for an advisory opinion submitted by the Committee of Ministers is within its competence as defined in Article 47.

Article 49 – Reasons for advisory opinions

1. Reasons shall be given for advisory opinions of the Court.

2. If the advisory opinion does not represent, in whole or in part, the unanimous opinion of the judges, any judge shall be entitled to deliver a separate opinion.

3. Advisory opinions of the Court shall be communicated to the Committee of Ministers.

Article 50 – Expenditure on the Court

The expenditure on the Court shall be borne by the Council of Europe.

Article 51 – Privileges and immunities of judges

The judges shall be entitled, during the exercise of their functions, to the privileges and immunities provided for in Article 40 of the Statute of the Council of Europe and in the agreements made thereunder."

Article 2

1. Section V of the Convention shall become Section III of the Convention; Article 57 of the Convention shall become Article 52 of the Convention; Articles 58 and 59 of the Convention shall be deleted, and Articles 60 to 66 of the Convention shall become Articles 53 to 59 of the Convention respectively.

2. Section I of the Convention shall be entitled "Rights and freedoms" and new Section III of the Convention shall be entitled "Miscellaneous provisions". Articles 1 to 18 and new Articles 52 to 59 of the Convention shall be provided with headings, as listed in the appendix to this Protocol.

3. In new Article 56, in paragraph 1, the words ", subject to paragraph 4 of this Article," shall be inserted after the word "shall"; in paragraph 4, the words "Commission to receive petitions" and "in accordance with Article 25 of the present Convention" shall be replaced by the words "Court to receive applications" and "as provided in Article 34 of the Convention" respectively. In new Article 58, paragraph 4, the words "Article 63" shall be replaced by the words "Article 56".

4. The Protocol to the Convention shall be amended as follows:

a. the Articles shall be provided with the headings listed in the appendix to the present Protocol; and

b. in Article 4, last sentence, the words "of Article 63" shall be replaced by the words "of Article 56".

5. Protocol No. 4 shall be amended as follows:

a. the Articles shall be provided with the headings listed in the appendix to the present Protocol;

b. in Article 5, paragraph 3, the words "of Article 63" shall be replaced by the words "of Article 56"; a new paragraph 5 shall be added, which shall read:

> "Any State which has made a declaration in accordance with paragraph 1 or 2 of this Article may at any time thereafter declare on behalf of one or more of the territories to which the declaration relates that it accepts the competence of the Court to receive applications from individuals, non-governmental organisations or groups of individuals as provided in Article 34 of the Convention in respect of all or any of Articles 1 to 4 of this Protocol."; and

c. paragraph 2 of Article 6 shall be deleted.

6. Protocol No. 6 shall be amended as follows:

a. the Articles shall be provided with the headings listed in the appendix to the present Protocol; and

b. in Article 4 the words "under Article 64" shall be replaced by the words "under Article 57".

7. Protocol No. 7 shall be amended as follows:

a. the Articles shall be provided with the headings listed in the appendix to the present Protocol;

b. in Article 6, paragraph 4, the words "of Article 63" shall be replaced by the words "of Article 56"; a new paragraph 6 shall be added, which shall read:

> "Any State which has made a declaration in accordance with paragraph 1 or 2 of this Article may at any time there-after declare on behalf of one or more of the territories to which the declaration relates that it accepts the competence of the Court to receive applications from individuals, non-governmental organisations or groups of individuals as provided in Article 34 of the Convention in respect of Articles 1 to 5 of this Protocol."; and

c. paragraph 2 of Article 7 shall be deleted.

8. Protocol No. 9 shall be repealed.

Article 3

1. This Protocol shall be open for signature by member States of the Council of Europe signatories to the Convention, which may express their consent to be bound by:

a. signature without reservation as to ratification, acceptance or approval; or

b. signature subject to ratification, acceptance or approval, followed by ratification, acceptance or approval.

2. The instruments of ratification, acceptance or approval shall be deposited with the Secretary General of the Council of Europe.

Article 4

This Protocol shall enter into force on the first day of the month following the expiration of a period of one year after the date on which all Parties to the Convention have expressed their consent to be bound by the Protocol in accordance with the provisions of Article 3. The election of new judges may take place, and any further necessary steps may be taken to establish the new Court, in accordance with the provisions of this Protocol from the date on which all Parties to the Convention have expressed their consent to be bound by the Protocol.

Article 5

1. Without prejudice to the provisions in paragraphs 3 and 4 below, the terms of office of the judges, members of the Commission, Registrar and Deputy Registrar shall expire at the date of entry into force of this Protocol.

2. Applications pending before the Commission which have not been declared admissible at the date of the entry into force of this Protocol shall be examined by the Court in accordance with the provisions of this Protocol.

3. Applications which have been declared admissible at the date of entry into force of this Protocol shall continue to be dealt with by members of the Commission within a period of one year thereafter. Any applications the examination of which has not been completed within the aforesaid period shall be transmitted to the Court which shall examine them as admissible cases in accordance with the provisions of this Protocol.

4. With respect to applications in which the Commission, after the entry into force of this Protocol, has adopted a report in accordance with former Article 31 of the Convention, the report shall be transmitted to the parties, who shall not be at liberty to publish it. In accordance with the provisions applicable prior to the entry into force of this Protocol, a case may be referred to the Court. The panel of the Grand Chamber shall determine whether one of the Chambers or the Grand Chamber shall decide the case. If the case is decided by a Chamber, the decision of the Chamber shall be final.

Cases not referred to the Court shall be dealt with by the Committee of Ministers acting in accordance with the provisions of former Article 32 of the Convention.

5. Cases pending before the Court which have not been decided at the date of entry into force of this Protocol shall be transmitted to the Grand Chamber of the Court, which shall examine them in accordance with the provisions of this Protocol.

6. Cases pending before the Committee of Ministers which have not been decided under former Article 32 of the Convention at the date of entry into force of this Protocol shall be completed by the Committee of Ministers acting in accordance with that Article.

Article 6

Where a High Contracting Party had made a declaration recognising the competence of the Commission or the jurisdiction of the Court under former Article 25 or 46 of the Convention with respect to matters arising after or based on facts occurring subsequent to any such declaration, this limitation shall remain valid for the jurisdiction of the Court under this Protocol.

Article 7

The Secretary General of the Council of Europe shall notify the member States of the Council of:

a. any signature;

b. the deposit of any instrument of ratification, acceptance or approval;

c. the date of entry into force of this Protocol or of any of its provisions in accordance with Article 4; and

d. any other act, notification or communication relating to this Protocol.

In witness whereof the undersigned, being duly authorised thereto, have signed this Protocol.

Done at Strasbourg, this 11th day of May 1994 in English and French, both texts being equally authentic, in a single copy which shall be deposited in the archives of the Council of Europe. The Secretary General of the Council of Europe shall transmit certified copies to each member State of the Council of Europe.

Titles already published in this series

Short guide to the European Convention on Human Rights, 1991,
ISBN 92-871-1981-3

People on the move – new migration flows in Europe, 1992,
ISBN 92-871-2021-8

Human rights in international law: Basic texts, 1992,
ISBN 92-871-2039-0

Blood transfusion in Europe: a "white paper"
ISBN-92-071-2508-2

Sales agents for publications of the Council of Europe
Agents de vente des publications du Conseil de l'Europe